Mr. Foster is assistant professor of history at Northern Illinois University. He received a Guggenheim Fellowship in 1971.

Yale Historical Publications

Miscellany, 94

THEIR SOLITARY WAY

The Puritan Social Ethic in the First Century of Settlement in New England

by Stephen Foster

New Haven and London, Yale University Press, 1971

Copyright © 1971 by Yale University.
All rights reserved. This book may not be
reproduced, in whole or in part, in any form
(except by reviewers for the public press),
without written permission from the publishers.
Library of Congress catalog card number: 76-151573
International standard book number: 0-300-01408-2

Designed by John O. C. McCrillis
and set in Garamond type.
Printed in the United States of America by
The Carl Purington Rollins Printing-Office of
the Yale University Press, New Haven, Connecticut.

Distributed in Great Britain, Europe, and Africa by
Yale University Press, Ltd., London; in Canada by
McGill-Queen's University Press, Montreal; in Mexico
by Centro Interamericano de Libros Académicos,
Mexico City; in Central and South America by Kaiman
& Polon, Inc., New York City; in Australasia by
Australia and New Zealand Book Co., Pty., Ltd.,
Artarmon, New South Wales; in India by UBS Publishers'
Distributors Pvt., Ltd., Delhi; in Japan by John
Weatherhill, Inc., Tokyo.

Baker & Taylor

7 1/3

June 72

2

44906

To my mother and the memory of my father

The World was all before them, where to choose
Thir place of rest, and Providence thir guide:
They hand in hand with wandring steps and slow,
Through *Eden* took thir solitary way.

Milton, *Paradise Lost*

Contents

Preface   xi

Acknowledgments   xix

List of Abbreviations   xxi

Introduction   1

Part One   Foundations   9
   1 Order   11
   2 Love   41

Part Two   Details   65
   3 Government: The Character of a Good Ruler   67
   4 Wealth: The Calling, Capitalism, Commerce,
      and the Problem of Prosperity   99
   5 Poverty: Affliction, Poor Relief, and Charity   127

Part Three   Potentials   153
   6 Puritanism and Democracy: A Mixed Legacy   155

Appendix A   The Massachusetts Franchise in the
                Seventeenth Century   173

Appendix B   The Nomination of Massachusetts Magistrates
                under the Old Charter   180

Appendix C   The Merchants, the Moderates, and
                Edward Randolph   182

Appendix D   Family Connections of Merchants, Ministers,
                and Magistrates   187

Bibliography   191

Index   209

Preface

When I first began this book I knew I was writing about the American Puritans but I had a difficult time selecting a suitable title for the specific subject of my study. "Puritan Social Theory" seemed to restrict me to summarizing sermons. "Puritan Social History" had something to do with ploughshares, probate records, and a machine capable of disposing in twenty minutes of "programs" that had taken three months of ingenuity to devise. I think I finally settled on "Puritan Social Ethic" because of its essential slipperiness. It permitted me to go beyond the learned treatises of divinity without trapping me in the rigors of the computer.

In retrospect the ambiguity seems a happy one and "social ethic" a coherent and discrete entity. Whatever the name, I have tried to get at the imperatives, aspirations, and inhibitions which collectively comprised the way a seventeenth-century New Englander thought he ought to act toward other seventeenth-century New Englanders when they came together in an organized civil society. Syntax may reel and diction waver under the strain of so painfully long a definition, but one word of it still stands out: *ought*. This book deals with norms and normative behaviour, that is, with the "ought" of a particular society. The "is," the actual social conditions of early New England, will have to wait for another historian. I am willing to admit that the influence of the norms may well have varied with changing material circumstances in New England, but I am far too prudent to attempt a history of these circumstances or the ways New Englanders responded to them. For the most part I am writing about what New Englanders habitually said they believed in, not what they habitually did about it.

Despite this disclaimer, I do not intend to limit myself to the formal records of Puritan intellection, those sermons, treatises, and controversial tracts that now seem less alive in their bulky totality than a single amusing paragraph on bestiality recounted in the journal of John Winthrop. A society's ethic lies as much in its diaries, law codes, government records, and letters as in its formal hortatory literature, though it would be as wrong to neglect the sermons as to leave out the bestiality stories. Both held interest for the seventeenth century, whatever the predilections of the twentieth.

Social historians would dismiss my use of the battery of sources associated with their discipline as unsystematic and "impressionistic," an old-fashioned substitution of the accessible fact for the typical. Such censure would be justified if my book were social history. But when I cite the Winthrop Papers or the *Records of the Governor and Company of the Massachusetts Bay* I do so simply to supplement the sermons and treatises in the work of defining social aspirations and determining their vitality in specific instances. I am not contending that a few recorded instances prove that behavior necessarily followed belief.

An example may make some sense of these abstractions. Both the Massachusetts and Connecticut general courts repeatedly attempted to regulate the amount of finery worn by the lesser sort in order to keep them from aping their betters in bravery of apparel. These sumptuary laws were only enforced sporadically, however, and finally were abandoned entirely. To cite them as proof that the poor in New England did not wear gold buttons would constitute very impressionistic social history indeed. (Since Old World societies had no better luck with their sumptuary regulation, to cite the failure of the legislation in America as proof of the irresistible egalitarianism of the New World would be equally impressionistic, though for some reason it might come in for less criticism). But I cited the laws for another purpose entirely: their enactment by two elected, partially representative bodies seems to confirm that a large part of the lay population shared the concept of hierarchy first enunciated in the sermon literature. The Puritan social ethic, then, was hierarchical, though New England society was not necessarily so.

Perhaps such an apology apologizes too much. At times, particularly in the chapters on political affairs, the distinction between social ethic and social organization blurs. For all their talk about polity, the Puritans had no idea what a convenanted state really was or how an aristocracy could be voluntary until John Winthrop and his company actually founded a state by contract and elected a ruling class by annual written ballot. Consequently, the Puritan imperatives dealing with the social covenant and a voluntary aristocracy cannot be studied without examining the origins, conflicts, and development of the political institutions of early New England. As an exposition of New England political practice this examination will be incomplete, but as an integral part of the study of the Puritan social ethic it may suffice and it must be attempted. In this instance theory literally had no meaning apart from the constitutional development that translated abstract European fictions into very concrete American realities.

Having admitted this much, there is a temptation to go just that little bit further. With almost no effort we find ourselves saying that there is no substance without context, that no idea can be understood apart from the social circumstances in which it was articulated. If the social context can add to the meaning of a given proposition, then it can also change it so that the most innocuous passages correctly read reveal a deeper and more significant meaning than their simple substantive propositions. Cotton Mather has no right to repeat in provincial Boston the dicta William Perkins first enumerated in late Elizabethan Cambridge, and if he does we can discover that he is really saying something different and far more appropriate to his surroundings; for we can make the plausible assumption that, while the words did not change much in the course of a century, their social context and therefore their meaning did. The actual social history of early New England being as yet little understood, we can then deduce the social context from the alleged hidden meaning (derived in turn from the social context) and congratulate ourselves on the remarkable symmetry of our interpretation. The gate is very wide and the way is very broad.

Without some sort of magic key we are admittedly left in a very curious situation. It has become a historiographical commonplace that New England society changed drastically between its foundation and the early eighteenth century, and in a setting of rapid social evolution towards modernity an archaic, partly static social ethic is undeniably inappropriate. But this very quality of the ethic, which is documented, should in itself cast some doubt on the commonplace about social change, which is not. Not even the law codes, the registers of social values most sensitive to the needs of a society in rapid transition, show much alteration until well into the eighteenth century.

The formal literature yields still less comfort: New England authors were not particularly unobservant and yet somehow they seem to have overlooked entirely the alleged transformation of their society, unless every minister in the migration and many of the lay participants, leaders and followers both, could produce evidence out of the High Commission and the diocesan courts to prove conclusively that they were Protestant nonconformists to the Church of England as by law established. They would have resented Laud's smear term of "Puritan"; but if any men were Puritans they were, if any set of values comprised a distinct Puritan social ethic theirs did.

As it happens, mucn that even the New Englanders professed was anything but unique. Chapter 1 on order contains little that is unfamiliar; but with all the emphasis on the radical and the creative in Puritanism, it is well to begin with a reminder of how many of its tenets were derivative, conservative, and traditional even in the most purely Puritan part of the Western world. There was also something new in the New England way, and it should be no less interesting to students of early modern Europe because it reveals some of what radical Protestantism was capable of when there was no need to adapt aspirations to the existing social structure. In particular, New England at peace anticipated England in revolution: congregational polity, the communitarianism of the New England town, the fixed codes of law, and the church-based franchises all foreshadowed similar developments in Cromwell's England. Historians trying to understand the Civil War fragmentation of English Puritanism, as well as the more exotic fragments, should remember that they are dealing with the second Puritan experiment in living without king and bishops; there was a first, in the New World, uncompromised by the inhibitions of traditional institutions or the exigencies of civil war.

This quintessential Puritanism of New England reveals above all that tensions and contradictions were an inherent part of the Puritan outlook, not mere products of its strained coexistence with traditional social forms. American Puritanism managed to combine the traditional and the radical, the voluntary and the authoritarian, as well as a host of other diametrically opposed impulses, into one organic whole that apparently thrived on its own internal conflicts. Failure to appreciate this curious trait accounts in large part for the unfortunate tendency of contemporary scholars to push back the date of the "declension" of the New England Way (one recent study putting it at 1636). With a movement whose essence was ambiguity, it is always possible to claim one half of the ambivalence as the defining trait and then to cite the existence of the other half as proof that Puritanism has collapsed. Contradictions within Puritanism produced tensions and schism but they also enabled it to embrace the most diverse kinds of individuals, from John Elliot to Robert Keayne, and to adapt to the most abrupt shifts in the fortunes of its adherents. In this it bears a marked resemblance to another and more modern idealogy whose internal tensions have also been productive of both fission and durability. I would prefer, however, to leave the analogies to others more inclined to cross-cultural generalizations than I am.

All I seek is to add a certain subtlety and precision to the historians' use of the word *Puritanism*. Yet history in the end remains the story of people, and at the conclusion of my last chapter some readers may still want to know the ways in which Puritanism affected the lives of the Puritans. Granted, I have spent my entire preface explaining why I have not answered the question and my entire text trying not to ask it. The final pages of a preface are still the moment for candor if any ever is, and I will venture a tentative suggestion—provided it is understood to be only tentative and suggestive.

In the first place we ought not to reduce the problem to correlating practice with preaching. Men may not always àct according to the rules, and yet the existence of accepted rules can influence their style of action even when they ignore virtue and apparently quite regularly practice vice. Too many medieval usurers devoted too much space in their wills to provisions for their souls for us to imagine that the ecclesiastical prohibitions on usury were without effect: they may not have stopped the practice or even diminished its intensity but they certainly bothered the usurer. A medieval man, he suffered from superstition; we moderns merely follow our consciences.

Call it what you like, the fear is the same, the knowledge that we are fragile creatures passing all to briefly through a cosmos all too large. The most hardened sinners have faced eternity at least once, and they have not all faced it the same way: at the end of his life Cortes regretted that he had succeeded in conquering half the world, Hitler that he had failed to conquer the other half. Intimations of mortality come more often to ordinary men, who usually take some comfort in knowing that they have followed their particular set of eternal verities part of the time and have not really enjoyed themselves the rest. The Puritan social ethic may have only made the New England tippler's hand tremble an extra little bit or it may have changed the nature of his tippling. Either way the rules remain important even to those who value deeds above thoughts, for we cannot really explain what was done without some reference to what was thought.

Assertions thus guarded probably annoy the nonscholarly reader at the same time that some of the scholarly ones find me presumptuous for spelling "Puritan" with a capital "P." Anyone who works in a discipline where the secondary sources threaten to outnumber the primary and where rival schools group into warring camps runs certain risks, not the least of them that of being misunderstood. I have lived with this book too long to have more than one wish for it: that it be judged on the basis of the answers it does give to the questions it does ask. To the readers—courteous and discourteous—who are willing to take me on these terms I commend both myself and the text that follows.

London   S. F.
Summer 1970

Acknowledgments

An author's most awkward moments are provided by his friends. He is embarrassed to ask for their criticism in the first place, winces visibly when they respond with enthusiasm, and finally never knows how to thank them without either falling into flattery or becoming impossibly cryptic. Very briefly then . . .

This book began as a doctoral dissertation directed by Professor Edmund S. Morgan of Yale University, whose combination of tolerance and guidance I shall always admire. Professor Sydney Ahlstrom of Yale and Professor David Hall, now of Boston University, provided detailed critiques of the dissertation that have had an obvious influence on subsequent revisions, including the final one. Professor J. H. Hexter made a substantial contribution, both intellectual and personal, to the shaping of this book and even to its ultimate appearance.

My fellow graduate students at Yale spent an unwarranted amount of time helping out a competitor. My thanks go especially to Professor Robert Zemsky, now of the University of Pennsylvania, and to Professor Timothy Breen, now of Northwestern University. Before leaving Yale, mention should also be made of the staffs of the Sterling and Beinecke libraries, whose patience matched the scholarly resources of their collections. Finally, I am especially grateful to whichever Yale committee it was that decided to bestow upon my dissertation the Theron Rockwell Field Prize, an award customarily reserved for works of poetry.

Since coming away from New Haven I have fallen under the spell of the Newberry Library and of the scholars who frequent it. Without the earnest efforts of Dr. Jan Rogozinski my sentences would be even longer, my syntax even more Teutonic. My debt to Professor Kenneth Lockridge, now of the University of Michigan, appears throughout my text. And I should never have finished the book at all without the assistance of the staff of the Newberry itself, and especially of its director, Dr. Lawrence Towner. Nor can I forget the many kindnesses of

Mr. David Stam and Mr. Arthur Miller of the Newberry and their unalterable good humor in the face of severe provocation.

My colleagues at the Department of History, Northern Illinois University, went over chapter 4 with a thoroughness that left me a bit shaken but a good deal wiser. Special thanks go to the ever formidable Professor C. H. George. Mrs. Darla Woodward and the clerical staff of the history department deserve high praise for typing and retyping the manuscript despite the obstacles of my somewhat disorderly methods of composition.

Chapter 2 owes a good deal to the thoughtful criticisms of Professor Martha E. François of Northeastern University; appendix A is similarly in debt to Professors Robert Wall and Richard Simmons. My thanks especially to these two gentlemen and to the *William and Mary Quarterly* and the *Journal of American History* for permission to reprint tables 1 and 2 respectively. And finally, but for my wife Verna Ann Foster this book would have had an inelegant title.

The enumeration of my accomplices appropriately ends at this point. There were others, too, responsible for a footnote here or a reference there and sometimes more: the influence of a casual remark can be far greater than its author realizes. All such are doomed to anonymity by reason of their numbers, but I hope this does not obscure my sense of their contribution and of the value of being part of a genuine intellectual community.

List of Abbreviations

Acts and Resolves	*Acts and Resolves, Public and Private, of the Province of the Massachusetts Bay,* ed. E. Ames and A. Cheney Goodell (Boston, 1869–1922).
Boston Rec.	*Boston Registry Department, Records Relating to the Early History of Boston* (Boston, 1876–1909).
Coll. MHS	*Collections* of the Massachusetts Historical Society. The number before the abbreviation indicates the series, the number after it, the volume. Thus 5 *Coll.* MHS, 4 is the fourth volume of the fifth series of the *Collections.*
Essex Cty. Ct. Rec.	*Records and Files of the Quarterly Courts of Essex County Massachusetts,* ed. George F. Dow (Salem, 1911–21).
Inferiour Court of Pleas	*Abstract and Index of the Records of the Inferiour Court of Pleas (Suffolk County Court) Held at Boston 1680–1698,* Historical Records Survey (Boston, 1940).
Mass. Rec.	*Records of the Governor and Company of the Massachusetts Bay in New England,* ed. N. B. Shurtleff (Boston, 1853–54).
Mather Diary	*The Diary of Cotton Mather, Collections* of the Massachusetts Historical Society, 7th ser., vols. 7–8 (1911–12).
NEH&GR	*New England Historical and Genealogical Register.*
Publ. CSM	*Publications* of the Colonial Society of Massachusetts (Boston, 1940).
Publ. MHS	*Publications* of the Massachusetts Historical Society.

Sewall Diary

The Diary of Samuel Sewall, Collections of the Massachusetts Historical Society, 5th ser., vols. 5–7 (1878–82).

Suffolk Cty. Ct. Rec.

Records of the Suffolk County Court, 1671–1680, Publications of the Colonial Society of Massachusetts (Boston, 1933), vols. 29–30.

Winthrop Journal

John Winthrop, *The History of New England from 1630–1649,* ed. James Savage (Boston, 1853).

THEIR SOLITARY WAY

Introduction

In the beginning God created the heaven and the earth and in the end he created New England. This was the course of human history from Genesis 1 : 1 to 5 *Carolus Rex* as viewed from the quarterdeck of the *Arbella* one June day in 1630 when the coast of the New World came into sight for the first time. On board the ship were Governor John Winthrop and his company, a group of English men and women now denominated "Puritans," though in their own estimation they were simply the most important body of people since the Apostles. The latter had brought true Christianity to the Old Israel, the Puritans would recreate it in a new.

Winthrop and the others on the *Arbella* would not have used the label "Puritan," but they did admit to advocating a thoroughgoing reformation of the church and society of their native England, the purging from both of their popish and "humane" corruptions, and their reorganization according to the Word of God. For the church this meant congregational polity and "Calvinist" doctrine, for society a strange mixture of some of the most commonplace of European ideals, and some of the most extraordinary.

In their homeland any kind of change except for the worse seemed impossible. King Charles I and his ecclesiastical advisor William Laud had just suspended Parliament and inaugurated the "Eleven Years Tyranny" that would end only with the Civil War and death on the scaffold for both men. But in 1630 the bloody and violent conclusion to the King's Peace lay years in the future: for many English Puritans the only alternative to Charles and Laud seemed to lie in following the lead of a company of English Separatists from Scrooby, men so dissatisfied with the Church of England that they had broken with it entirely, going into exile at Leyden and then in 1620 forsaking even the relative comfort of Holland for the arduous but unrestricted life of pilgrims in the "wilderness" of New Plymouth Colony. A new land, separated from king and bishops by three thousand miles of Atlantic

I

Ocean, offered Winthrop's company their only chance of creating the kind of world they wanted.

The thousands of settlers who poured into New England after 1630 founded not one colony there but four, in addition to the earlier settlement at New Plymouth. Winthrop himself established Massachusetts Bay, the largest of the five, which grew so steadily in population that some of its settlers, under the leadership of the Rev. Thomas Hooker, found themselves overcrowded and moved south to found Connecticut in 1636. Two years later Theophilus Eaton and the Rev. John Davenport, skeptical even of the godliness of the Bay colony, established New Haven to the south of Hooker's settlements and maintained a separate existence from the rest of Connecticut until 1664. Rhode Island, the fifth colony, grew out of four separate towns built by a variety of heretics expelled from Massachusetts between 1636 and 1643. All told, the combined policies of Charles I and Laud had made England seem unattractive enough for over fifteen thousand of their Puritan countrymen to emigrate to the more congenial environment of New England in the decade 1630 to 1640.

Yet the new immigrants were not the sort who combatted error by fleeing it; at least, the more reflective of them were not. Just before leaving England the leaders of the 1630 expedition had declared their firm allegiance to the Church of England, and Winthrop himself had written earlier that:

> he which would have suer peace and joye in Christianitye, must not ayme at a condition retyred from the world and free from temptations, but to knowe that the life which is most exercised with tryalls and temptations is the sweetest, and will prove the safeste. For such tryalls as fall within compasses of our callinges, it is better *to arme and withstande them* than to avoid and shunne them.[1]

1. *Winthrop Papers* (Boston, 1929–   ), 1 : 209; 2 : 231–33. The refusal of the Massachusetts Bay settlers to become Separatists like their brethren at Plymouth is treated by Perry Miller in *Orthodoxy in Massachusetts* (Cambridge, Mass., 1933) and by Edmund Morgan in *The Puritan Dilemma* (Boston, 1958).

I have retained the original spelling and punctuation in this and all subsequent quotations, except for the minor changes of the "expanded method" explained in Oscar Handlin et al., *The Harvard Guide to American History* (Cambridge, Mass., 1963), pp. 98–99. Similarly, I have kept all dates in the Old Style, following the Julian Calendar and double dating between 1 January and 24 March (as in 26 January 1634/35).

They had crossed an ocean and come to a strange and unsettled land, but they founded a society designed to benefit England and all Christendom by serving as a model for the reformation of other churches and other states in what Puritans and non-Puritans alike commonly considered "these last times" before the Second Coming of Christ. While the *Arbella* still rode the Atlantic midway between the Old World and the New, Winthrop composed and delivered his *Model of Christian Charity*, concluding with a warning quoted in whole or part many times afterwards:

> we must Consider that wee shall be as a Citty upon a Hill, the eies of all people are uppon us; soe that if wee shall deale falsely with our god in this worke wee have undertaken and soe cause him to withdrawe his present help from us, wee shall be made a story and a by-word through the world, wee shall open the mouthes of enemies to speake evill of the wayes of god and all professours for Gods sake; we shall shame the faces of many of gods worthy servants, and cause theire prayers to be turned into Cursses upon us till wee be consumed out of the good land whether wee are going.[2]

If the Lord carried them safely through the journey, he had signified his consent to a covenant with the people of New England, promising them temporal prosperity in return for their attempting to live in conformity with his will. All societies had such covenants, but New England would be unique in that its people must live not only a good life but an exemplary one that would display the true way for others, so that "men shall say of succeeding plantacions: the lord make it like that of New England." Exemplary failure would bring exemplary punishment.

> he hath taken us to be his after a most strict and peculiar manner which will make him the more Jealous of our love and obedience soe he tells the people of Israell, you onely have I knowne of all the families of the Earthe therefore will I punishe you for your Transgressions.

The covenant did not end with the correct way to conduct services on Sunday and the proper moral conduct for the other six days of the

2. *Winthrop Papers*, 2 : 295.

week, nor did Winthrop restrict "the worke we have in hand" to church polity: "it is by a mutuall consent through a speciall overruleing providence, and a more than an ordinary approbation of the Churches of Christ to seeke out a place of Cohabitation and Consorteshipp under a due form of Government both civill and ecclesiastical."[3] God had rules for civil policy as well as for ecclesiastical, and the Puritans intended to follow all of them.

They could scarcely have picked a better time or place in which to try it. Distracted by internal conflicts, the English government had to allow the Puritan colonists to rule themselves as they pleased for over half a century, while the new land itself presented equally few obstacles to the Lord's work. In coming to America, the Puritans not only escaped a tyrannous king and meddling bishops, they escaped every European institution whatsoever, except such as they chose to resurrect in a form suitable to their purposes. As Englishmen reacting to new circumstances they often used traditional English techniques, but they could not and would not try to recreate English society in its entirety: if they had been happy with life in England they never would have left in the first place. In the New World they could build as God had commanded without having to accommodate social theory to any preexisting social reality; they had brought their reality with them.

God had not, however, supplied all the details. The only precedents Puritan theorists could point to in their blueprints for church and state were, by modern standards, mythical: the congregational polity of the apostolic church, the voluntary covenants of some primeval era in which all civil government had its origin. When the American Puritans founded their new world on this magnificently incorrect version of human history they operated in effect without a past, and the meaning of their present lay hidden in the future—in the form their new institutions would take in the course of time after the conflicts and contributions of many men had hammered out their ultimate definition. Winthrop said far more than he intended in 1630 when he told the *Arbella's* passengers, "That which the most in theire Churches maineteine as a truthe in profession onely, wee must bring into familiar and constant practise."[4]

3. Ibid., 2 : 293.
4. Ibid.

Today the profession in question seems too esoteric ever to have held much interest for the bulk of ordinary New Englanders, who must have been exclusively concerned with the more visceral needs of accumulation, procreation, and nourishment. In the midst of our own contemporary confusion of voices it is not easy to imagine the impact of some One True Way repeatedly inculcated by an official priestly caste *without competition*. The average New England farmer had a mind as well as an intestine. Three times a week, once on Thursdays and twice on Sundays, every week of every year of his allotted three score and ten he heard his local minister preach the received doctrine. He may not have appreciated all its subtleties, his leaders may even have had to remind him of its main tenets now and then when he grew rebellious, but he heard it, he believed it, and—once reminded— he sometimes even managed to follow it.

At other times, to be sure, he did as he pleased, but the effect of a bad conscience can be overlooked only by overlooking all consciousness. Historians must not think that the ordinary seventeenth-century New Englander could not understand complicated doctrine because they cannot; that Puritanism was relevant only to theology, and theology was irrelevant; that whatever the leaders may have thought, the followers did not think at all. Even ordinary men made some effort to order their lives according to principles laid down by men who were quite extraordinary; they did not just react to their environment with a series of emotional responses that were semiconscious at best. When William Ames, professor of theology at Frenkeur in the Netherlands, found that puppeteers, magicians, and jugglers had no valid callings and wrote as much in his *Conscience with the Power and Cases Thereof*, he gave Samuel Sewall an argument with which to convince Captain John Wing, no theologian but the proprietor of a tavern in Boston's Hudson Street, that he ought not to rent a room "for a Man to show tricks in."[5] Captain Wing was not a man of profound education and his visceral parts presumably worked as well as anyone's in Massachusetts.

5. *The Diary of Samuel Sewall*, 5 *Coll*. MHS, 5 : 196. Volumes 5, 6, and 7 of the fifth series of the *Collections* will be cited hereafter as *Sewall Diary*, 1, 2, and 3 respectively.

PART ONE

Foundations

For the Puritans the proper study of mankind was God. If we are to understand the way they thought about themselves, singly or collectively, we must begin where they began: not with the created, but with the attributes of the Creator. God was order and God was love; the godly society must therefore rest on these twin foundations.

Proceeding from the general to the specific, the chapters in the next section will discuss the implications of order and love for the details of political, economic, and social activity as well as some of the changes Puritan social thought underwent in its first century in the New World. First, however, come the foundations themselves: order, which recapitulated the most orthodox of European orthodoxies, and love, which radically altered them.

1 Order

THE RULES OF THE UNIVERSE: BEAUTY AND EFFICIENCY

At the opening of act four of *King Lear* Gloucester, blinded, betrayed, and deserted, tells what he has come to know of man's role in the universe:

> As flies to wanton boys, are we to the gods;
> They kill us for their sport.

William Perkins, fellow of Emmanuel College, Cambridge, considered all stage plays immoral and all stage players vicious, so he presumably would never have gone to *Lear* even if he had not died in 1602, three years before the first performance. Had he heard them, Gloucester's words would only have confirmed his opinions of the theater: like most other English Protestants, Perkins lived in a world governed neither by chance nor malicious fate, but by a divinity who ordered all things for his own good ends, from the courses of the greatest stars in the heavens down to the smallest detail of the meanest man's daily life on earth.

> In regard of God there is no chance, neither any event by it; in regard of men indeed who know not the causes of things, many chances may be: but God's providence, and chance are contrary; he having all things written before him with their causes . . . . nothing comes to passe without the decree of God, no not the wicked actions of men. Which God not onely forseeth, but decreeth . . . and then even that which is against the will of God cometh not to passe without his will, God willing the being of that which he willeth not to effect; and though he esteeme not evil to be good, yet he accounteth it good that evil should be.[1]

Seventy-three years after Perkins's death another minister, a New Englander named William Hubbard, reiterated this doctrine in a ser-

---

1. *An Exposition of the Epistle of Jude* in *Works* (London; 1631), 3 : 516. Unfortunately, I used a mixed set: vol. 1 was printed in Cambridge in 1608.

mon before the Massachusetts General Court and applied it in time-
honored fashion to social relationships:

> It is not then the result of time or chance, that some are
> mounted on horse-back, while others are left to travell on foot.
> That some have with the Centurion, power to command, while
> others are required to obey. *The poor and the rich meet together
> the Lord is the maker of them both.* The Almighty hath ap-
> pointed her that sits behind the mill, as well as him that ruleth
> on the throne.

God had not given men varied attributes and talents without having
a benevolent purpose behind this variety, a cosmic division of labor in
which each man had his own peculiar function suited to his particular
talents, and in which every man contributed to the good of all in his
appointed way. The doctrine was as old as civilization, but the assembled freemen, deputies, and magistrates took special comfort in hearing it anew each year at election time, especially when the preacher
was as eloquent as Hubbard:

> Herein hath he as well consulted the good of humane nature, as
> the glory of his own wisdome and power: Thoase of the supe-
> riour rank, but making a supply of what is wanting in the other:
> otherwise might not the foolish and the ignorant be like to loose
> themselves in the Wilderness, if others were not as eyes to them.
> The fearful and the weak might be distroyed, if others more
> strong and valiant, did not protect and defend them. The poor
> and the needy might starve with hunger and cold, were they not
> fed with the morsells, and warmed with the fleece of the wealthy.
> Is it not found by experience, that the greatest part of mankind,
> are but as tools and Instruments for others to work by, rather
> than any proper Agents to effect any thing of themselves [?][2]

The modern reader curious enough to look through three-hundred-
year-old sermons may wonder why God did not simply endow all men
with all virtues instead of giving them only one or two each, but the

---

2. *The Happiness of a People in the Wisdome of their Rulers Directing and
in the Obedience of their Brethren Attending Unto what Israel ought to do*
(Boston; 1676), pp. 9–10.

Puritans thought they knew the reason. Aside from pointing out that he *had* made men different, and that whatever he did was good by definition, they invoked what Arthur Lovejoy calls the principle of plenitude: the concept that God most increased his glory and created most beautifully when he created in infinite variety.[3] John Winthrop reminded the prospective settlers, while they were still on the *Arbella* in 1630, that "God almightie in his most holy and wise providence hath soe disposed of the Condicion of mankinde, as in all times some must be rich some poore, some highe and eminent in power and dignitie; others meane and in subjeccion" in order "to hold conformity with the rest of his workes, being delighted to shewe forthe the glory of his wisdome in the variety and differance of the Creatures and the glory of his power, in ordering all these differences for the preservacion and good of the whole and the glory of his greatness . . . counting himselfe more honoured in dispenceing his guifts to man by man, then if hee did it by his owne immediate hand."[4]

Cosmology joined social theory in defense of rank. The basic science text used at Harvard from 1687 to 1727 explained that the world had "Perfection, both of parts and vertues," meaning that it already had the maximum possible number of species and that each had a suitable virtue assigned to it.

> So that tho we may fancy greater perfections, (as that man should fly as birds dive as fishes, be Invisible as the Angels etc:) yet in reality these would not be mans perfections because the Infinitely Wise God has ordered for Every Thing what is best; his will and wisdom being the measure of all perfection.
> The World of parts perfection is Possest.
> and Every part of Vertues which are best.[5]

3. Arthur O. Lovejoy, *The Great Chain of Being* (New York; 1960), pp. 50–55 and passim. For the political implications of the great chain in Elizabethan times see E. M. W. Tillyard, *The Elizabethan World Picture* (New York; 1944), pp. 82–84, 87–91. A recent study concerned with English Puritanism prior to the Civil War argues, however, that Puritan doctrine destroyed the traditional concept of the great chain, replacing it with a more egalitarian philosophy (Michael Walzer, *The Revolution of the Saints* [Cambridge, Mass.; 1965], pp. 151–71).

4. *The Model of Christian Charity, Winthrop Papers*, 2 : 282–83.

5. Charles Morton, *Compendium Physicae, Publ. CSM*, 33 : 210.

God, as Hubbard had said, "is the God of peace, of order, and not of confusion." Having made all those various species, he arranged them in an order where each fulfilled its assigned function most effectively for the benefit of the whole. The stars followed fixed courses, the angels stood in serried ranks, the very birds of the air followed a due pattern of deference. So should men regulate their society, "for Order is as the soul of the Universe, the life and health of things natural the beauty of things Artificial." Borrowing from the "Schools," Hubbard defined order as "such a disposition of things in themselves equall and unequal, as gives to every one their due and proper place." Those to whom God had given the talent to govern should become the governors, the rest should each serve in that place best suited to them.[6]

The Puritans, like many others before and after them, envisioned a society of specialists bound together by mutual need and believed that any other arrangement would inevitably lead to chaos. Daniel Dennison, himself called to be a ruler, put it graphically:

> we must not pervert the order of God and nature, why should I
> expect my fellow-traveller should direct my way better than my
> guid[e]? why then do I employ him? that my comrade should
> give a command more advantageous than my captain, that a sheep
> . . . should lead the flock into better Pasture than the shepherd;
> that my Brother should have a greater care for me than my
> Father[?][7]

The concept of order served equally well to defend all sorts of servile relationships between masters and servants, and even, when the need arose, the existence of human slavery itself. Answering Samuel Sewall's spirited attack on slavery, *The Selling of Joseph*, in 1700, John Saffin had only to reiterate the traditional theories and then accuse Sewall of attempting "to prove that all men have equal right to Liberty, and all outward comforts of this life,"

> which Position seems to invert the Order that God hath set in the
> World, who hath Ordained different degrees and orders of men,

6. *The Happiness of a People*, p. 8. Cf. Thomas Hooker's definition of order, *A Survey of the Summe of Church-Discipline* (London; 1648), p. 2.
7. *Irenicon or a Salve for New-England's Sore*, printed with William Hubbard, *The Benefit of a Well-Ordered Conversation* (Boston; 1684), p. 216.

some to be High and Honourable, some to be Low and Despicable, some to be Monarchs Kings, Princes and Governours, Masters and Commanders, others to be subjects, and to be commanded; servants of sundry sorts and degrees, bound to obey; yea, some born to be slaves, and so to remain during their lives, as hath been proved. Otherwise there would be a meer parity among men.[8]

Most of the Puritan ministry would probably have balked at carrying the doctrine of order to the point where slavery became a "natural" attribute: this was too Aristotelian a position for anyone other than slaveholders. Few would have doubted, however, that inequality in general was not merely natural but beneficial, of value to superior and inferior alike. "Order" insured that each man performed that function in which he best served the good of all men, not just the good of the upper classes or the dictates of his own unstable whims. *Salus populi* depended on subjection and subordination: if any man were to follow his individual desires then every man would ultimately suffer for it. Thomas Hooker developed the point with what the Puritans must have thought irresistible logic:

> For if each man may do what is good in his owne eyes, proceed according to his own pleasure, so that none may crosse him or controll him by any power; there must of necessity follow the distraction and desolation of the whole, when each man hath liberty to follow his owne imagination and humerous devices and seek his particular, but oppose one another, and all prejudice the publike good.
>
> In the building, if the parts be neither mortised nor braced, as there will be little beauty so there can be no strength. It[']s so in setting up the frames of societies among men, when their mindes and hearts are not mortified by mutuall consent of subjection one to another, there is no expectation of any successefull proceeding with the advantage of the publike. . . .

8. John Saffin, *A Brief and Candid Answer to a Late Printed Sheet Entitled The Selling of Joseph* (Boston; 1700), reprinted in part in George H. Moore, *Notes on the History of Slavery in Massachusetts* (New York; 1866), pp. 251–52.

Mutuall subjection is as it were the sinewes of society, by which
it is sustained and supported.

. . . .

Hence every part is subject to the whole, and must be serviceable to the good there of, and must be ordered by the power
thereof.

Salus Populi suprema lex.

It is the highest law in all Policy Civill or Spirituall to preserve
the good of the whole; at this all must ame, and unto this all
must be subordinate.[9]

The doctrine bound with equal rigor those it made members of the
upper ranks and those it consigned to the lower. Men who had great
gifts, be they of government, of preaching, or even of wealth, lay
under an inescapable injunction to use them for the public welfare and
not just for their own advancement or pleasure. "We ought Every One
of us to *Serve our Generation*, before we fall *asleep*, or it will be but
an uncomfortable Sleep that we shall fall into. We are, in Publico
Discrimine, and that man is a *Wen* or a *Scab*, rather than a *Member* of
this *Body Politic*, who shall decline the service of his countrey."[10]

A Puritan gentleman had always to convince himself that his current mode of life allowed him to employ his talents and estate in the
most serviceable way. He could not, like the contemporary English
ascetic Nicholas Ferrar, conclude that a public career was corrupting
and retire to Little Gidding to pursue a life of prayer, fasting, and
bookbinding. That was not only to flee temptation instead of over-
coming it but, worse yet, to fail the Lord's trust by not employing the
talents he had given for use as his steward, a crime no Puritan wanted
to stand accused of on that awful day when he must render up his
final accounts to his master.

Before moving to New England John Winthrop had been obliged
to convince himself that the most useful field for his talents lay there
and not at home in England. His friend Robert Ryece had warned that
"the church and common welthe heere at home, hathe more neede of
your beste abyliytie in these dangerous tymes, then any remote plantation, which may be performed by persons of lesser woorthe and

9. *A Survey of the Summe of Church-Discipline*, p. 188.
10. Cotton Mather, *The Serviceable Man* (Boston; 1690), p. 55.

apprehension," to which Winthrop replied that financial reverses would curtail his usefulness in England in any case, "and if I should let passe this opportunitye, that talent which God hath bestowed on me for publike service, were like to be buried."[11]

Once established in New England, Winthrop and his associates showed little sympathy for anyone who did not manifest the same desire for public service. The Massachusetts General Court considered fining men who were qualified to become freemen (that is, entitled to vote and hold office) but failed to, and declared that "the Countrye wanteth the use of their gifts in public service, and others are thereby the more burdened."[12] Most men of "parts," however, were as willing as Winthrop to assume public duties appropriate to their stations, and the colony benefited from it—so much so that the government thought the fact of "ships safely arrived with persons of spetiall use and quality" in 1633 sufficient grounds to declare a day of thanksgiving.[13]

If the upper ranks had obligations, the lower ones had rights. In return for respecting their superiors and deferring to their special qualities, inferiors deserved to be treated with respect themselves, not with contempt or haughtiness.[14] While no Puritan wanted to encourage too much familiarity between the various social orders for fear of undermining discipline, no one approved of pride or an overbearing carriage even in men in the highest positions of power. Royal Governor Joseph Dudley's curt order to two young farmers one day in 1707 to get out of the road on which he was traveling, and his subsequent attack on them with his sword when they failed to obey, shocked his eminently respectable and conservative council. When Dudley charged the two with contempt of authority, the Massachusetts Superior Court summarily dismissed the case.[15] The man who used high rank to abuse those beneath him had forgotten the reason God raised him up in the world: to serve all men for His glory.

11. *Winthrop Papers*, 2 : 105–06, 126.
12. Ibid., 5 : 190. The actual act as passed by the General Court was considerably milder. *Mass. Rec.*, 2 : 208. Failure to accept public office was also liable to ecclesiastical censure: cf. the case of Ensign Richard Morris in 1634, *Winthrop Journal*, 1 : 152.
13. *Mass. Rec.*, 1 : 109.
14. Superiors, William Perkins insisted, must honor their inferiors as well as the other way around. (*Cases of Conscience* in *Works*, 2 : 152).
15. *Sewall Diary*, 2 : 144–46, 144n–47n, 148, 152, 158.

Sin and the Need for Regulation

Mutuality, subordination, and public service constituted a kind of
sacred trinity of all respectable societies, Puritan or otherwise. Any
other kind of arrangement would have impressed the seventeenth century as downright unnatural. Henry Peacham, the author of *The Compleat Gentleman,* was no Puritan but he struck a note common to all
educated men when he insisted that human society must follow the
same divinely ordained pattern of hierarchy found in nature.

> Can we be curious in descerning a counterfeit from the true
> Pearle; to choose our siens [scions] of the best fruit, buy our
> Flowers at twenty pounds the foote or slip: and not regard or
> make difference of linage, nor bee carefull into what Stocks we
> match our selves, or of what parents we chose a servant?
>
> Surely, to beleeve that Nature (rather the God of Nature)
> produceth not the same among our selves, is to question the rarest
> worke-mistris of ignorance or partiality, and to abase ourselves
> beneath the Beast.[16]

A century and a half later, in 1776, other men would appeal to
nature's God to justify their claims for the equality of all men, and of
Americans and Englishmen in particular, but this only indicates the
intellectual distance traveled in America in that period of time. Every
Puritan theorist could still feel the anarchist Anabaptists of Muenster
breathing down his neck even after a century and could hear their dia-
bolical argument that, since government came about as a device to
control man's sinful nature, Christ in taking away sin had taken away
government too. The Puritans had to rejoin that God had created men
unequal, that there had been superiors and inferiors before the Fall,
and that the divine will would have naturally ranked men in an orderly hierarchy even if they had remained innocent. Government
would not in that case have been needed to restrain men's lusts, "yett
it might tend to the ornament of the universe, and be a trial of our
obedience to this Precept [the fifth commandment]: And we have

16. *The Compleat Gentleman,* ed. G. S. Gordon (Oxford; 1906), pp. 1–2.
This is a reprint of the edition of 1634.

good footing in the Word of God, that God hath placed an order between the very Angels of Light."[17]

But the case for order did not rest with uncorrupted nature. Eve had given Adam that apple, and ever after men needed order not only for beauty and efficiency but as a check on the limitless atrocities that they might be tempted to commit at any time. The Puritan minister waxed unusually eloquent, not to say enthusiastic, when he tried to depict the effects of sin. Thus Thomas Hooker:

> It crosseth the whol course of Providence, perverts the work of the Creature and defaceth the beautiful frame, and that sweet correspondence and orderly usefulness the Lord first implanted in the order of things; the Heavens deny their influence, the Earth her strength, the Corn her nourishment, thank sin for that. . . . This makes crooked servants in a family no man can rule them, crooked inhabitants in towns, crooked members in congregations, ther's no ordering nor joynting of them in that comly accord and mutual subjection. . . . Man was the mean betwixt God and the creature to convey all good with all the constancy of it, and therefore when Man breaks, Heaven and Earth break all asunder, the conduit being cracked and displaced there can be no conveyance from the Fountain.[18]

While sin had not overthrown divine order, it had crippled man's ability to conform to it by warping his affections and clouding his reason. In Puritan cosmology man had occupied a central place in the universe before the Fall, using all the "creatures" for the glory of God and his own comfort.[19] Within human society each man stood ranked

17. Samuel Willard, *A Compleat Body of Divinity* (Boston; 1726), p. 619 (2d pagination). Cf. William Perkins, *Exposition of Jude, Works*, 3 : 536–37; Ebenezar Pemberton, *A Christian fixed in his Post* in *Sermons and Discourses on Various Occasions* (London, 1727), p. 39, and *The Divine Original of Government Asserted* (Boston; 1710), pp. 15–16. In the first of these two sermons Pemberton wrote that "it is highly probable had man retained his first state of unblemisht integrity, there would yet have been *different degrees of men*" and deduced from that, that "it is no presumption to assert that Levilism is contrary to nature, and the intention of the *God of Nature.*"

18. *The Application of Redemption* (London; 1657), p. 59.

19. On man's role in the universe before the Fall see Urian Oakes, *A Seasonable Discourse Wherein Sincerity & Delight in the Service of God is earnestly pressed upon Professors of Religion* (Cambridge, Mass.; 1682), p. 27.

in an ascending order, but one he submitted to gladly and willingly. Sin had destroyed all this: man now valued the creatures for themselves, not realizing in his Fall-induced stupidity that they were empty and useless without him who made them, and in his sinful state he would not obey authority without the threat of coercion. Left to his own devices man would run amuck—at least in their own view Puritans would.[20] Grace restored some of the primitive integrity of the human reason and will, but regeneration would always remain imperfect this side of Jordan: "The best of the Saints have flesh as well as Spirit, they have something of the *Old Man, as well as of the New; they know but in part* and are *Sanctified but in part;* and hence many weaknesses in managing the cause of God."[21]

Perfection of the works of the regenerate, like celibacy and the holy nature of poverty and solitude, amounted to little more than a popish conceit. The existence of crime in itself did not alarm or dishearten the Puritan: more than any other man he was no perfectionist. In his old age Judge Samuel Sewall, with an air of delivering the most elementary of commonplaces, began his charge to the Suffolk County grand jury, "since men's departure from Gode, there was such an aversion in them to return, that every kind of Authority was necessary to reclaim them."[22]

The key phrase was "every kind of authority." Puritan speculations on the necessity of government seem only innocent, if obvious, refu-

20. On the eve of the execution of three criminals in Boston in 1681, Cotton Mather wrote in his diary: "It was the holy [John] *Bradford's* Custome when hee heard of any atrocious Iniquity perpetrated, hee would lay his Hand on his Breast, and Say, *There is that in this Heart of mine, which would make mee as vile as the Vilest, if sovereign Grace did not prevent it.* Alas, I have the seed of all corruption in mee. My Heart naturally departs from God; it is not any vertue of my own, that keeps mee from the most enormous Villanies" (*The Diary of Cotton Mather,* 7 *Coll.* MHS 7 : 30). Volumes 7 and 8 of the seventh series of the *Collections* will be cited hereafter as *Mather Diary,* 1 and 2, respectivley. Cf. Thomas Shepard, *The Sincere Convert,* 5th ed. (London; 1650), p. 31.

21. John Higginson, *The Cause of God and his People in New England* (Cambridge, Mass.; 1663), p. 6. Cf. John Cotton, *A Brief Exposition on Ecclesiastes* (Edinburgh; 1868), p. 74. The date of composition of this work is uncertain; it was printed in England in 1654, two years after Cotton's death.

22. *Sewall Diary,* 3 : 379.

tations of anarchism until it becomes clear that for them as for all seventeenth-century Europeans "government" meant "subordination" and that they did not restrict the concept simply to the political state. Every kind of relationship—between magistrate and subject, master and servant, minister and people—consisted of inferior and superior, and in each the superior made the decisions and the inferior obeyed.

> Take away this order, and how shall peace, or the society continue? This truth of a ministerial Judge, is reckoned among the Fundamentals . . . if it be in matters of Religion, there is the Priest; if in matters civil, there is the Magistrate, and he that stands not, or sumbits not to the sentence of these, *let him be cast out from Israel: so requisite a thing is order.*

John Norton, the man who wrote that, reminded his readers that whatever their opinions they must follow the dictates of authority, which while they might not be the "Truth Positive," were nevertheless that which "the God of Truth hath made . . . for to keep societies in peace; and if it were not for this Institution, there could be no sitting in Judgement, or any Polity among men." Authority might make a mistake, but "better an innocent and a good man suffer, than order, for that preserves the whole."[23]

Norton founded his remarks on the Puritan's basic distrust of man's capacity to rule himself since the Fall: "where there is liberty and the Old man, there must needs be much controversie." Doing battle with the alleged right of the individual conscience to judge truth for itself, he argued that men must submit their lives to the ordering of recognized specialists in the church and the state. In an earlier time and another place the Elizabethan Puritan Peter Wentworth had replied to the bishops' claim to determine religious dogma with the stirring cry, "make you popes who list . . .for we will make you none"—and gone to the Tower for it. That affair, however, occurred in an England not controlled by Puritans, and in any case bishops and popes could claim only a usurped authority. Rulers of church and state in New England, invested with authority in a lawful manner, could determine the truth and enforce it whenever the "Old Man" prompted some of the ruled

23. John Norton, *Sion the out-cast healed of her Wounds* (Cambridge, Mass.; 1664), pp. 8–10.

to resist. Whether it was toward magistrates, ministers, masters, or
even parents, disrespect for authority of the Wentworth variety met
just as severe a punishment in New England as in the old.[24]

A few would make the decisions for all, but the agenda they were
to decide on was much broader than in contemporary society. Salus
populi then as now remained the end of government, but European
theorists of every religious stripe conceived of the "public" as a sum
far greater than the simple total of its individual parts and of the public's welfare as something entirely separable from the collective well-
being of its individual members. For Puritans in particular, salus
populi denoted a positive pattern of virtue determined by God's unalterable and eternal law and ratified by a covenant between God and
society. If society failed in its obligations, if it let any kind of overt sin
flourish anywhere, it failed in its covenant and would suffer for it.

By consequence the New England magistrates had an even greater
obligation to use the formidable powers the seventeenth century always
assigned the state than did their equally traditional counterparts in
England and the other colonies. The New England governments
passed regulations covering some of the most intimate and personal

24. Instances of punishment for contempt of government, magistrates, the
clergy, masters, and parents occur very frequently in the Massachusetts court
records throughout the whole of the seventeenth century. See, for example,
Mass. Rec. 1 : 84, 86, 97, 114, 133, 177, 220, 222, 234, 315; 2 : 36, 37, 42.
Cf. *Winthrop Journal,* 1 : 9, 67–68, 73. Even the ministry felt the might of
the state: in 1646 the court of assistants fined the Rev. Peter Hobart £20 when
"the jury found that he seemed to be ill affected to this government, and that
his speeches tended to sedition and contempt of authority." *Winthrop Journal,*
2 : 313.

The county courts took over the main burden of the prosecution of such
offenders in the latter part of the century, and their records abound with cases.
For particulars, consult the indexes of the published editions of the files of
the Essex and Suffolk County Courts under the heading "Crimes" and a
variety of subheadings, including "Contempt," "Slander," "Abuse," and "Speaking against Magistrates" (*Essex Cty. Ct. Rec.; Suffolk Cty. Ct. Rec.,* Vols.
29–30). See also the cases of Francis Stepney and Charles Lemmons in
Suffolk County in 1685 and 1691, respectively, and of Peter Bussaker in
Connecticut in 1648, in *Inferiour Court of Pleas,* pp. 131, 135; and *Records of
the Particular Court of Connecticut 1639–1663, Collections* of the Connecticut
Historical Society, 22 (1928): 54–55.

details of their subjects' lives: laws requiring men to be industrious, laws supervising the disciplining of their children, laws forbidding them to live beyond their means, and even laws controlling the amount of lace and gold braid they could wear.[25] Displaying a passion for the elimination of "masterless men" that did credit to their Tudor heritage, the leaders of New England even attempted to place all single

25. Passing a law and enforcing it are two different things, especially in an area with as dispersed a population and as primitive communications as New England. Some statutes, such as those dealing with contempt of authority, were enforced constantly; some, like the sumptuary regulations, only very sporadically; and still others, like the price and wage regulations, rarely if at all, particularly in the latter part of the seventeenth century. In general, though occasionally revived with new ferocity, the legal regulation of the inhabitants' personal lives seems to have grown less in the second half of the century. Yet a partial list of the criminal charges heard by the Essex County Court in the years 1680–83 gives some approximation of the extent to which statutes still sought to supervise people's lives and also indicates both the good and the bad in this kind of regulation: absence from public ordinances, abuse on board ship, abusing a servant, abusing another, abusing her husband, abusing his wife, abusive carriages, abusive speech to authority, accusing a minister of theft, base words against the minister, bastardy, breach of the Sabbath, contempt of authority, cruelty to animals, defaming authority, disorderly company-keeping, drunkenness, entertaining servants, folding and frizzling hair, fornication, kissing another's wife, lascivious conduct, living away from wife, lying, neglect (of a town) to provide a schoolmaster, neglect of family, night walking, posting books on the Sabbath, reproaching ministers, parents, and relations, running away from master, sailing out of a harbor on the Lord's day, smoking tobacco, speaking against authority, against the government, the magistrates, the elders, and the form of worship, speaking reproachfully, swearing, traveling on the Sabbath, uncivil carriage, wearing silk scarfs, and witchcraft. Not all these charges resulted in convictions, but they do indicate the large number of things then considered subject to legal restriction (*Essex Cty. Ct. Rec.*, 8, passim).

As late as the 1730s a large portion of the cases heard before the Worcester County Court involved charges of profane swearing, working, or traveling on the Sabbath, failing to attend public worship, or fornication before marriage. The last charge referred to married couples who had cohabited before the actual marriage ceremony, a circumstance often arising out of the formal and binding character of betrothals (*Records of the Court of General Sessions of the Peace for the County of Worcester, Massachusetts, From 1731 to 1737, Collections* of the Worcester Society of Antiquity, 5 (1883): no. 10, passim).

men under family supervision and then to regulate all families.[26] As late as 1682 the Massachusetts General Court ordered each town's "tythingmen" (the seventeenth-century version of block wardens) to report to the selectmen for legal action all persons who neglected their callings or who "mispend their Time and that little which they earn, to the Impoverishing, if not utter undoing of themselves and Fami-

26. In 1636 the Massachusetts General Court ordered the towns to "take care to order & dispose of all single persons and inmates with their towne to service, or otherwise," and Connecticut and Plymouth passed specific statutes against single men living alone without official permission. Massachusetts adopted a nearly identical law under the New Charter in 1703. *Mass. Rec.*, 1 : 186; Nathaniel B. Shurtleff et al., eds., *Records of the Colony of New Plymouth in New England* (Boston, 1855–61), 11 : 223; J. H. Trumbull and C. J. Hoadly, eds., *Public Records of the Colony of Connecticut* (Hartford; 1850–90), 1 : 8; *Acts and Resolves, Public and Private, of the Province of the Massachusetts Bay* (Boston; 1869–1922), 1 : 538.

The Massachusetts towns seem to have done as they were ordered. Cf. *The Records of the Town of Cambridge* (Cambridge, Mass.; 1901), 2 : 160, 161; *Boston Rec.*, 4 : 158–60, 168, 181–82, 208; Don Gleason Hill, ed., *The Early Records of the Town of Dedham* (Dedham, Mass., 2 : 1886–99), 5 : 53; *Watertown Records* (Watertown, Mass., 1894), 2 : 134.

The Massachusetts county courts also took steps to regulate families and to insure that all single men belonged to a family (*Essex Cty. Ct. Rec.*, 4 : 160, 5 : 104; Middlesex Cty. Ct. Rec., MS transcript in the office of the clerk of court, Middlesex County Court House, Cambridge, Mass., 3 : 24).

The county courts also oversaw local regulation of families, occasionally taking action when the town selectmen were remiss in their duties. In 1679, for example, the Essex County Court presented the towns of Salem, Beverly, and Manchester for not inspecting all their families to see if all children had been brought up to read and to practice a lawful calling. The court did not dismiss the presentment until the towns gave written accounts of their efforts to comply with the laws (*Essex Cty. Ct. Rec.*, 5 : 378). As in the case of placing single men, the courts also sometimes bypassed the town selectmen, and regulated family order directly (*Suffolk Cty. Ct. Rec.*, 1 : 302, 411; 2 : 940; *Inferiour Court of Pleas*, p. 137). For other instances of regulation by this court see the index to the *Suffolk Cty. Ct. Rec.* under "Husband and Wife."

The Suffolk and Essex county courts passed numerous orders for couples living apart to reunite, for specific cases of which see the indexes of their printed records under "Living Away from Wife (or Husband)" and "Husband and Wife, Living Apart," respectively. The state supervision of family life and the role of the family in maintaining social order are discussed in Edmund S. Morgan, *The Puritan Family*, rev. ed. (New York; 1966), chap. 6.

lies."[27] If the authorities deemed a family improperly ordered they could (and sometimes did) break it up and disperse its members among households more in line with official standards.[28] Conceiving of order as restriction, Puritans constantly used military analogies in writing of social organization. Each man was engaged in daily battle with sin, and all men together with Antichrist; to change one's calling in this "Christian Warfare" (as John Downame called it) broke the discipline and formation necessary for the struggle. "As in the Campe every man hath his place appointed him, and his proper colours under which he is to keep him; so all Christian Soldiers have their stations, that is, their vocations whereunto they are called of God, within the limits whereof they are to containe themselves."[29]

Having put men in their appropriate places, the Puritans tried to insure that they and everyone else knew what these places were. A properly ordered society, according to Samuel Willard, would "take care, that all orders of Men have their due Honour and respect paid to them," and that "due Distances be maintained between Superior and Inferiors."[30] The magistrate especially, if he was to impress his sub-

27. *Mass. Rec.*, 5 : 373. The tythingmen were established by the General Court in 1677 to see that tavern-keepers obeyed the laws regulating their trade and also that their patrons did not spend too much time drinking, to the neglect of their families and professions. The office lapsed under the Dominion of New England, but the General Court revived it and gave it new powers in 1693 and after (*Mass. Rec.*, 5 : 240–41; *Acts and Resolves*, 1 : 59, 60, 155, 329, 679).

28. *Suffolk Cty. Ct. Rec.*, 1 : 647; *Essex Cty. Ct. Rec.*, 8 : 344. This kind of action was reserved for extraordinary cases, and official regulation was obviously never completely successful, but it was put into practice often enough to be more than a sporadic annoyance. The selectmen of the various towns repeatedly subjected the families of the poor in particular to inspection and broke them up when they found them unsatisfactory. Cf. below, chapter 5, pp. 143–44.

29. John Downame, *The Christian Warfare* (London, 1634), p. 20. Cf. William Perkins, *A Treatise of Callings* in *Works*, 1 : 727.

30. *A Compleat Body of Divinity*, pp. 623–24. Cf. the introduction to Daniel Dennison's *Irenicon*: "emulation about wisdom, wealth and holiness have put the whole Earth into combustion. This is the root of bitterness to all other evils of self-love, malice and envy, of all which covetousness is an inseparable companion: and is either chief in the first enterprize, or over-rules in carrying all wayes of commotion" (contained in *The Benefit of a Well-Ordered Conversation*, n.p.).

jects with his authority, must assume in his bearing and costume some semblance of the majestic divinity whose vicegerent on earth he was. In 1583, while Philip Stubbes was anatomizing England's abuses—his list took up one hundred and twenty pages—he digressed long enough to note that:

> Familiaritie, or coequalitie doth ever bring contempt. And therefore take awaye authoritie and honor from the magistrates either temporall or spirituall, and over throwe the same altogether. If authoritie should not be dignified, as well with glorie and eternall pompe the better to score the same, & to shew forth the majestie thereof, would it not soone grow to be dispised, vilipended, and naught set by?[31]

During the next one hundred and fifty years Puritan writers would reiterate that point and New England magistrates would act upon it.[32] On 18 January 1635/36 the Massachusetts magistrates, conscious that their internal feuding had weakened their standing with the people, agreed to act with more unity in the future "that their vote in public might bear (as the voice of God)," and to "appear more solemnly in public, with attendance, apparel, and open notice of their entrance into the court."[33]

Social order involved more than these stage tricks to maintain the prestige of public officials. In the orthodox view, men with socially useful endowments, men of talent and virtue, deserved wealth and social status in proportion to the extent to which they contributed to the public good. The Aristotelian concept of "distributive justice"—the idea that the whole should distribute its benefits to its parts in proportion to their worth—[34] gave a classical facade to a basically medieval

31. F. J. Furnivall, ed., *The Anatomy of Abuses* (London, 1882), 2 : 102–03.
32. Cf. below, chapter 3, pp. 68–70.
33. *Winthrop Journal*, 1 : 214.
34. William Ames's account of distributive justice in his *The Marrow of Sacred Divinity*, the single most basic statement of the whole of Congregational Puritan theology, differs little if at all from similar sections in Aquinas's *Summa*—or from the *Nichomachean Ethics* for that matter—except that Ames adds the fifth commandment to the authority of Aristotle (Ames, *Works* [London, 1643], pp. 308–10. *The Marrow* is paged separately from the rest of the book). Cf. Ames's *Conscience with the Power and Cases thereof* in ibid., pp. 112–13 (3d pagination).

conception of society as an interlocking series of political, social, and economic hierarchies in which rank in one implied the eqivalent rank in the others. If there was an objective ranking of vocations, then men in the lower ranks, though they might move into the upper, should not ape the prerogatives of the latter until they had done so.

Whatever the pride of any mean persons may prompt them to think, whatever is not according to order, is very indecent; *sc.* [to wit] for the peasant to equal the prince, or imitate him in garbe or in gate, or for the handmaid to emmulate her mistriss. Will not this occasion the base to behave themselves proudly against the Honourable, a forerunner of sad confusion breaking in upon a degenerating people.[35]

In England the distinguishing privilege of aristocracy until the mid-nineteenth century was embodied in the hunting laws. Certain circles in Suffolk considered dilatory enforcement of these laws as much a sign of declining times in its way as the rise of Arminianism.[36] Hunting in New England was a mode of survival, not the distinguishing sport of a privileged class, but the Puritans found other ways to give "serviceable" men their due honor. Though each New England town decided on its own how it would distribute its land among its inhabitants, many chose some sort of system that tried to preserve existing economic and social distinctions by varying the size of allotments in direct proportion to the recipient's wealth or social status. A Dedham town meeting in 1642 went so far as to vote explicitly to apportion land to the townspeople, not only according to the size of their families and their existing state of wealth, but also "According to their Ranke and Qualitie and desert and usefullness either in church or common weale."[37]

35. William Hubbard, *The Happiness of a People*, p. 56. For other Puritan statements on the need to fit outward show to rank, see William Perkins, *Works*, 2 : 134–36, 3 : 11; Downame, *The Christian Warfare*, pp. 510–13.
36. *Winthrop Papers*, 1 : 307–08.
37. *Dedham Records*, 3 : 92. Boston, Sudbury, and Charlestown all seem to have followed some sort of land distribution scheme that gave out lots in proportion to social standing, existing estate, "ability to improve the land," or general serviceableness to the commonwealth—all of which, given the Puritan way of thinking, amounted to the same thing. See Darrett B. Rutman,

Superior worth could also expect certain external signs of social deference. The order on school and college class lists, the seating in many
churches, and the use of honorifics ranging from "goodman" upwards
to "esquire" all registered an individual's place in the social scale, and
both the Massachusetts and Connecticut governments lent a hand by
passing sumptuary legislation restricting fine apparel to men of quality.[38] The Massachusetts General Court declared "our utter detestation
and dislike that men or women of meane condition, educations, and
callings should take upon them the garbe of gentlemen, by the wear-
inge of gold or silver lace, or buttons, or points at their knees, or to
walke in greate bootes, or women of the same rank to weare silk or
tiffany hoodes or scarfes, which though allowable to persons of greater
estates, or more liberall education, yett wee cannot but judge it intol-
lerable in persons of such like condition." After 1651 a statute would
restrict the privilege of wearing such finery to those possessing a total
estate greater than £200. The list of persons exempted from the law
was also significant: magistrates and public officers, certain military
officers, soldiers in time of military service, "or any other whose education and imployments have binn above the ordinary degree, or whose
estates have binn considerable, though now decayed."[39]

Winthrop's Boston (Chapel Hill, N.C., 1965), pp. 75–82, 87–92; Sumner C.
Powell, *Puritan Village* (Garden City, N.Y., 1965), p. 108. Richard Frothingham,
The History of Charlestown, Massachusetts (Boston, 1845–49), p. 56. Springfield allotted its house lots in proportion to "every ones quality and estate,"
its planting ground in proportion to the recipient's ability to use it, and its
meadow and pasture according to his cattle and estate ("because estate is like
to be imployed in cattel"), which tended to preserve existing class distinctions.
The Connecticut River towns of Hartford, Wethersfield, and Windsor also
had similar systems, though Wethersfield divided one lot of common land
equally in 1670. See *The First Century of the History of Springfield*, ed. Henry
M. Burt (Springfield, 1889), 1 : 156, 158; Charles M. Andrews, *The River
Towns of Connecticut, Johns Hopkins University Studies in Historical and
Political Science* (Baltimore, 1889), seventh series, 7–9 : 55–63. Cf. John
Cotton, "Moses, his Judicials," in Peter Force, ed., *Tracts and Other Papers,
Relating Principally to the Origin, Settlement, and Progress of the Colonies
in North America* (Washington, 1844), vol. 3, no. 9, p. 8; Edmund Browne to
Sir Simon D'Ewes, 7 September 1639, *Publ.* CSM (Boston, 1905), 7 : 75.
  38. Cf. below, chapter 6, pp. 158–59.
  39. *Mass. Rec.*, 4 : pt. 1, 60–61, pt. 2, 41–42; 5 : 59–60. Massachusetts had

Salus populi remained suprema lex in Puritan theory, at least officially, and those able to contribute to it most effectively would remain a superior class. A very traditional theoretical edifice received its equally traditional capstone, a hereditary aristocracy, with the assumption that virtuous parents passed on their gifts to their descendants:

For the Lord having bestowed some heroicall gifts and graces upon some speciall men, as wisdome, magnanimitie, fortitude, magnificence, courtesie, liberalitie and the rest; doth also for the good of common-wealthes usually vouchsafe, that there should be certaine seeds of these virtues derived after a secret and unknowne manner, from them successively unto their posteritie, whereby being come to maturitie, they resemble their ancestors in these special graces.[40]

VARIATIONS ON THE THEME: THE NEW WORLD

The concept of social order did not suffer much of a sea change in its transfer to the New World. If anything, the American Puritans sometimes seem a little old-fashioned in their ideals. English sumptuary regulation had reached its greatest proliferation in late Tudor times and disappeared on or shortly after the death of Elizabeth in 1603, never to be reestablished.[41] Massachusetts did not even pass its first class-biased law on apparel until 1651 and strengthened it again in 1662 and 1675. A recent description of Tudor social policy would

---

a number of sumptuary laws before 1651, but none of them discriminated by classes, applying equally to all, and all of them were repealed in 1644 (*Mass. Rec.*, 2 : 84). Connecticut copied the Massachusetts law almost verbatim in 1676, lowering the £200 to £150 (*Conn. Rec.*, 2 : 283). In 1641 Connecticut had passed a much less specific regulation empowering town constables to restrain "all such as they judge to exceed their conditions and ranks" by their apparel (*Conn. Rec.*, 1 : 64).

40. Downame, *Christian Warfare*, p. 490. Cf. Ruth Kelso, *The Doctrine of the English Gentleman in the Sixteenth Century, Univ. of Illinois Studies in Language and Literature* (Urbana, 1929), 14 : 35–36.

41. For Tudor sumptuary regulation and its fall see Francis E. Baldwin, *Sumptuary Legislation and Personal Regulation in England* (Baltimore, 1926), pp. 192–225.

serve almost as well as a summary of the ruling assumptions of the
magistrates and ministers of New England:

> The ideal of Tudor statesmen was organic: society was made up
> of members performing different functions for the common
> good. The ideal was also hierarchical: though all parts of the com-
> monwealth were indispensable, they were not equal, but differed
> in degree and excellence as well as in kind. The role of policy was
> to maintain and support good order as good order had been
> understood for several centuries—social peace and harmony in a
> status-based society.[42]

Yet much that was present in Puritanism and much that was lacking
in New England had a strange effect on European doctrine called on
to function on the Atlantic's leeward shore. The Puritans never wanted
for paradoxes, but most paradoxical of all was their insistence that,
while men must do only the good, they must do it voluntarily. "Where
the Lord sets himselfe over a people he frames them unto a willing
and voluntary subjection unto him, that they desire nothing more then
to be under his government. . . . Thus when the Lord is in Covenant
with a people they follow him not forcedly, but as farre as they are
sanctified by grace, they submit willingly to his regiment. Therefore
those that can be drawne to nothing that is good, but by compulsion
and constraint, it is a signe that they are not under the gracious government of the Lord God."[43] Coercion might be necessary; it would
never be moral.

The attraction of salvation by grace lay in its restoration of freedom
of choice and action without any of the dangers that ordinarily went
with it. Reborn through the effects of saving grace, the regenerate
would *want* to do good because of their love for God whereas before
they had acted only out of fear of punishment. Any lapse from virtue
could be attributed to the imperfections of the process of regeneration
in an imperfect world, and coercion would be called in again to deal

---

42. J. H. Hexter, *Reappraisals in History* (New York, 1963), p. 108.

43. Peter Bulkeley, *The Gospel-Covenant* (London, 1651), pp. 219–20. Cf.
Ebenezar Pemberton, *A True Servant of His Generation Characterized* in
Sermons and Discourses on Various Occasions, pp. 219–20.

with the remnant of the Old Man that still lingered inside the new. Though bordering on the jesuitical, this doctrine had unpredictable consequences when applied to social theory. Massachusetts leaders sometimes divided their commonwealth into the traditional three categories (ministers, magistrates, and people), carefully neglecting, however, to mention that in Massachusetts the third estate elected the first two—or rather, the regenerate part did, for only church members might become freemen and (at least after about 1636) only the regenerate might become church members. The ministers never tired of telling the people that they must elect only men of wisdom and virtue to the offices of magistrate and pastor and that, once elected, rulers—civil and spiritual—ceased to be responsible to the electors; yet nothing forced either church members or freemen to follow those injunctions—nothing except the traditional sense of order regularly inculcated by these same ministers and magistrates.[44] Such subordination as existed in Massachusetts rested on mutual consent. The Dedham land system noted earlier was passed at a town meeting attended by fifty-two men, easily the majority of adult males then living in the town, and the sumptuary laws were enacted by both houses of a legislature elected by the very men whose freedom was abridged.

Since it depended so heavily on consent, the system did not always function smoothly: not every town was as consistently generous as Dedham,[45] not every freeman always chose to respect the prerogatives of the magistrates. Often, however, events went as magistrates and ministers said they ought to go, because the people accepted their claims to a superior status and because all orders held the goals of New England, the sense of mission, in common. Puritan voluntarism really made a virtue of necessity in a state where the law not only permitted but required every adult male to bear arms, and where the ultimate police power rested exclusively on local militias made up of all

44. This theme is treated at length in chapter 3.

45. Clashes over the restrictive land system occurred among the inhabitants of both Sudbury and Boston, for example, and in the case of Sudbury ended in the founding of Marlborough, Massachusetts, where land was allotted approximately equally. Rutman, *Winthrop's Boston*, pp. 65, 78–82, 85–87, 96, 157; Powell, *Puritan Village*, pp. 150–77.

the male inhabitants, free and nonfree.[46] No one has yet discovered a way to oppress a society of armed men unless they want to be oppressed, and then the word *oppression* loses all meaning. Fact, then, could agree with theory only so long as men agreed to let it. And yet from the earliest days of settlement many facts about New England contradicted the accepted European social classifications enunciated in terms of a hierarchy of varying ranks. Sir Thomas Smith wrote in his celebrated *De Republica Anglorum* that "the commonwealth of England, it is governed, administered, and manured by three sorts of persons": the monarch, the gentlemen (subdivided into barons, knights, esquires, and simple gentlemen), and the yeomanry. At the bottom of the heap came "the fourth sort of men which doe not rule," comprising "day labourers, poore husbandmen, yea merchants or retailers which have no free lande, copiholders, and all artificers."[47] The commonwealths of New England were constructed on rather different principles. They did not have the upper and lower extremes of the English social scale, most men owned their land in fee simple, and Massachusetts, at least, had a larger electorate than contemporary England.[48] Sir Thomas's four categories were reduced to two: simple gentlemen and a combined class of yeomen and the fourth sort, most of whom did own land and many of whom could rule after a fashion.

---

46. For the militia laws, see *Mass. Rec.*, 1 : 84, 85, 125, 190, 2 : 222; *Plymouth Rec.*, 1 : 15; *Acts and Laws of His Majesty's Colony of Rhode-Island and Providence-Plantations in America* (Boston, 1719), p. 86. Cf. Michael Zuckerman, "The Social Context of Democracy in Massachusetts," *William and Mary Quarterly*, 3d ser., 25 (1968) : 523–44.

47. L. Alston, ed., *De Republica Anglorum* (Cambridge, 1906), pp. 31–47.

48. On the extent of the Massachusetts freemanship see appendix A. The law permitting selected nonfreemen to serve on juries and hold local offices is in *Mass. Rec.*, 2 : 197. The extent of the Connecticut franchise is even less clear than that of Massachusetts, but a recent study indicates that a majority of the adult males probably were *eligible* to become freemen, though perhaps only half those who could, actually did take the freemen's oath. The size of the Plymouth franchise is conjectural: such evidence as exists—and there is not much of it—points to a wide franchise, at least before 1672. David H. Fowler, "Connecticut's Freemen: the First Forty Years," *William and Mary Quarterly*, 3d ser., 15 (1958): 312–33; George D. Langdon, Jr., "The Franchise and Political Democracy in Plymouth Colony," *William and Mary Quarterly*, 3d ser. 20 (1963): 513–26.

When it came down to talking about New England society in concrete terms rather than about man or angels, even the theorists described it more in terms of a duality than an ascending hierarchy. Winthrop's *Model of Christian Charity* divided men into just two sorts, the rich and the poor, meaning those who could support themselves and those who could not.[49] The New England sumptuary laws also replaced the complicated gradations of their Tudor equivalents with a simple two-part division. "To distinct ranks we willingly acknowledge, from the light of nature and scripture," John Cotton informed Lord Say and Sele in 1636, "the one of them called Princes, or Nobles, or Elders (amongst whom gentlemen have their place), the other the people."[50]

Perhaps Cotton was not just tailoring theory to reality. Puritans, more than most people, tended to see things in bipolar terms. He who is not with the Lord is against him, after all, and men do not receive grace by degrees. Besides, if civil societies were analogous to ecclesiastical ones, to allow a graded chain of lay superiors might have dangerous consequences for congregational polity.[51] In any case, for all the talk of graded ranks of angels in heaven, New England society came to be viewed as split into only two major ranks, and the gulf between them would by no means prove unbridgeable.

Here social mobility received a boost from, of all disciplines, formal logic. The American Puritans had avidly adopted the logical system of the French Protestant humanist Petrus Ramus (1515–72), who satisfied their penchant for dichotomy with a vengence. Breaking with scholastic Aristotelian logic, Ramus had adopted the Platonic tenet

49. *Winthrop Papers*, 2 : 283.

50. "Certain Proposals made by Lord Say, Lord Brooke, and other Persons, of quality. as conditions of their removing to New-England, with the answers thereto," in Thomas Hutchinson, *History of the Colony and Province of Massachusetts-Bay*, ed. L. S. Mayo (Cambridge, Mass., 1936), 1: 410.

51. Thomas Hooker admitted that the same logic applied to all associations founded by covenant, the church as well as the state: "in all voluntary covenants, which arise from the free consent of party and party, there is no difference to be found in those covenants, but in the peculiar and Individuall formalities of speciall ingagements, which passe betwixt party and party, and therefore the difference is there alone to be sought, and there alone it can be found" (*A Survey of the Summe of Church-Discipline*, p. 66).

that all universals exist as eternal ideas in the mind of God, and then proceeded to divide and subdivide God's mind ad infinitum. The basic unit of thought he called an "argument," meaning anything that indicated the relationship between things, and the method by which arguments could be combined into coherent discourse he named "judgment." Arguments and judgment in turn were subdivided many times over to lay bare the fundamental structure of the cosmos and the Bible alike. Both could be understood by use of the same logical method, the Ramist Dialectic. "Truth therefore becomes for the Ramist, and through him for the Puritan, clear-eyed perception of immutable essences, beauty becomes correspondence to them, virtue becomes conformity to them."[52]

Somehow, after Ramus had finished his classification of subsets within subsets, at the end of all the dichotomies the basic arguments turned out to be the categories of Aristotle. One of these was the "relatives," which Ramists defined more narrowly than Aristotle as "contraries affirming; the one whereof consists by the mutual relation to the other." They meant that relatives were any two terms which could only be defined by reference to each other. Ramists commonly gave as examples, "Priest and people, Maister and Servant, Mistress and maid, etc.," and pointed out that "because of this mutual relation, Relatives are said to be together in nature: so that he which perfectly knowes the one knoweth the other also."[53]

For Aristotle relatives were merely one of ten classes of predicates, one of ten types of things men could say about a subject; Ramists looked upon them as one of the central principles by which the uni-

52. Perry Miller and Thomas H. Johnson, *The Puritans* (New York, 1963), p. 31. Reference is to the Harper paperback edition. Miller treats the significance of the dialectic for Puritans briefly in ibid., pp. 27–40 and at much greater length in *The New England Mind, The Seventeenth Century*, especially in pp. 111–80. The Ramus Dialectic in itself and in its place in European history is the subject of Walter J. Ong's *Ramus: method, and the decay of dialogue* (Cambridge, Mass., 1958). For the social implications of the dialectic I am in debt to Edmund S. Morgan, particularly to his discussion in *The Puritan Family*, pp.21–25.

53. Samuel Wotton, *The Art of Logick* (London, 1626), pp. 55–58. This is one of many English translations of Ramus's *Dialecticae libri duo* with a detailed English commentary. Cf. Abraham Fraunce, *The Lawiers Logike* (London, 1588), pp. 48 recto–49 recto.

verse was organized. Most Puritans (and some non-Puritans) consequently felt it necessary to classify all social obligations in terms of relative duties, the mutual duties between father and son, minister and people, magistrate and subject, master and servant, and superior and inferior in general.[54] Thomas Hooker (following the lead of Ramus himself) made the whole concept particularly appealing to Congregationalists by pointing out that if minister and people were relatives, then a man could not be a minister apart from the particular people with whom he stood in a relationship, and Anglican and Presbyterian claims for a continuous and independent status for the minister consequently fell to the ground.

> The Proposition is supported by the *fundamental* principles of reason, so that he must rase out of the received rules of Logick that must reject it: *Relata sunt, quorum unum constat e mutua alterius affectione* [those things are related, one of which springs from mutual affection to the other]: and hence all men that will not stifle and stop the passage of rationall discourse, forthwith infer, that therefore they are *simul natura*, are together in nature one with another.[55]

The modern reader who will not stifle and stop the passage of rational discourse should understand that if pastor and congregation were true relative terms, then the pastor could not come into existence before or apart from his ordination over a particular congregation, though, of course, he who became the pastor still existed *as a man* before ordination.

The same fundamental principles of reason negated any kind of social class in an absolute sense. No man was a superior or an inferior by nature, but only as he stood in relation to some other man. Both

54. The relative duties are summarized in Willard, *A Compleat Body of Divinity*, pp. 600–31 (2d pagination). The Anglican writers William Sherlock, Dean of St. Paul's, and Jeremy Taylor, chaplain to Laud and later Lord Bishop of Down and Comer, both used the concept. Sherlock, *A Discourse on Divine Providence*, 2d ed. (London, 1694), pp. 355, 356; Taylor, *Ductor Dubitantium*, 4th ed. (London, 1696), pp. 304, 739.

55. *Survey of the Summe of Church Discipline*, p. 68 (2d pagination). Cf. Robert Kingdon, *Geneva and the Consolidation of the French Protestant Movement, 1564–1572* (Madison, Wisc., 1967), pp. 96–111.

Hooker and Samuel Willard pointed out that a man might conceivably be a superior in one relation and an inferior in another: he might, for example, be the father of a family but the subject of a ruler. Two men could even simultaneosuly be each other's inferior and superior, depending on which relationship applied to them at any given time. A magistrate stood superior to a minister when the latter appeared as one of his subjects but inferior to him when he himself functioned as a member of the minister's congregation.[56] In parodying the Presbyterian claims of an independent ministerial status, Thomas Hooker also incidentally demolished the concept of a master class or caste:

> Should a man come to a servant, and tell him, I am a master of servants. . . . *Therefore thou art my servant, and must do the work of my family.*
>
> Should people of one congregation come to the Pastour of another, and tell him; come and bestow your pains constantly with us, for its all one as if you did it with your own people, for its folly to seek for differences in *covenant*, betwixt *Pastor* and *people*, for that makes no difference, since the covenant is common to all. . . . Therefore you are our Pastor, and must do the work of our congregation.
>
> That *a man* should be a generall Husband to all women, or a woman a *generall wife* to all men, because *marriage covenant is common* to all. It seems strange at the first sight, and therefore, [if] its counted folly on our part to seek any difference here. . . . [then] we are content to bear *the charge of folly for it.*[57]

Even Puritans did not construct their social system out of textbooks of logic; but in any case the Ramist Dialectic was descriptive, not prescriptive. It purported to be a description of the actual nature of the world and so gave its advocates in New England a way to accept social mobility and the partial failure of their plan to give wealth to those with political power and political power to those with high social status.

56. *Survey of the Summe of Church Discipline*, p. 62 (2d pagination); Willard, *Compleat Body of Divinity*, p. 600 (2d pagination).

57. *Survey of the Summe of Church Discipline*, pp. 66–67 (2d pagination).

Despite the eternal principle of distributive justice, the New England colonies never found an effective way to compensate their magistrates for the time they spent away from their business affairs, caring for the state. The early governors, including Winthrop and Endecott, developed a distressing tendency to die almost bankrupt. On Endecott's death in 1665, John Hull, Boston mintmaster and merchant, jotted down in his diary:

> He died poor, as most of our rulers do, having more attended the public than their own private interests.
> It is our shame: though we are indeed a poor people, yet might better maintain our rulers than we do.[58]

Government was not a source of profit in early Massachusetts, which could compensate its magistrates for the costs of their office only by large grants of land. These in turn could not be developed without capital, just what governors and government did not have. Nor did the grants have much speculative value while other land was still available for free: many magistrates ended up, in effect, land poor. Followed to its logical conclusion, the Puritan social ethic would have produced a Ferris wheel mobility, with the poor enjoined to grow rich and the rich enjoined, in effect, to grow poor by taking on the responsibility of government. Samuel Symonds, later deputy governor of Massachusetts, was not attempting whimsy when he wrote John Winthrop in 1647 that God had brought His people to New England "to exercise the graces of the ritcher sort in a more mixt condiccion, they shall have the liberty of good government in their hands yet with the abatement of their outward estates. And that the poorer sort (held under in England) should have inlargement."[59]

Even the characteristic form of land tenure in New England compromised traditional social distinctions. Some people owned much more land than others, but almost everybody owned it by right of

58. *The Diary of John Hull, Archaeologia Americana* (Boston, 1857), 3 : 215. The same thing happened to an extent to Hull himself. When he died, Massachusetts was in debt to him for £1700, only £450 of which was ever repaid. On the problem of renting land cf. below, chapter 5, p. 138n.

59. Samuel Symonds to John Winthrop, 11 January 1646/47, *Winthrop Papers*, 5 : 126.

freehold.[60] Traditional social distinctions depended on differences in
the ways men made their income as well as in differences in income
itself. In a society of freeholders status was a good deal cloudier than
in an Old World collection of tenants and landlords. Plymouth's governor, William Bradford, had discovered in his colony's early days
that similarity of economic status damaged a due social order:

> Upon the poynte of all being to have alike, and all to doe
> alike, they thought them selves in the like condition, and one as
> good as another, and so, if it did not cut of those relations that
> God hath set amongest men, yet it did at least much diminish
> and take of the mutuall respects that should be preserved
> amongest them. And it would have been worse if they had been
> men of another condition.[61]

But social order suffered from more than the land and the land system; forms of government established by men affected it in unwanted
ways. A small farmer or tradesman in Massachusetts could vote if he
was in full communion with some church, but the owner of a forty-
shilling freehold or a gentleman who lacked this qualification could
not. Lord Say and Sele, Lord Brook, "and other Persons of Quality"
appreciated the peculiarities of the Massachusetts franchise well
enough to demand that the colony establish a hereditary upper house
of its legislature as the condition on which they would immigrate.
John Cotton, assigned the unenviable job of answering them, charac-
teristically hedged on most of the demands and did his best to mis-
represent the magistracy as a house of lords. But even Cotton balked at
identifying hereditary social status with political privilege: "Though
we receive them [gentlemen] with honor and allow them pre-eminence

60. Jackson Turner Maine provides the most complete survey to date of the
social structure of New England and the middle colonies in *The Social Structure
of Revolutionary America* (Princeton, N.J., 1965), chapter 1. His conclusions,
however, seem more appropriate to the seventeenth and early eighteenth century than to the New England of the American Revolution. Biases inherent in
his sources led him to overlook the possibility of an increasing polarization
of late eighteenth-century society because of overpopulation. Cf. Kenneth
Lockridge, "Land, Population and the Evolution of New England Society
1630–1790," *Past and Present* 39 (April 1968): 62–80; Kenneth Lockridge,
"Communication," *William and Mary Quarterly*, 3d ser., 25 (1968): 516–17.
    61. *History of Plymouth Plantation* (Boston, 1912), 1 : 302–03.

and accommodations to their condition, yet we do not, ordinarily, call them forth to the power of election, or administration of magistracy, until they be received as members into some of our churches. . . . Hereditary honors both nature and scripture doth acknowledge . . . but hereditary authority and power standeth only by the civil laws of some commonwealths." Besides, "if God should not delight to furnish some of their posterity with gifts fit for magistracy, we should expose them rather to reproach and prejudice, and the commonwealth with them, than exalt them to honor, if we should call them forth when God doth not, to public authority."[62]

For all its adherence to time-honored social doctrine, Puritanism on both sides of the ocean contained a strong radical streak that set up an absolute standard by which even traditional authority and the authority of tradition must be judged and discarded if found wanting.[63] In England this fact cost Charles I his head; New England had less trouble with wicked rulers or ungodly authority and so less need to invoke the unsettling slogan, "resistance to tyranny is obedience to God." But even Massachusetts took only a short time to discover that in carrying out a holy mission in a corrupt world not even gentlemen who *were* church members could be automatically entrusted with all the powers that went with their rank in England. When Henry Vane, Esq., son of the comptroller of the royal household, came over in 1636 he quickly joined the Boston church, and on the basis of his lineage the freemen just as quickly elected him governor. During the crisis over Ann Hutchinson's Antinomian heresies a few months after his election, Vane, to Winthrop's horror, sided with the Hutchinsonians and actually led a move with two other magistrates to censure the Rev. John Wilson for his dogged defense of orthodoxy. Winthrop soon learned the awful lesson that superiors govern by bad example as well as good:

> It was strange to see, how the common people were led, by example, to condemn him [Wilson] in that, which (it was probable) divers of them did not understand, nor the rule which he was supposed to have broken; and that such as had known him so long, and what good he had done for that church, should fall

62. Quoted in Thomas Hutchinson, *History of the Colony and Province of Massachusetts-Bay*, 1 : 411–13.
63. See below, pp. 162–65.

upon him with such bitterness for justifying himself in a good cause; for he was a very holy, upright man, and for faith and love inferior to none in the country, and most dear to all men.[64]

The Antinomians were overcome and banished, and Vane was dropped from the magistracy in 1637. He returned to England in disgust, but the experience had been a painful one for the Bay Colony: mere rank coupled with professed piety did not always qualify a man for government. The Rev. Thomas Shepard of Cambridge, preaching the election sermon in 1638, made sure to point out to the assembled freemen the appropriate moral of Vane's apostacy. In one mordant breath he destroyed the whole of the tenuous structure of qualification and prevarication that John Cotton had constructed to bedazzle Lord Say and Sele and Lord Brook:

> let any come over among us never so nobly descended never so pious. Let men seeme to be never so fayre some good estate, it may be their judgments or harts may be so corrupt and apt to be caryed by private respects that [they are] troublers not keepers of vineyards: and hence: none chosen till the freemen know and give their voluntary assent thereto: known for wisdom holiness publicke spirit[.][65]

In the future the freemen would exercise more caution in their choice of magistrates but they would not abandon their attachment to order or to distributive justice. New Englanders remained Europeans as well as Puritans, traditionalists as well as innovators, and most of their assumptions about hierarchy and order would have gone down as well with William Laud as with William Ames. Yet Ames did live his life in exile in Holland, Laud did end his on Tower Hill, and twenty thousand Englishmen did find it necessary to migrate to New England. Shepard's words on Vane revealed revolutionary potentials that had almost been released in 1638 and that would explode with murderous (if ultimately futile) violence at home in England in 1649. In America the same potentials would lie dormant until long after Shepard, Vane, and Winthrop had vanished from the scene—until, in fact, the role of Charles I could obligingly be filled by George III.

64. *Winthrop Journal*, I : 250–51.
65. "Thomas Shepard's Election Sermon," *NEH & GR* 24 (1870): 366.

2 Love

Of of the three divine sanctions for inequality with which the *Model of Christian Charity* begins, the first sounds absurd today, the second rings sophistical, and the third seems cynical. Yet John Winthrop undoubtedly believed them; he was not trying to defend the interests of his class in preaching the *Model*, he was taking up the age-old problem of theodicy, the justification of God's ways to man. He knew inequality existed, he could not believe that God did not—therefore, God must have had reasons for making men as he had, and those reasons had to be good.

The first of them, the argument from plenitude, has already been discussed. The second Winthrop mentioned briefly and then passed on: God had made men imperfect in order to give himself something to do after their creation and in order to allow them an opportunity to manifest certain graces (mercy, gentleness, temperance, faith patience, obedience) that they would not need if all were equal. The bulk of the *Model* concerns the third reason: God created inequality as an inducement to love. Men of unequal talents would "have need of [each] other, and from hence they might be all knitt more nearly together in the Bond of brotherly affeccion."[1] It was to be almost a century before John Wise pointed out that men can cooperate most effectively when they all have an equal right to ask assistance of each other; but by that time Man had become a very different creature than in 1630[2]

The "charity" of Winthrop's title referred not to alms but to love, the concept contained in the Greek word *agape*, translated *caritas* in the Vulgate and rendered as *charity* in some sections of the Geneva and King James Bibles. Winthrop explicitly declined to defend sub-

1. *Winthrop Papers*, 2 : 283. William Perkins also founded society on love and inequality (*Works*, 1 : 732).
2. John Wise, *A Vindication of the Government of the New England Churches*, ed. Perry Miller (Gainesville, Fla., 1958), p. 41. This is a reprint of the edition of 1717.

ordination as the only proper division of labor or as the most beautiful and natural scheme. Such arguments appealed only to the reason, and after the Fall the reason was unreliable.

> the way to drawe men to the workes of mercy is not by force of Argument from the goodnes or necessity of the worke, for though this course may enforce a rationall minde to some present Act of mercy as is frequent in experience, yet it cannot worke such a habit in a Soule as shall make it prompt upon all occasions to produce the same effect but by frameing these affections of love in the hearte which will as natively bring forthe the other, as any cause doth produce the effect.

Men "walked" toward one another by two rules, justice and mercy, but Winthrop intended "to omitt the rule of Justice as not propperly belonging to this purpose." Similarly, though both "the law of nature" ("the morrall law") and the "law of grace" ("the law of the gospell") regulated human conduct, he chose to concentrate on the latter, abandoning any intention to call on men to love their neighbors as themselves while the self remained corrupt. In the *Model*, social dinstinctions rest exclusively on love.

Many thinkers both before and after the Reformation had considered love an essential, even the essential basis of society, but they all talked of the love of the law of nature, the command given to man in his innocency, and Winthrop knew that men had lost their innocence. The rule he would have his listeners obey did not propound "one man to another, as the same fleshe and Image of god" but "as a brother in Christ allsoe, and in the Communion of the same spirit and soe teaches us to put a difference betweene Christians and others."[3]

He said Christians but he meant regenerate Christians, men who had experienced saving grace. Love in Puritan logic sprang from faith and faith from God's mere and free grace.[4] Before the Fall Adam had the principle of love in him naturally, but by his disobedience he rent not only himself from his creator but "all his posterity allsoe one from another."[5] The self and self-love were two of the results. Win-

3. *Winthrop Papers*, 2 : 283–84, 288.
4. William Perkins, *A Commentary upon the Epistle to the Galatians* in *Works*, 2 : 313; John Downame, *The Christian Warfare*, p. 125.
5. *Winthrop Papers*, 2 : 290.

throp would undoubtedly have followed Thomas Hooker in defining the self as "those Principles and Opinions which by Nature, now corrupted, are in every one, and incline him to establish his own independecie of any other whatsoever, yea even of God Himselfe, and to crook every thing toward himself, so making himselfe the sole end of his thoughts, words and actions," or more briefly as "*our owne will to be or have any thing contrary to the will of God.*" Many generations later, men would dignify that emotion with the title of "individualism" but for Hooker and his contemporaries it was "the Devils first *Handsale,* his *Masterpiece* that *Grand Fundamentall Designe* on which he has built his *Kingdom* ever since."

By contrast "Self-Denyal," the realization that nothing existed apart from God, Hooker called "the very Foundation of Christianity, yea the *Grand Designe* of all *Theologie.*" All vice proceeded from self-love, all virtue from self-denial, and charity rested totally on the latter. Only grace could enable men to conquer self-love. By themselves they had an "utter Imbecility, to subdue it."[6] Winthrop summarized the doctrine concisely: "every man is borne with this principle in him, to love and seeke himselfe onely and thus a man continueth till Christ comes and takes possession of the soule, and infuseth another principle love to God and our brother." Regenerate men recognized the same gracious principle in other regenerate men, they themselves possessed and loved them for it, realizing they were now reunited, however imperfectly, with each other and with the body of God.

> soe the ground of love is an apprehension of some resemblance in the things loved to that which affectes it, this is the cause why the Lord loves the Creature, soe farre as it hath any of his Image in it, he loves his elect because they are like himselfe, he beholds them in his beloved sonne. . . . Thus it is betweene the members of Christ, each discernes by the worke of the spirit his owne Image and resemblance in another, and therefore cannot but love him as he loves himselfe.[7]

While men retained what Hooker called "this vile, vain *Body* of ours," regeneration was imperfect and so consequently was love and

---

6. *Heautonaparnumenos or a Treatise of Self-Denyall,* pp. 22, 24–25, 5–7, 56.
7. *Winthrop Papers,* 2 : 290.

reunion in one mystical body; but even on earth men were in some
sense knit together by love with one another and with Christ. "Christ
and his church make one body: the severall partes of this body considered aparte before they were united were as disproportionate and
as much disordering as soe many contrary quallities or elements but
when christ comes and by his spirit and love knitts all these partes to
himselfe and each to other, it is become the most perfect and best
proportioned body in the world."[8]

This doctrine of an almost physical tie between members of the
Invisible Church gave new meaning and impact to the Puritan's use
of the time-worn organic metaphors of society and church. When they
spoke of community (a concept some modern writers have strangely
seen fit to praise them for) they did not mean the truism that society
consists of more than a collection of atomized individuals, they meant
Communion in the sacramental sense. Love was a kind of socialized
Eucharist.

The emphasis on regenerate love turned Christian charity in the
neighborhood of Boston into a very different thing from the kind
practiced in London and Lincolnshire. Traditional Christian doctrine
enjoined men to love their neighbors because of their common humanity and because of the image of God that still remained in every
man despite the Fall. Gracious men might deserve an extra share of
love because "that image is renewed and restored in them by the Spirit
of Christ," but grace merely heightened an existing obligation of the
law of nature. It did not (as it did for Winthrop) create an entirely
new obligation peculiar to the saints. William Perkins, in most other
things second only to Moses as a lawgiver to the New England Israel,
had explicitly denied that the "Law of Christ" propounded any new
kind of love, and John Calvin had emphatically rejected any concept
of charity that distinguished between Christians and other men:

> But I say that the whole human race, without exception, are to
> be embraced with one feeling of charity: that here is no distinc-
> tion of Greek or Barbarian, worthy or unworthy, friend or foe,
> since all are to be viewed not in themselves, but in God.[9]

8. Ibid. 288–89.

9. Perkins, *Works*, 2 : 362. Cf. ibid., 1 : 704, 754, 2 : 322, 3 : 310. John
Calvin, *The Institutes of the Christian Religion*, trans. Henry Beveridge, book 2,
chap. 8, par. 55; Cf. ibid., book 3, chap. 7, par. 5–6.

The image of the saints united together in one body with Christ at its head traditionally symbolized the church, visible or invisible. Conceiving of civil society in the same terms, the New England Puritans accomplished their first significant break with European precedent, as the Europeans themselves were quick to note. English contemporaries rightly considered the most peculiar feature of the New England Way the Bay Colony's singular insistence on communion in some established church as the sole qualification for freemanship. Winthrop and his associates had chosen to base their civil commonwealth on principles strikingly similar to those that gave form to their ecclesiastical societies. Like any orthodox New England church, the state in the Bay Colony was founded through a voluntary covenant, admission to voting rights was restricted to the elect, and members were expected to feel the same bonds of communion that united the saints within each of the individual congregations in the colony. Bay Colony Puritans may have completely rejected the idea of a national church and deprived their clergy of formal political power, but in a sense their colony was a true "theocracy."[10] In an age when every progressive polity solved the problem of church and state by methods at least Gelasian and preferably Erastian, the New Englanders chose to found dominion on grace in a manner so literal that they outdid *Unam sanctam.* They were thoroughly reactionary, highly original, and, by consequence, uniquely American.

The New England practice did have a pedigree—a long one—and it had parallels, but it did not have a European equivalent. Much of medieval political thought certainly posited a "theocratic" ideal of sorts. Church and state were really just two different organic forms for one society, the *corpus christianum,* in which priest and prince proceeded to the same end by different means.[11] The Continental Reformers took the concept a step further in the compact, highly cor-

10. Cf. John Cotton's use of "theocracy" in his 1636 letter to Lord Say and Sele, Hutchinson, *The History of the Colony and Province of Massachusetts-Bay,* 1 : 415.
11. Robert C. Walton, *Zwingli's Theocracy* (Toronto, 1967), chap. 2; Otto F. v. Gierke, *Political Theories of the Middle Ages,* trans. Frederic William Maitland (Cambridge, 1900), pp. 9–30. The latter work is Maitland's translation of Gierke's *Das Deutsche Genossenschaftsrecht,* vol. 3, chap. 2, sec. 11. My thinking on this whole subject owes much to Professor Kenneth Lockridge of the University of Michigan.

porate city-states of Switzerland and Germany, where it was literally possible to speak of the city assembly and the Christian congregation as the same group of people. Zwingli used the word *theocracy* to describe the government of Zurich in much the same way John Cotton did in speaking of the ideal of the Bay Colony. Both men meant a commonwealth openly avowing God as its source of authority, but ruled in his name through officers, lay and clerical, chosen in their turn by popular assemblies. Neither Zwingli nor Cotton had in mind an hierocracy, a government by priests alone; both reserved distinct and separate functions for ministers and magistrates; and both men would have objected to either group acting outside is rightful sphere of activity.[12]

Zwingli and Cotton shared a common Reformed Protestantism and, equally important, a similar physical situation: early New England resembled the Swiss and German city-states in the size, compactness, and homogeneity of its population. Some similarity in official aspirations as well is hardly surprising. But history is not made by sermons alone. No one ever actually became a voting citizen of Zurich or Geneva merely by joining its church. While the Reformers intensified the ideals of medieval Christianity, the Puritans heightened the zeal of the Reformation almost beyond recognition. New England Puritanism really was Protestantism purified, freed of any of the compromises required by inherited medieval institutions or the need to govern a mixed multitude of inhabitants born rather than selected by their own act of immigration. At the founding of the Puritan colonies and in their earliest decades of existence, New Englanders could be enjoined to love their neighbors as fellow saints, not fellow men; and the New England body politic could be defined as another more literal body, not just the *corpus christianum* but the *corpus christi.*

The continent could at least offer the New Englanders analogies if not precedents; the England of their birth offered neither. Not even

12. Walton, *Zwingli's Theocracy*, chaps. 1, 13, and passim. In addition to Walton's book several other studies in English have recently appeared that deal with the relationship of church and state in the Reformation cities: E. William Monter, *Calvin's Geneva* (New York, 1967); Gerald Strauss, *Nuremberg in the Sixteenth Century* (New York, 1968); Miriam U. Chrisman, *Strasbourg and the Reform* (New Haven, 1967).

the Levellers had so radical a conception of society, if the word *radical* is not taken as synonomous with *democratic*.[13] For a brief moment, in the Barebones Parliament of 1653, there was a hint of the practice New Englanders had been employing for over two decades, but it was a moment only. The only consistent English advocates of the immediate restriction of political power to "God's freemen" were the Fifth Monarchy Men, a universally execrated fringe group led in part by former New Englanders.[14] Englishmen for the most part identified church membership with residence and the franchise with property. The electoral laws of Massachusetts, by contrast, took no cognizance of property until 1664 and then only recognized it as a minor *alternative* to church membership. While the old charter stood, the right to vote in Massachusetts functioned not as a means to protect property rights but as the vehicle through which the regenerate expressed their union with each other and with the New England Way.

On the local level this same tight communitarianism—half Christian charity, half tribal bond—became even more important. The organization of the town of Dedham, Massachusetts, for example, also approximated that of a congregational church. The inhabitants incorporated themselves into a social unit by drawing up a written town covenant in which they promised to walk with one another according to the laws of God and the rule of love:

13. The Leveller program or programs are a matter of considerable dispute. It is clear, however, that some of the Levellers continued to identify voting with some sort of property qualification, and it is not clear that any of the Levellers advocated unqualified universal manhood suffrage. C. B. MacPherson argues that all the Levellers advocated a property franchise steep enough to exclude the majority of adult males in *The Political Theory of Progressive Individualism* (Oxford, 1962), pp. 107–36 and appendix. For criticisms of MacPherson, cf. J. C. Davis, "The Levellers and Democracy," *Past and Present* 40 (July 1968): 174–80; Roger Howell, Jr. and Donald E. Brewster, "Reconsidering the Levellers: the Evidence of the Moderate," Ibid. 46 (February 1970): 68–86.

14. Thomas Venner, one of the most extreme leaders of the Fifth Monarchists, and William Aspinwall, one of their most prolific publicists, had both lived in New England. The most recent study of the Fifth Monarchy Men is P. G. Rogers, *The Fifth Monarchy Men* (London, 1966), but Louise F. Brown, *The Political Activities of the Baptists and Fifth Monarchy Men in England during the Interregnum* (Washington, 1912) remains useful.

1 We whose names are here unto subscribed. doe. in the feare
and Reverence of our Allmightie God, Mutually: and severally
promise amongst our selves, and each to other to proffesse and
practice one trueth according to that most perfect rule. the
foundacion where of is Everlasting Love:[15]

To insure that the inhabitants really did carry themselves lovingly,
Dedham employed a mechanism very like the "gospel procedure" by
which church members were supposed to settle their differences. As a
matter of deliberate policy incorporated into the town covenant, the
townspeople agreed to refer their controversies to two or three im-
partial "arbitrators" chosen by the town or by the parties involved,
and for a full half-century the rule of love did take substantial business away from the rule of the law courts. As the seventeenth century
waned so did the practice; the ideal would remain long afterward in
Dedham, and in New England at large, to make the quarrelsome
inhabitants' ordinarily bad consciences a little worse.[16]

The restrictive application of "love thy regenerate neighbor" gave
the imperative an unusual vitality and also a distinctly ominous potential—for not all one's neighbors were regenerate. Winthrop could
not separate the spiritual sheep from the goats aboard the *Arbella*
and probably had no desire to. But once they had established their
Congregational polity in fact as well as in theory, the American Puritans grew more confident of their ability to bring about some sort of
conformity between the invisible and visible churches. By 1636 they
were restricting church membership to those who could provide a reasonable proof of having experienced a work of saving grace. It seems
likely that many, possibly most, of the first settlers could comply;
future generations would not be so fortunate.[17]

Winthrop did not have to face that problem. To him and his generation love to God and man was not just the English translation of
some New Testament Greek, but a real, vivid passion in which *agape*,
philos, and *eros* were all combined. When it came to writing of love,

15. *Dedham Records*, 3 : 2.
16. Ibid., pp. 2–3; Kenneth Alan Lockridge, *A New England Town, The
First Hundred Years* (New York, 1970), pp. 6, 13–15.
17. The development of the concept of restricted church membership is the
main subject of Edmund S. Morgan's *Visible Saints*, especially pp. 94–106.
Statistics on the church membership of adult males are given in appendix A.

the governor, whose literary style was ordinarily sobriety itself, sought his images in the Song of Solomon. To his God he prayed, "Let us heare that sweet voice of thine, my love my dove, my undefiled . . . make us sicke with they love," and on taking final leave of an old friend, Sir William Springe, he wrote:

> I loved you truely before I could think that you took any notice of me: but now I embrace you and rest in your love: and delight to solace my first thoughts in these sweet affections of so deare a friend. The apprehension of your love and worth togither have overcome my heart, and removed the veil of modestye, that I must needes tell you, my soule is knitt to you as the soule of Jonathan to David: were I now with you, I should bedowe that sweet bosome with the teares of affection: O what a pinche will it be to me, to parte with such a friende! If any Embleme may expresse our Condition in heaven, it is this Communion in love.[18]

If communion meant anything at all, it meant unity. "The Kingdom of God," Thomas Shepard wrote, "is not divided against itself."[19] The rich would not oppress the poor, men would deprive themselves to aid others and not follow their own interests, inferior would not rise against superior, superior would have respect for inferior, and everyone would find his satisfaction in the prosperity of the whole of which love made him an inseparable part.

> Wee must be knitt together in this worke as one man, we must entertaine each other in brotherly affection, we must be willing to abridge our selves of our superfluities, for the supply of others necessities, wee must uphold a familiar Commerce together in all meekenes, gentlenes, patience and liberallity, wee must delight in eache other, make others Condicions our owne rejoyce together, mourne together, labour, and suffer together, allwayes haveing before our eyes our Commission and Community in the worke, our Community as members of the same body, soe shall wee keepe the unitie of the spirit in the bond of peace.[20]

18. John Winthrop to Sir William Springe, 8 February 1629/30, *Winthrop Papers*, 2 : 205–06.

19. Election Sermon of 1638, *NEH&GR*, 24 : 364

20. *Winthrop Papers*, 2 : 294.

"Unitie" often included sheer physical closeness. "Society in all sorts of human affairs is better than solitariness" wrote John Cotton, who had no use for "popish anchorites and hermits who think solitary life a state of perfection."[21] Massachusetts Bay may have been originally planned as a single enormous town,[22] and the leaders of both the Bay and Plymouth colonies viewed geographical dispersion with suspicion. Winthrop tried to block the removal of Thomas Hooker and his Cambridge congregation to Connecticut on the grounds "that, in point of conscience, they ought not to depart from us, being knit to us in one body, and bound by oath to seek the welfare of this commonwealth."[23] Winthrop's Plymouth counterpart, Governor William Bradford, thought extensive farming would be the ruin of New England:

> no man now [1632] thought he could live, except he had cattle and a great deale of ground to keep them; all striving to increase their stocks. By which means they were scattered all over the bay, quickly, and the towne, in which they lived compactly till now, was left very thine, and in a short time allmost desolate. And if this had been all, it had been less, though to much; but the church must also be divided, and those that had lived so long together in christian and comfortable fellowship must now part and suffer many divisions. . . . And this, I fear, will be ruine of New England, at least of the churches of God there, and will provock the Lords displeasure against them.[24]

From Bradford to Timothy Dwight, one wing of the Puritan intel-

21. *A Brief Exposition of Ecclesiastes*, pp. 44–45.
22. On this point see Rutman, *Winthrop's Boston*, pp. 280–83, and on the effects of geographical dispersion on the Puritan ideal, ibid., pp 96–97.
23. *Winthrop Journal*, 1 : 167.
24. *History of Plymouth Plantation*, 2 : 152–53. Like Plymouth from 1624 to 1632, Massachusetts Bay from 1636 to 1640 had laws in effect forbidding the inhabitants to live more than half a mile from the meeting house of a settled town, although given the dates of the Massachusetts law this may have been simply for the purpose of defense against the Indians rather than to keep community. The laws have no preambles (*Mass. Rec.*, 1 : 157, 181, 291).

ligentsia regarded dispersion with hostility no matter how inevitable it became in a land of expanding population and unsettled areas.[25]

In such a scheme of values the most serious social misconduct had to consist in the clearest breaches of the organic fabric of society: covetousness (seeking the self over the common good), faction, and contentions, especially that "spiritual pride" that caused inferiors to resist their superiors. "A going aside to make a party" and "disturbance of unity" Winthrop called "sedition," and promptly banished the Antinomians to Rhode Island as seditionists.[26] That remedy was usually reserved for extreme cases. The real cure for all divisiveness, economic and political, William Hubbard reminded the Massachusetts General Court in 1676, was a renewal of Christian charity:

> Could we but get our hearts stored with this Christian virtue, it would prove as a Balm out of Gilead, a sovereign remedy against all our troubles. This grace of charity in the compleat and perfect exercise thereof would heal all our divisions, reform all our vices, root out all our disorders, make up all our breaches. . . . So for other Maladies and Distempers in our minds, or distresses in our outward Estates, charity would be like the Widows Oyle, that would never cease running till it had filled all the vessels.[27]

New Englanders turned out to be a contentious lot, but they thought enough of love to make it the basis of their church and town covenants and to try to live by it, even if with mixed success. God did

25. Increase Mather managed to tie in geographical dispersion with covetousness, and both themes with his favorite subject, the degeneration of New England (*An Earnest Exhortation to the Inhabitants of New England* [Boston, 1676], pp. 9–10). Alan Heimert has argued convincingly that the Puritan attitude toward frontier expansion included a good deal of satisfaction and enthusiasm for the spreading of the gospel in previously uninhabited parts and the "conquest" of the wilderness. Only their appreciation of the divisiveness of the westward expansion kept New Englanders from all-out praise of the movement ("Puritanism, the Wilderness and the Frontier," *The New England Quarterly* 26 [1953]: 361–82).

26. Charles Francis Adams, ed., *Antinomianism in the Colony of Massachusetts Bay, 1636–1638* (Boston, 1894), pp. 204–07, 214–16.

27. William Hubbard, *The Happiness of a People*, pp. 61–62. Cf. Thomas Walley in the Plymouth election sermon of 1669, *Balm in Gilead to Heal Sions Wounds* (Cambridge, Mass., 1669), pp. 17–19.

not expect regenerate men to abandon all their sinful ways; he only required them to try and to understand their own disobedience. "We are to *Hate* our *selves* and *ours* when they are contrary to *Christ*," Thomas Hooker had written; and his readers managed to turn self-hate into an art form, denouncing their own failings with staggering eloquence. They were not really any more sinful than other men, though they delighted to claim they were; they were only more conscious of the extent and ugliness of their sins.[28]

Just misbehaving at the same rate as other men put the Puritans' love to a severe test. Given their insistence on voluntarism and their own confessedly imperfect natures, occasions for divisions were inevitable, especially when it came to settling matters of religion or land distribution. Each dispute, each instance of contention brought forth from society fresh exclamations of outrage, fresh claims to be scandalized at the lack of communion, fresh lamentations over the decay of the ideals on which the colonies were founded. No one seemed to appreciate that the very cries that New England had lost its original values testified to continuing vitality of those values. To practice completely as they preached the Puritans would have had to be something more than human—or something less. They paid their standards honor enough in codemning themselves every time they fell short of them.

Indeed, the Puritans were too attached to unity ever to be able to achieve it. Often enough the need for unity itself encouraged the hated geographical fragmentation because Puritan society could maintain its homogeneity only by the expulsion or withdrawal of dissidents. The settlement of Rhode Island by Gortonists, Hutchinsonians, and followers of Roger Williams, all of them exiles from the Bay Colony, is a familiar story; but the same fissiparous tendencies occurred on the local level for reasons more mundane than disagreements over God's free grace or the nature of the Trinity. When a large minority of the townspeople of Sudbury in 1655 opposed a more liberal system of land distribution, its proponents removed and founded Marlborough eight miles away. Both parties were "united"

---

28. *Heautonaparnumenos: or a Treatise of Self-Denyall*, p. 26. On the "Jeremiad" and its significance see below, chapter 4.

after that and both remained under the jurisdiction of Massachusetts Bay, but the covenant that bound them together as townsmen had been rent, and two towns stood where one had before.[29]

Love could and did justify conciliation as well as separation, and unity could be achieved through inclusion as well as exclusion. By the end of the seventeenth century many men were arguing for religious toleration on the basis of charity, which "makes us not only love God, but those whom God loves; he that loves him that begat, loves him also that is begotten, because he is a son of God, not because he is of the same opinions, or that this or that quality in him is pleasing."[30] Even in the first decades of settlement the mature and perceptive Winthrop sometimes convinced his fellow magistrates to give in to the people on disputed points, though still convinced of their own opinions, because this would preserve unity.[31] But from the founding of New England the Puritans tended to identify love and exclusiveness, to avoid disunity simply by eliminating or excluding all potentially divisive members. Following the provision on love in the Dedham town covenant came a second term that, together with the first, might have served as the basic program of the whole Bay Colony:

> 2 That we shall by all means Laboure to keepe of[f] from us all such. as are contrarye minded. And receave only such unto us as be such as may be probably of one harte, with us that we either knowe or may well and truely be informed to walke in a peaceable conversation with all meekenes of spirit for the edification of each other in the knowledg and faith of the Lord Jesus: And the mutuall encouragement unto all Temporal comforts in all

29. Sumner C. Powell, *Puritan Village*, pp. 169–70. Interestingly, a council of Sudbury's neighbors unsuccessfully attempted to intervene in the dispute in 1655 in order to determine "such further course . . . as may most conduce to the Glory of God and the Unity of their hearts to Unity in truth and praier, according to the rule of the Gospel" (Ibid., pp. 166–69).

30. Daniel Dennison, *Irenicon*, p. 211. Cf. John Oxenbridge, *New England's Freemen Warmed and Warned* (Cambridge, Mass., 1673), pp. 37–38; Cotton Mather, *The Way to Prosperity*, printed with *The Wonderful Works of God* (Boston, 1690), pp. 30, 32.

31. See below, chapter 3.

things: seekeing the good of each other out of all which may be derived true Peace.[32]

No one at the time realized that this statement sounded inappropriate in the mouths of men who refused to separate from the Church of England for fear of breaking charity, and who justified their coming to the New World on the grounds that they would provide a beacon and a model for all men in the Old. As time passed and fewer people could claim an experience of saving grace and the privileges that went with it, "love" came more and more to be a tribal devotion to the offspring of the elect alone, and "unity" the preservation of their purity without reference to the rest of mankind. When Thomas Shepard denounced religious diversity in 1648 and declared that "I would not have a godly man to go into the company of an erroneous person; his words are infectious";[33] he failed to see that in keeping the godly joined together in orthodoxy he simultaneously broke their ties with humanity.

This feature of "tribalism" has received considerable attention elsewhere,[34] but it had another, neglected aspect, uglier though less obvious. Members of the tribe remained the only legitimate objects of love just so long as they kept strictly to its rules. Once expelled, their former brethren regarded them with a hate stronger than any feeling they had toward the mixed multitude who had never shared in the privileges of the elect in the first place. John Winthrop, more moderate than most, could invoke the rule of mercy in 1643 to justify aid to the French Catholic La Tour in his struggle against a rival governor of Acadia, but he denied that the same rule applied to suspected Antinomians in 1637. "A man is not a fit object of mercy except he be in miserye," and a Catholic nobleman with a fleet and soldiers was

32. *Dedham Records,* 3 : 2. Nathaniel Ward defended Ipswich's policy of exclusion in 1635 on the grounds that in their isolated condition the settlers "had need to be strong and of a homogeneous spirit and people, as free from dangerous persons as we may" (*Winthrop Papers,* 3 : 216).

33. *Wine for Gospel Wantons* (Boston, 1668), pp. 8–11, 14.

34. Edmund S. Morgan named the phenomenon "tribalism" and delineated its symptoms, an exclusive devotion to the offspring of the elect, in *The Puritan Family,* chapter 7.

somehow more miserable than an Antinomian immigrant desiring permanent resident in Massachusetts.[35]

The Antinomian crisis of 1637 to 1638 displayed the concept of love at its best and worst, before it became totally corrupted. In the name of love the orthodox majority of the Bay Colony at first tried to accommodate the heretical minority and only reluctantly made up its mind to cast them out; but once the Antinomians were outside the tribal bond, the orthodox turned on them with a fury approaching outright sadism. The General Court convicted the Antinomian leader John Wheelright, brother-in-law of Anne Hutchinson, of sedition in May 1637 but deferred sentence, "having now power enough to have crushed them [the Antinomians], [so that] their moderation and desire of reconcilliation might appear to all." The same session of the court passed an order "to keep out all such persons as might be dangerous to the commonwealth" and then allowed Winthrop to administer it very leniently.

By July, Winthrop was writing in his journal that "the differing grew so much here, as tended fast to a separation." When a synod convened on 30 August managed to squeeze into line John Cotton, whose theology the Antinomians claimed to follow, the orthodox party found it had gone as far toward comprehension as it could. Wheelright's party continuing obstinate despite their having been (in Winthrop's opinion) "clearly confuted and confounded," the General Court on 2 November 1637 "finding upon consultation that two so opposite parties could not contain in the same body, without apparent hazard of ruin to the whole, agreed to send away some of the principal." The Antinomian leaders and their most ardent followers were ejected from the Bay Colony, the Boston Church first admonishing and then excommunicating the prophetess of the movement, Anne Hutchinson. Two of Mrs. Hutchinson's sons cast the only votes against the admonition, whereupon the church immediately admonished them too for "a breach upon the honour of Christ." Boston would have unanimity one way or another.[36]

35. *Winthrop Journal*, 2 : 136–37; "A Declaration in Defense of an order of the Court Made in May, 1637," *Winthrop Papers*, 3 : 424.
36. *Winthrop Journal*, 1 : 265, 267, 278, 277, 291–92, 306. Adams, *Antinomianism in Massachusetts Bay*, pp. 223–24.

After the expulsion of the Hutchinsonians Winthrop eagerly collected information on their subsequent misfortunes, devoting over
several pages of his journal to detailed descriptions of the monstrous
children born to Anne Hutchinson and to Mary Dyer, one of her followers, as the Almighty's confirmation of the monstrousness of the
women's heresies.[37] Earlier, on 31 October 1636, when affairs were
still being carried "lovingly" in the Boston Church, Winthrop had
addressed John Wheelright, his fellow church member, as "brother"
and "professed that he did love that brother's person, and did honor
the gifts and graces of God in him."[38] But if Wheelright was Winthrop's brother, Mary Dyer was his sister. She became a member of
the Boston Church in 1635 and, despite her removal to Rhode Island
in 1638, the church held that the ties of love still bound her and
never dismissed or excommunicated her,[39] not even in 1660 when
she was hanged on Boston Common as a Quakeress. Such inconsistent
behavior did not make Winthrop a hypocrite: his feelings were real,
both his love for Wheelright in 1636 and his deep satisfaction at
Mary Dyer's monster in 1638. During the year and a half between
the two journal entries the Antinomians had ceased to be erring men-
bers of the tribe who were worthy of conciliation, and had become
rebels against it, to be cast out and left to Jehovah's vegeance.

37. *Winthrop Journal*, 1 : 313–17, 326–28. The fact that Mrs. Hutchinson
later ran afoul of some Indians in Westchester County, New York, and had
her head bashed in was received with considerable jubilation by the orthodox
(Adams, pp. 93–94).

38. *Winthrop Journal*, 1 : 241–42.

39. For Mary Dyer's admission to the Boston Church see *The Records of
the First Church in Boston 1630–1868*, Publ. CSM, 39–41, ed. Richard D.
Pierce (Boston, 1961), p. 90. The church records do not show any trace of a
sentence of excommunication on her. She was certainly still considered a
member in 1639 when the church sent messengers up to Rhode Island to
inquire into questionable behavior on the part of individuals still bound to
them by covenant in the ties of love. One of the Antinomians, Francis Hutchinson,
even sent a letter requesting a formal dismissal and was refused on the grounds
that there was no church to dismiss him to. In 1645, on hearing that one Rhode
Island exile was accused of adultery, the church sent for him and excommunicated him when he naturally failed to come (Rutman, *Winthrop's Boston*, p.
155). When John Winthrop exulted over Mary Dyer's monstrous child, he
was as formally bound to mourn and rejoice with her as with Wheelright.

In the seventeenth century individuals of the most varied religious persuasions shared the tendency to see the misfortunes of their enemies as divine judgments, but it took Winthrop to identify his opponents' sins with crimes against the tribe and to record their punishments in his diary as proof of "the presence and power of God in his ordinances, and his blessing upon his people, while they endeavor to walk before him with uprightness."[40] He did not limit the scope of the Lord's wrath to outright heretics and profane scoffers, but went on to include "others, though godly, who have spoken ill of his country, and discouraged the hearts of his people." John Humphrey, one of the original members of the Massachusetts Bay Company, abandoned the people of God in 1641 and advocated abandoning New England for Providence Isle: he subsequently suffered great financial hardships, one of his daughters went mad, and two others, both under ten, were discovered to have been repeatedly "abused by divers persons." Similar misfortunes befell others who deserted New England "upon like grounds." Such people had earned their fates, in Winthrop's view, because they violated the tribal bond:

> For such as come together into a wilderness, where are nothing but wild beasts and beastlike men, and there confederate together in civil and church estate, whereby they do, implicitly at least, bind themselves to support each other, and all of them that society, whether civil or sacred, whereof they are members, how they can break from this, without free consent, is hard to find, so as may satisfy a tender or good conscience in time of trial.[41]

Massachusetts as a whole was no less a covenanted society than John Cotton's First Church of Boston; deserting the one or the other

---

40. *Winthrop Journal*, 1 : 387. Winthrop was talking about some remarkable prodigies "discovering hypocrites and other lewd persons, and bringing them their deserved punishment." He tended to reserve his greatest wrath, not for outright sinners or even heretics, but for those within the tribe who were secretly hostile to it.

41. Ibid., 2 : 13–16, 104–05. Cf. Winthrop's comments on the fate of Capt. Daniel Patrick (2 : 182). Winthrop always connected an individual's downfall with God's love for the people of Massachusetts. He recorded such things in his journal "so that it will appear how the Lord hath owned this work and preserved and prospered his people here beyond ordinary ways of providence" (2 : 13).

violated communion sufficiently to provoke one form of judgment or
another. Everything Winthrop wrote about the unfortunate Humphrey tallied exactly with the descriptions Cotton gave of the ways in
which the Lord punished *church* members who similarly removed
from their brethren for selfish or frivolous reasons:

> But when men thus depart, God usually followeth them with
> a bitter curse: either taking away their lives from them, or blast-
> ing them with povertie, or exposing them to scandall where they
> come, or in entertaining them with such restlesse agitations, that
> they are driven to repent of their former rashnesse, and many
> times to desire to returne to the Church, from which they had
> broken away.[42]

Tribal thinking received additional force from the inclination to
identify with the Israel of the Old Testament, especially as the size of
the twelve Puritan tribes dwindled with the passing of the first generation and the coming to maturity of a second far less disposed to
see in itself the workings of saving grace. Puritans realized that external pressure brought about internal cohesion centuries before so-
ciologists announced it, and used their knowledge to strengthen the
internal bond, love.[43] Even Winthrop in his *Model of Christian
Charity* had spoken of New Englanders as united through a "Community of perill": because the stakes in their venture were so high,
the potential rewards and punishments so great, they must be knit
together as one man in their work if they were to avoid the most ap-
palling calamities.[44] Later writers, inclined to build the community by

---

42. *The Way of the Churches of Christ in New England* (London, 1645),
p. 105. Cf. Larzer Ziff, "The Social Bond of the Church Covenant," *American
Quarterly* 10 (1958): 454–62.

43. The Rev. John Higginson of Salem wrote Winthrop about the Pequot
War in May 1637:" whether now the Lord begins not to send (as shepards
use to do their dogs to fetch in their stragling sheep so he) the Indians upon
his servants, to make them cleave more close together, and prize each other,
to prevent contention of Brethren which may prove as hard to break as Castle
barres, and stop their now beginning breaches before they be as the letting out
of many waters that cannot be gathered in againe, etc." (*Winthrop Papers,*
3 : 404).

44. Ibid., 2 : 293–95.

emphasizing the peril, quickly converted New England from the promised land to the wilderness where the twelve tribes must wander until purged of worldliness and unified together in the Lord's work. "God in his infinite wisdom did train them up to encounter with Marches and Journeyings in the wilderness, and then acquainted them with the difficulties of a long War, that they might learn obedience by what they underwent."[45]

When William Hubbard delivered his *Happiness of a People* to the assembled freemen, magistrates, and deputies of Massachusetts on election day in 1676, the country was well acquainted with the difficulties of a long war—the massive Indian uprising of King Philip—and Hubbard played the analogy for all it was worth. He took as his ideal only one of the twelve tribes, Issachar, which he considered particularly outstanding for its order and unity. The brethren elected their wisest men as "Heads" and then followed them loyally: "Guidance belongs to their leaders, Obedience to their followers, whose wisdom it is to obey rather than dispute the commands of their Superiors." Issachar in Hubbard's description came out as united, militarized, spirited, tough, disciplined, and hierarchical, the tribe King David found most dependable in war.

Hubbard's sermon included the paeans to order quoted in the preceding chapter; but, like Winthrop in the *Model*, the pastor of Ipswich waived any appeal to a natural order comprehensible to the reason. Issachar did not learn its good order from a prudent observation of the seasons and "God in nature"; rather the tribe became exemplary through "long experience of the calamities and service of Warr."[46] If New England would have the virtues of Issachar, Hubbard explained at the end of the sermon, it must cultivate Christian charity and the good order that went with it.[47] The community of peril had reached its ultimate development: agape had become a military virtue, the tie that united Israel's judges with Israel's people in the fear-induced discipline necessary to control a hostile population of Philistines.

45. William Hubbard, *The Benefit of a Well-Ordered Conversation*, pp. 53–54. Cf. Alan Heimert, "Puritanism, the Wilderness and the Frontier," pp. 361–62.
46. Pp. 1–7 passim.

The wars of the Lord could not last forever: even the children of Israel entered Canaan after forty years in the wilderness. All the military analogies, all the perils of New England life, all the instances of God's condign punishment of apostates could not stop the number of church members from declining to the point where the larger part of society ceased to be under the moral obligations of regenerate love. Then it became necessary to reinvoke order and to remind men of the rule of justice Winthrop had so casually omitted in 1630.

But order in the eighteenth century was a far different thing from what it had been in the seventeenth. The charter of Massachusetts, the foundation of its holy commonwealth, had fallen in 1685 with the inauguration of royal government in the colony under the short-lived Dominion of New England. When a local version of the Glorious Revolution overthrew the dominion in 1689, the new charter Massachusetts received saddled the colony with a royal governor and required religious toleration. At the same time a new suffrage law in the Bay Colony substituted a simple property qualification for the old requirement of church membership as the prerequisite for freemanship. Connecticut and Rhode Island were able to resume their old charters in 1689, but in all of New England the government could not, and eventually would not, cooperate as closely with the church in establishing the Puritan social ideal as it had before 1685.[48]

No longer certain of their ability to call on the power of the state, Puritan thinkers had to construct a variety of new, extralegal institutions to take the place of coercive legal power in enforcing social discipline. Of all those who applied themselves to the problem, Solomon Stoddard, minister of Northampton, proved the most thoroughgoing. Since the requirement of actually having experienced saving grace kept most men from coming to full communion, and thereby from

47. God sent the war to purge New England of its divisions and to bring about love and unity. "He uses to sit as a Refiner over his fire. And when he hath prepared the Soyle by ploughing and harrowing he will cast in the precious Seed. . . . God doth not at any time willingly afflict the Children of men, but at no time over afflict them" (p. 60).

48. The changes in the New England mentality that took place after 1685 form the subject of Perry Miller's *The New England Mind, From Colony to Province* (Boston, 1961), chapters 11-28. The final section of this chapter is heavily indebted to this book, especially to the discussions of Stoddard and Mather in chapters 15 and 24.

being subject either to the duties of love or to church discipline, the solution lay in dropping the requirement by redefining the sacrament as a saving ordinance rather than as a mere seal of conversion. All but the most reprobate could then be gathered into the bosom of the church, subject to godly discipline and exhortation and to a minister whose administration of the Lord's Supper gave him the keys to heaven. The new members probably discovered that ecclesiastical order did not differ much from civil: "A church is not a confused body of people, but they are brought into order, and each one must observe his proper station: It is compared to a natural body, wherein there are divers organs appointed to their peculiar services." Stoddard also compared it to an army.[49]

"Stoddardeanism," opening the communion service to all, flourished in the Connecticut River Valley, but eastern Massachusetts under the leadership of Increase and Cotton Mather rejected the western innovations. Cotton Mather was prepared to go part way with Stoddard, for all the fury with which he and his father denounced the minister of Northampton. He advocated admitting individuals who were free from scandal and willing to "own" the church covenant into a halfway membership where they could secure baptism for themselves and their children and be under church discipline; but he still denied them the right to come to the Lord's Supper without the traditional requirement of saving grace.[50] Yet at the same time he tried to make it easier for the members of his congregation to have the requisite experience by emphasizing the part their own efforts played in the process.[51]

---

49. Solomon Stoddard, *The Way for a People to Live Long in the Land that God hath given them* (Boston, 1703), pp. 4–5.

50. For Mather's stand on this question see *Mather Papers*, 4 *Coll.* MHS, 8 : 397–401. This should not be confused with the Half-Way Covenant, which applied only to the children of parents already baptized and themselves the children of church members. Over the opposition of some of the leading members of his church Mather wanted to extend halfway privileges to all professing adults living a godly life.

51. "If men did in Religion more than they do, & *All* that they could by a *Natural Power* do, there would be a greater likelihood (I say not, a *Certainty*, but a *Likelihood*,) that God would grant them that *Higher Power*; they would be much more in the likely way, of *Coming to a Saviour*" (*A Conquest over the Grand Excuse of Sinfulness and Slothfulness* [Boston, 1712], pp. 28–29).

Mather's main labors for social regulation lay outside the church entirely, in the creation of purely secular organizations independent of either civil or ecclesiastical authorities though cooperating with both. The need to increase good works justified such a step in Mather's view. For all their insistence on salvation by faith alone, Puritans had never slighted good works, but Mather carried the exhortation to do good, as he carried most things, to extremes:

> Tho' the Assertion fly never so much like a *Chain Shot* among us, and Rake down all before it, I will again Assert it; *That we might every One of us do more Good than we do.* And therefore, This is the FIRST PROPOSAL, to be made unto us; *To be Exceedingly Humbled, that we have done so little good in the World.*[52]

The best way to do good was to do it together in an organized fashion through various appropriate community organizations, many of which Mather actually helped found. Doctors, lawyers, and others could form professional associations to aid good works in the course of their callings: physicians by taking advantage of their position to advise their wealthy or powerful patients to do good and their poor ones to repent, lawyers by prodding wealthy clients to leave money for pious uses in their wills, landlords by requiring tenants to read the Bible and hold family worship as part of the terms of their leases. For the better governing of individual neighborhoods Mather recommended the establishment of local, voluntary *"Reforming-Societies"* which should each include at least one minister and one justice of the peace as members. Modeled on the English societies for the reformation of manners, these organizations and similar young men's associations for the voluntary ordering of youth could admonish scandalous and contentious individuals, advise the ministers about special services to religion and the local justices on "the further Promoting of *Good Order*," uncover "*oppression* or *Fraudulence*, in the *Dealings* of any sort of people," humbly suggest laws for public benefit, and succor

52. *Bonifacius* (Boston, 1710), p. 24.

those under sore affliction by giving charity to the poor, medicine to the sick, and comfort to the bereaved.[53]

The functions and methods of these proposed organizations had a familiar ring to them, and when it came to their internal organization the resemblance to the churches became explicit. If any one of the membership fell "into a *Scandalous* Iniquity," the association should first admonish him and then, if he failed to repent, cast him out "until he bring Suitable Expressions and Evidences of *Repentance* with him."[54] Once every four months the association would go over the membership rolls and similarly discipline habitual absentees. This marked the difference between Stoddard and Mather: the former's church sounded like the old conception of civil society, and the latter's civil societies sounded like the older conception of the church.

Mather had chosen to replace both minister and magistrate by voluntary associations exercising coercive power through the force of public opinion alone. To modern sensibilities this program may seem a continuous incitement to busybodyism, one more unpleasant feature of a thoroughly unpleasant man who lived his life in italics and whose ideas of literary style was the exclamation point. Yet for all his incredible bathos Mather at least did something few Puritans before him had even attempted: he said something to the mixed multitude. He may have kept the unregenerate out of full membership in the church but at least he brought them back into society. Perhaps he had to at a time when church membership had ceased to be a requirement for the franchise and when most males, voters and otherwise, did not think

53. Ibid., pp. 127–28, 133, 147, 164. Mather was very active in organizing and directing the activities of his three Boston societies for the reformation of manners. See his *Diary*, 1 : 418, 500, 517. Nothing if not methodical, Mather prepared a "Catalogue of Young Men, who visit wicked houses" for the benefit of the societies so that they might send the errant youngsters written admonitions, and he also made up a "List of the wicked Houses in the Town" (*Diary*, 2 : 160).

54. *Bonifacius*, pp. 85–88. Cf. his proposed organization of "associated families" into private religious societies complete with ministers (ibid., pp. 82–85). Because of Boston's size, Mather could restore the community that came with geographical proximity only by fragmenting the town into neighborhoods.

themselves qualified for full communion. Whatever his motives, when he talked of love he did not restrict it to the elect. The members of his neighborhood religious societies in the midst of minding each other's business were to "look upon themselves, as bound up in one *Bundle of Love;* and count themselves obliged, in very Close and Strong Bonds to be serviceable to one another."[55]

Thanks to Mather and Stoddard and to general human inertia, men could still be exhorted to acknowledge their natural inequality as a basic part of the cosmic order. But Stoddard had destroyed the principle of voluntarism in both church and state, replacing the covenants by exercises of naked power; and Mather, in his own devious way, had also dealt the older ideals a fatal blow by substituting a flaccid moralism for the intense Augustinian piety that had originally given Puritanism its energy and strength. One concept of love had founded New England and another had nearly wrecked its ecclesiastical and social system. In the name of a charity extending to all Christendom, Winthrop and his followers had founded New England to reform a benighted world through the force of their example. Yet they built their exemplary society on a charity so narrowly defined that it restricted the bonds of love to the regenerate, and then even insisted on identifying the regenerate as the ever-dwindling number of New Englanders able to supply clear testimony of a work of saving grace. Ultimately by their own standards, the Puritans failed to convert the world because they failed to convert themselves.

PART TWO

Details

Once the generalities of the treatises are exchanged for the specifics of life in New England, it becomes increasingly difficult to separate the Puritan social ethic from the institutional context in which it functioned. Poverty has no meaning apart from the poor, government no real significance without the governors, and both were often different from their European counterparts. But if the American Puritans broke with their European heritage, they did so inadvertently and for the most European of reasons, assuming all the while that they were building their society according to unchanging divine decrees applicable on either side of the Atlantic. The unprecedented in the New England Way still could find a justification in an English treatise; its originality was the accidental product of inherited misconceptions about the nature of the past. There was simply no one to tell the New Englanders that Christ had not necessarily been a Protestant nor his Apostles Congregationalists.

3 Government: The Character of a Good Ruler

Human society in Puritan thought was an organic union among men created unequal. Differences existed everywhere, in riches, in birth, in intellect, and most importantly in power. A few led, the many followed, and no set of "relative duties" needed or received more attention than those concerning ruler and ruled.[1]

By using the rhetorical device of synecdoche to transform "honor thy father and mother" into "obey thy governors," Puritan exigeticists gave government the status of a divine command and rulers the right to claim their power from God. At the same time so orthodox a minister as John Cotton could also write of "the people, in whom fundamentally all power lyes."[2] That paradoxical being, the Puritan God, instead of establishing government and governors by direct deputation, decided to work through men. Along with saving grace, the regenerate received the inclination to live under government; they formed social covenants to establish civil societies and to choose the men who would run them. The office of ruler came by way of divine command but the form of the office and the choice of the man to fill it lay at the discretion of the people.

The people, however, could not set up any government they found convenient. A state's powers and ends had to conform to the purposes for which God had established all government, and all rulers had to meet the standards he set. If men founded a government by contract, God wrote the terms. When the people of Connecticut actually were founding a government, in 1638, Thomas Hooker reminded them of this point:

> Doctrine. I. That the choice of public magistrates belongs unto the people by God's own allowance.

---

1. On relative duties see above, chapter 1.
2. *An exposition upon the 13th Chapter of the Revelation* (London, 1656) in Perry Miller and Thomas H. Johnson, eds., *The Puritans*, 1 : 213.

II. The privilege of election, which belongs to the people, therefore must not be exercised according to their humors, but according to the blessed will and law of God.[3]

In both Connecticut and Massachusetts election sermon after election sermon for over a century outlined in detail exactly what the blessed will and law of God prescribed. The ruler should not typify the people who elected him but the God whose deputy he became. He must be better than his constituents, a man able to promote public peace, prosperity, and godliness by virtue of his wisdom, learning, piety, religious orthodoxy, courage, integrity, and, above all, his public spirit—"one who prefers the publick Benefit above all private men and separate Interests whatsoever."[4] In 1676, William Hubbard gave his description of a ruler under seven heads: piety and grace, "humane learning," constantcy, moderation, peaceableness (the ability to avoid contention), "condesencion" (humility, a willingness to yield on nonessentials), and deliberation. By "humane learning" Hubbard meant intelligence, education, and experience. "Such as by the benefit of natural parts, Experience, Education, and Study, have advantage above others to be acquainted with the affairs of the world abroad, as well as with the Laws and Customes of their own people at home."[5]

Hubbard's emphasis on the good ruler's moderate and amiable disposition typified Puritan thought on the subject. While the actual New England magistrates sometimes seemed more concerned about testifying to their own personal righteousness than about governing a colony, the magistrate of the Puritan ideal shunned excessive severity. Cotton Mather could think of nothing more praiseworthy in the character of John Winthrop than the governor's ability to temper resolution with condescension and "MODERATION."

> Indeed such was the *mixture* of distant qualities in him, as to make a most admirable temper; and his having a certain great-

3. *Collections of the Connecticut Historical Society*, 1 (1860): 20.
4. Samuel Willard, *The Character of a Good Ruler* (Boston, 1694), pp. 8–13. Cf. Increase Mather, *The Excellency of a Publick Spirit* (Boston, 1702), pp. 2–11.
5. *The Happiness of a People*, pp. 27–33.

ness of soul, which rendered him grave, generous, courageous, resolved, well-applied, and every way a *gentleman* in his demeanour, did not hinder him from taking sometimes the old Roman's way to avoid confusions, namely *Cedendo* [by yielding the point].[6]

On one subject the magistrate should not be moderate: he must hate "covetousness," defined by the Rev. John Oxenbridge as "an earnest intentiveness upon wealth and increase of estate." Oxenbridge added grimly:

> Magistry is not . . . a trading and merchandize but a Ministry, he that dispiseth the gain of oppression, that shaketh his hands from holding of bribes . . . shall hold up his head when all the world is on fire, and such a fire seems kindling now.[7]

Apart from injunctions to avoid using public office as a means for private gain, the writers of election sermons paid very little attention to wealth. Not that a good ruler either could or should be poor; everyone simply assumed that any man elected to high public office would have to be rich to discharge his duties effectively. As early as 1641, William Hawthorne, John Winthrop's most outspoken opponent in the lower house of the Massachusetts legislature, advocated removing Winthrop and another magistrate from their offices "because they were grown poor, and spake reproachfully of them under that motion."[8]

The ministry did not find it necessary to caution against the election of poor magistrates until the very end of the seventeenth century. In 1693, however, the Rev. Increase Mather reminded the freemen that "persons Nominated for Councillors should be men of Estate and some Port in the World" or they would render government contemptible for lack of an "Estate to support the place and

---

6. *Magnalia Christi Americana* (Hartford, 1855), 1 : 120, 128–29.

7. *New England's Freemen Warmed and Warned* (Cambridge, Mass., 1673), pp. 45–46. Cf. Thomas Bridge, *Jethro's Advice Recommended to the Inhabitants of Boston, in New-England, viz. to Chuse Well-qualified Men and Haters of Covetousness, for Town Officers* (Boston, 1710).

8. *Winthrop Journal*, 2 : 67. Cf. Samuel Symonds's letter to John Winthrop quoted above, chapter 1, p. 44.

Dignity of a Ruler." Thereafter the same warning was repeated periodically.[9]

Similarly, most discussions of the character of a good ruler never mentioned the most obvious qualification for public office, superior social standing.[10] Social rank and political power had been so long associated that the people rarely had to be told they must choose only the better sort. The founding generation elected to high office the same sort of gentlemen who had made public service their exclusive prerogative in England (or what would pass for this class in New England); succeeding generations chose either the first magistrates' descendants or men who had managed to attain the same elevated social status by their own efforts in America.[11]

The perfect New England magistrate turned out to be virtuous, prudent, religious, well-educated, wealthy, devoted to the commonweal and, preferably, well born. Puritan speculation had combined Exodus 18 : 20 with the *Nichomachean Ethics* to produce a social ideal not very different from the contemporary English one, that of the country gentleman dedicated to public service, though the Puritan variant was possibly more austere and intensely religious.[12] The real difference lay in the political systems in which the two functioned. An English gentleman in government either inherited his position or received it by commission from some higher power; even if he ran for Parliament he usually had to appeal only to a comparatively select group of electors. In Massachusetts, during most of the lifetime of

9. Increase Mather, *Primitive Counsellors, A Great Blessing* (Boston, 1693), p. 19. Cf. John Barnard, *The Throne Established by Righteousness* (Boston, 1734), pp. 33–34.

10. An exception is John Cotton, who held that the people should "make choice of men of greatest worth for wisdom, for sufficiency, for birth" (*A Brief Exposition on Ecclesiastes* [Edinburgh, 1868], p. 108).

11. If social status was high enough, youth was no bar to public office. In 1636 Henry Vane was elected governor of Massachusetts Bay at the age of twenty-four because his father was comptroller of the King's household. Of the remaining thirteen magistrates in 1636, one was in his twenties and four were in their thirties. Of those four, three had originally been elected while still in their twenties.

12. A comprehensive survey of the contemporary English concept of the gentleman is Ruth Kelso's, *The Doctrine of the English Gentleman in the Sixteenth Century* (Urbana, Ill., 1929), *Univ. of Illinois Studies in Language and Literature*, 14 (1929).

the old charter (1630-86), a much larger number of people could vote, and vote for all the main officers of government. If the number of elective officers narrowed under the new charter (1692-1774), the franchise broadened considerably.[13] The American Puritans assumed that the people of New England would continue in the customary English patterns of political deference towards social superiors even though the political power that would have been held by right of birth and class in England was held only through the suffrage of that very same people in New England.

For more than a century the ideal of political leadership in Massachusetts remained aristocratic in the sense of rule by the best, a group of men selected for their moral and intellectual virtues, not their opinions. "Popularity," electing a man because he favored or opposed a given scheme, not only ignored the valid criteria for a leader, it breached the fifth commandment. Samuel Willard warned the freemen in 1694:

> When a people are divided into Factions; Just, and Wise, and good Men are renounced, & not thought worthy to be made use of, because they favor not the Party that can sway; and such as are hotly zealous for the design, are counted, mer[e]ly by that zeal sufficiently qualified, and to be of all men worthy; this will not promote the Public Good, but only gain to the one side a little more advantage to do hurt.[14]

Elections for magistrates were held annually, but no one spoke of voting as an instrument for the enactment of the popular will. When a voter cast his ballot for a magistrate and an elected magistrate accepted office, both signified their assent to a covenant, an agreement

13. The franchise under the Old Charter is discussed in appendix A. Since the Massachusetts franchise was almost certainly declining during the seventeenth century and the English franchise may have been rising, there very likely came a point about 1680 when, for a brief period, a greater proportion of the population could vote in England than in America. For England, cf. J. H. Plumb, "The Growth of the Electorate in England from 1600 to 1715," *Past and Present* 45 (November, 1969): pp. 90–116. For the franchise in Massachusetts under the new charter see Robert E. Brown, *Middle Class Democracy and the Revolution in Massachusetts, 1691–1780* (Ithaca, N.Y., 1955), pp. 21–52.

14. *The Character of a Good Ruler*, p. 24.

to give obedience in return for government according to the laws of God. The people had the right to remove a ruler only if he broke the covenant by clearly violating God's law—then he could be voted out of office or when necessary eliminated by more drastic means. In this sense and no other a ruler was accountable to the people; otherwise, though they elected him, he did not represent them. It was this system, not some form of representative democracy, that John Cotton meant by the word *aristocracy* in his letter to Lord Say and Sele:

> [Jean] Bodine confesseth, that though it be *status popularis,* where a people choose their owne governors; yet the government is not a democracy, if it be administered, not by the people, but by the governors, whether one (for then it is a monarchy, though elective) or by many, for then (as you know) it is aristocracy.[15]

For the Puritans "democracy" was a question of the relationship between the ruler and the ruled. By the time Cotton wrote his letter (1636) the Bay Colony did have an institution generally regarded as "democraticall": the deputies, elected four times a year to represent the freemen in the quarterly General Courts that made all laws for the colony after 1634.[16] Since the magistrates also sat in the General Court, contemporaries described the system as "mixd" or a "mixd aristocracie," a fair enough name, given their definition of terms.

> Our Civill Government is mixt: the freemen choose the magistrats everye yeare . . . and at 4 Courts in the yeare 3 out of each towne (there being 8 in all) doe assist the magistrats in making of lawes, imposing taxes, and disposing of lands.[17]

An anonymous "small treatise" of 1643, possibly written by John Norton, defined aristocracy as that system "where majesty or su-

15. Thomas Hutchinson, *The History of the Colony and Province of Massachusetts Bay*, 1 : 416–17. B. Katherine Brown argues by contrast, in "A Note on the Puritan Concept of Aristocracy," *Mississippi Valley Historical Review*, 41 (1954): 105–12, that Cotton's and Winthrop's concepts resembled modern notions of representative democracy.

16. During a later political controversy Winthrop noted that both he and his opponent, Richard Saltonstall, agreed "that the Deputyes are the Democraticall parte of our Government" (*Winthrop Papers*, 4 : 383).

17. John Winthrop to Sir Nathaniel Rich, 22 May 1634, *Winthrop Papers*, 3 : 167.

preame civill power is committed by the people to the nobles or superior sort of the people as Gentry," and democracy as a system in which the people committed "majesty" to "any sort of the people." The author called the "present forme of government with us" a mixture of aristocracy and democracy and endorsed the controversial theory that, in order for the government to remain truly mixed, the people must not only elect both the inferior and superior sort of men, but in addition neither sort must be able to act without the other.[18]

The idea of mixed government did not originate with the Puritans, nor did the theory of the social covenant, and they were hardly the first people to face the problem of the source of authority: medieval and Tudor theorists would have found most of their thinking familiar. But in Europe before 1630 most of these ideas and the controversies over them were literally academic, or at best provided justification and some guidance for the contending sides in rivalries between already existing political institutions—pope and emperor, king and parliament. The New World of 1630, by contrast, was really new: the king with historically derived prerogatives and the parliament whose advocates could cite and miscite precedents going back to Edward I were both three thousand miles away. Aside from a few Indians, the American continent offered only a total void in which a disciplined and talented people could create new institutions in conformity to theories of church and state which had been elaborated and debated at length in the Old World but which had never been tried before. For this very reason the details and even many of the ultimate implications of Puritan theory remained fluid and undetermined until given definition by the results of the theory in action. Winthrop explained it quite simply to that incorrigible collector of precedents, Sir Simon D'Ewes:

> what you may doe in England where things are otherwise established, I will not dispute, but our case heere is otherwise: being come to clearer light and more Libertye, which we trust by the good hand of our God with us, and the gratious indulgence of our Kinge, we may freely enjoye it.[19]

18. *Proc.* MHS, 46 (1912–13): 280–81.
19. 21 July 1634, *Winthrop Papers*, 3 : 172. Cf. John Cotton, *A Discourse About Civil Government in a New Plantation whose Design is Religion* (Cambridge, Mass., 1663), pp. 9–11. Sometimes attributed to John Davenport.

The attempt to let the clearer light of Massachusetts dictate political organization began almost as soon as the main body of colonists landed. Winthrop defined a commonwealth as "the counsent of a certaine companie of people, to cohabite together, under one government for their mutual safety and welfare," and such a commonwealth he intended to establish.[20] Although his definition might have come straight out of Sir Thomas Smith's *De Republica Anglorum*,[21] there was one major difference: Queen Elizabeth's principal secretary of state never had the opportunity to establish a government on the principle of consent. For John Winthrop, first governor of Massachusetts Bay, the case was otherwise.

The Charter of the Massachusetts Bay Company gave the governor, assistants, and freemen of the company meeting in a general court absolute authority over the government of the colony. Winthrop, Deputy Governor Thomas Dudley, and the six assistants who had come over with them were also the only freemen of the company then in Massachusetts, so they could have ruled the colony as they pleased. Instead, on 19 October 1630 "for the establishinge of the government," Winthrop and the assistants threw open the freemanship, membership in the Company, to almost all the free adult males then in the colony. In return the freemen would elect their rulers, the assistants, once a year, and the rulers "should have the power of makeing lawes and chuseing officers to execute the same." When this "was fully assented unto by the generall vote of the people, and erreccion of hands," Massachusetts Bay had become a commonwealth with a government established on the principle of consent. A myth of the Old World had come true in the New.[22]

The following May the General Court required that all future freemen belong to one of the colony's churches, but this law did not drastically restrict the franchise at first: a majority of the men in the first

20. "A Declaration in Defense of an Order of Court Made in May, 1637," *Winthrop Papers*, 3 : 423.

21. "A common wealth is called a society or common doing of a multitude of free men collected together and united by common accord and covenauntes among themselves, for the conservation of themselves aswell in peace as in warre" (*De Republica Anglorum*, p. 20).

22. *Mass. Rec.*, 1 : 70. Cf. Edmund S. Morgan, *The Puritan Dilemma* (Boston, 1958), pp. 93–94. Reference is to the paperback edition.

generation probably were church members.[23] Yet by contemporary definitions Massachusetts was not a "democracy." Once a year the people elected their rulers, not their representatives. The same ten or eleven individuals who had filled the posts of "magistrates" (governor, deputy-governor, and assistants) before the covenant of October 1630 continued to fill those posts in subsequent years (with suitable additions from newly arrived individuals of equally high social rank). Massachusetts government for a time exhibited the paradox of a "popular aristocracy."[24]

While the same men held office, however, the nature of their offices became a subject for heated controversy. Extension of the freemanship opened the way for fifteen years of spectacular political and constitutional conflict between freemen and magistrates which has obscured the solid basis of fundamental social assumptions they held in common. No one had ever founded a state like Massachusetts before; its real meaning had to be worked out through years of experimentation. Tension and contradiction within a shared political ideology had somehow to be resolved within the very frame of government itself. The colony avoided a wilderness version of the English Civil War in large measure because magistrates and people agreed on most major articles of political faith and came into conflict only over their application.[25]

The first serious clash occurred in 1634 when representatives of the freemen requested a look at the Massachusetts-Bay Company charter and discovered that it gave the governor and assistants only vague supervisory powers between meetings of the General Court. This body and this body alone, consisting of governor, assistants, *and* all the freemen, had the sole and exclusive power under the charter to enact

23. *Mass. Rec.*, 1 : 87. Cf. appendix A.

24. The complete lists of the governor and assistants of Massachusetts Bay under the Old Charter are in William H. Whitmore, *The Massachusetts Civil Lists for the Colonial and Provincial Periods, 1630–1774* (Albany, N.Y., 1870), pp. 16–17, 21–26.

25. The story of this conflict has been told often and sometimes well, and I do not intend to retell it, except to explain the constitutional conflicts in relation to the Puritan concepts of social class. A good summary of the issues involved is George L. Haskins, *Law and Authority in Early Massachusetts* (New York, 1960), pp. 25–42.

laws, appoint officers, and admit new freemen. On 14 May 1634 the General Court voted to resume its charter powers, changing the colony from a pure aristocracy into a mixed one. The rule of the magistrates would be tempered by the freemen four times a year when the two groups met jointly to make the colony's laws.[26]

By "freemen" the authors of the charter had contemplated the limited body of stockholders of a trading company, not the one thousand or more citizens of a commonwealth denoted by the term in 1634. Because so numerous a body could not meet as a legislative assembly, the freemen created the office of "deputy," a device they understood far more clearly than many of the Bay Colony's later historians. Even in the seventeenth century the word *deputy* meant an individual delegated by another to take his place and exercise his function.[27] There would be no ambiguities about the origins of the deputies' power: the order establishing them stated that they "shall have the full power and voyces of all the said freemen, deryved [i.e. transferred] to them."[28] Winthrop stated that "in their first institution they were appointed as the representative body of the Freemen," and during a later political controversy he wrote of their power:

> If it be in the Deputyes it is in the people . . . for they are but the representative body of the people, and the matter lyes not in the number Assembled, but in their power: Againe the people are not bounde to send their Deputyes [to the General Court] but they may come themselves, if they will.

The deputies were not magistrates nor rulers; when they sat in the General Court they were the body of freemen incarnate.[29]

26. *Mass. Rec.*, 1 : 117.

27. Lord Kensington wrote in 1624: "But this case is now different, sayd she, for there the Prince was in Person, heer is but his deputy. But a Deputy, answered I, that represents his person." Quoted in *The Oxford English Dictionary* (Oxford, 1961), 3 : 224, col 1.

28. *Mass. Rec.*, 1 : 118–19.

29. *Winthrop Papers*, 4 : 359; "Defense of the Negative Voice," *Winthrop Papers*, 4 : 382–83. For later views of the representativeness of the lower house of the General Court, see the instructions of the town of Boston to its deputies in 1679 (*Boston Rec.*, 7 : 134) and "Americanus," *A Letter to the Freeholders and other Inhabitants of the Massachusetts Bay, Relating to their Approaching Election of Representatives* (Newport, R.I., 1739), p. 3.

Jealous of their newly gained rights and under no obligation to follow English precedents, the freemen might have followed the example of most of early modern Europe and severely limited the deputies' power.[30] Instead, apparently without much discussion, the deputies received *plena potestas,* the right to pledge their constituents' binding consent to a law without consulting them for prior approval.

Elaborate safeguards probably seemed unnecessary while the deputies stood for the small corporate towns whose members could and did instruct their representatives in detail on important issues—and this in matters of general concern to the whole colony as well as in purely local demands. Propositions of peculiar gravity, especially changes in the fundamental form of polity, were simply referred directly to the towns themselves, the deputies serving only as intermediaries between the court and the people. As institutions go, the deputies were a decidedly casual creation, developed in response to a geographical inconvenience and not according to some theoretical imperative. Not surprisingly, their creators failed to articulate a fully developed doctrine of the nature and mechanics of representation.[31] New England political writers in the seventeenth century had little to say about the representativeness of the deputies beyond assuming they would remain representative; theorists and controversialists alike devoted themselves primarily to the really important figure in government, the godly magistrate.

Superficial similarities between magistrates and deputies should not lead to a confusion of their functions. The freemen did elect both: the

30. On contemporary European theories of representation cf. G. R. Elton, *"The Body of the Whole Realm," Parliament and Representation in Medieval and Tudor England* (Charlottesville, N.C., 1969); H. G. Koenigsburger, "The Powers of Deputies in Sixteenth Century Assemblies," *Album Helen Maud Cam* (Louvain-Paris, 1960–61), 2 : 213–43.

31. For pre-Revolutionary representation in Massachusetts, cf. J. R. Pole, *Political Representation in England and the Origins of the American Republic* (New York, 1966), pp. 33–75. On instructions, cf. ibid., pp. 70–72; Kenneth Colegrove, "New England Town Mandates," *Publ.* CSM, 21 (1919) : 411–19. Pole and some other authorities to the contrary, instructions were quite common in seventeenth-century Massachusetts and covered general issues as well as purely local matters. For examples of instructions on questions of colonial policy in general see *Boston Rec.,* 7 : 110–11, 133–34, 160; W. H. Upham et al., eds., *Town Records of Salem, Massachusetts* (Salem, 1868–1934), 2 : 37.

magistrates at large, the deputies by towns. Both sat in the General Court, which served as the colony's legislature and supreme judicial tribunal. But there the resemblance ended. The magistrates remained a select ruling council of the wise and virtuous not accountable to the electorate. The deputies by comparison were a mechanical convenience for transmitting the freemen's wishes. Winthrop explained in 1642 that "our magistrates doe represent the Authoritye of all the people as well as the deputyes doe that power and Libertye which they [the people] have reserved to themselves."[32]

The order creating the deputies indicated both the degree of conflict between freemen and magistrates and the extent to which they agreed on fundamental ideas. If the freemen had not recognized the magistrates' claim to be a nonrepresentative body of superiors, they would not have needed deputies in the first place. They could simply have voted out of office magistrates not conforming to their wishes. Instead, while the old charter lasted, the freemen refrained from making any major changes in the composition of the magistrates, even during the periods of stormiest conflict.

These conflicts involved in the main the nature and power of the magistrate's office. Winthrop contended that the magistrates had absolute legislative, executive, and judicial powers limited only by the moral restrictions of their oath of office and the covenants of their churches, and by the word of God as interpreted by themselves with occasional advice from the ministers. In opposition to this the freemen tried to establish clear limits on the magistrates' power, first by instituting the deputies and by denying the magistrates' claims to a legislative veto and life tenure, then by attacking the magistrates' executive authority, and finally by insisting on a written code of laws with fixed penalties as the basis of judicial decisions. Most of the time the magistrates won, but with only one exception neither freemen nor the deputies ever attempted to limit the magisterial office by control-

---

32. *Winthrop Papers*, 4 : 387. Here neither Winthrop nor Puritan theory was completely consistent. He seems to be saying that even the magistrates' authority comes from the delegation of powers originally residing in the people. At other times he would argue that the authority of the office came directly from God, the people only choosing the men who would exercise it. Cf. John Bulkley, *The Necessity of Religion* (New London, Conn., 1713), p. 14.

ling the men in it. By 1645, when the political system finally gained a degree of stability, fifteen years of controversy had gone a long way toward resolving the problem of maintaining the political power of a socially superior class within the framework of an elective state.

At the very court that established the deputies the issue of life tenure came up in dramatic fashion. John Cotton, preaching the election sermon, chose that moment to announce that the magistrate had a property right to his office and ought never to lose it except for gross wickedness. The freemen reacted by relegating John Winthrop, who had served as governor for the previous four terms, to the rank of assistant, replacing him with Deputy Governor Thomas Dudley. Israel Stoughton, a leading deputy, wrote his brother not long after "we desire to change yeare by yeare the governorship: but the assistants more rarely, yet sometimes least it be esteemed hereditary."[33]

The clause about the assistants proved nothing more than a pious hope, but the ministers (Cotton excepted) also favored a rotating governorship and opposed the whole idea of a governor distinct in power from the other magistrates. They repeatedly "laboured" to see that Winthrop did not serve more than one term in the governorship at a time, though the freemen, left to their own devices, would have reelected him to that office almost every year.[34]

Life tenure for the office of magistrate received more sympathy from the ministry. When General Court established a special select standing council of magistrates for life with extraordinary powers, the ministers gave it their approval. The deputies, however, though they initially acquiesced in creating the council always suspected it, and its career proved short and ill-fated.[35]

Like the controversy over office for life, conflict over the "negative voice" began early. At the General Court of 3 September 1634, by a peculiar construction of one clause in the charter, the magistrates claimed that an act of the court needed their approval before it became a law. The deputies countered that an act needed only a majority of the whole court, deputies and magistrates together, in order to

33. *Winthrop Journal*, 1 : 157; *Proc.* MHS, 58 (1924–25): 456–57.
34. *Winthrop Journal*, 1 : 363, 2 : 3, 41–43, 119.
35. At least that was the way Winthrop remembered the matter in 1642. *Winthrop Journal*, 2 : 78. Cf. Ellen Brennan, "The Massachusetts Council of the Magistrates," *New England Quarterly*, 4 (1931): 54–93.

pass. Matters reached such an impasse the court had to adjourn temporarily. When it reconvened John Cotton preached a sermon in
which he declared that the magistracy by virtue of its authority, the
ministry by virtue of its purity, and the people by virtue of their
liberty had *each* a negative voice. This "gave great satisfaction": the
issue was put aside and then lost entirely in the furor that John Endicott succeeded in provoking by ripping the cross out of the king's
ensign on the grounds that it was a popish emblem.[36]

The controversies over the negative voice and the cross left the
whole colony weary of contention. Winthrop noted that at the General Court of 6 May 1635, "divers jealousies, that had been between
the magistrates and deputies, were now *cleared*, with full satisfaction
to all parties." This session and subsequent ones passed legislation
designed to satisfy the magistrates' demands for the power appropriate to superiors and the people's insistence on the limitation necessary
on all power. Magistrates and deputies both received a negative voice
on all legislation and judicial acts, and the court also set up the standing council of life magistrates. At the same time the process of cur-
tailing the magistrates' discretionary judicial powers began with the
appointment of committees to draw up a written code of fundamental
law. Winthrop did not like prescribed laws and he liked prescribed
penalties even less, but here he found himself at variance with both
the ministers, who usually supported him, and many of his fellow
magistrates. In their attempts to bring magisterial power under control the freemen achieved their greatest success on the matter of a
written code of fundamental law.[37]

This reconciliation put a temporary halt to the problem of defining
the relationship between ruler and ruled, and then the Antinomian
crisis of 1636 to 1638 submerged the question entirely. Three magistrates who supported Anne Hutchinson were voted out in 1637, but
this required no theoretical innovations: heretical rulers deserved to
lose their offices at the very least. Massachusetts had had enough controversy of any sort for a few years, and when Winthrop assumed the
governorship again in 1637 he held it (except for two years) until
1644. Final settlement of the debate over the nature and extent of the

36. *Winthrop Journal*, 1 : 166–69.
37. Ibid., 1 : 190–91, 388–89; *Mass. Rec.*, 1 : 167, 168, 174, 175.

good ruler's prerogatives came only at the conclusion of the prolonged constitutional crisis of 1642 to 1645.

In those four years all the issues of the past twelve came to a head almost simultaneously. The "sows case," originating in 1642, renewed the struggle over the negative voice for another two years. At the same time Richard Saltonstall, one of only two magistrates to oppose the negative voice, decided to attack the standing council too. The court had stripped the members of this institution of their authority as magistrates following a controversy in 1639,[38] and its powers remained ephemeral after that date, but Saltonstall's criticisms helped inspire the deputies from his hometown of Salem to head-on assault on all the magistrates' executive powers.

With legislative and executive functions under fire, the magistrates' judicial powers could hardly escape. The freemen had obtained a written body of liberties and a statement of capital offenses, but they were still agitating for a codified fundamental law and fixed penalties for other crimes. Winthrop found it necessary to write a "Discourse on Arbitrary Government," a brief for leaving penalties at the discretion of the judges, and then to defend it against an outraged body of deputies. Assailed on all sides, the magistrates acquitted themselves well and in the process firmly established their status and authority.

The sow's case opened the struggle. In June 1642, Goody Sherman of Boston, unable to win a favorable judgment in the lower courts against Captain Robert Keayne for allegedly misappropriating her stray sow six years before, appealed the case to the General Court. A plurality of the deputies supported her, the majority of the magistrates Captain Keayne, and the case was deadlocked for two years. Trifling as the issue was, it still set the deputies to reconsidering their concession of the negative voice in 1636.[39] Under Richard Saltonstall's leadership an aroused body of freemen and deputies once more demanded majority rule in the General Court, only to be overwhelmed by Winthrop assisted by some of the ministers.

In discussing the "sow business" and the disputes arising out of it, Winthrop made some significant statements about the differing natures of the deputies and the magistrates. He noted in his journal that

38. *Winthrop Journal*, 1 : 360–64. *Mass. Rec.*, 1 : 264.
39. *Winthrop Journal*, 2 : 86.

most of the deputies realized the triviality of the case and also that
the evidence, such as it was, stood in favor of Captain Keayne. Still,
they continued to press for further review, carried along "in this
course as it were in captivity" because their constituents emphatically
supported Goody Sherman.

> the deputies stood only upon this, that their towns were not sat-
> isfied in the cause (which by the way shows plainly the demo-
> cratical spirit which acts our deputies, etc.).[40]

The power of the people to force the "democratical" deputies to tie
up the General Court for months at a time in taking repetitive testimony about the number of spots under a pig's ear epitomized for
Winthrop the weakness of democracy.

The magistrates suffered from no such disability, or at least should
not have. Winthrop registered genuine alarm when he heard rumors
that the people had become so incensed over the negative voice that
they would purge the body of magistrates to put in men more con-
formable to their own opinions. This threat Winthrop called not simply dangerous but "dishonourable" because it violated the fifth commandment. Magistrates qualified for office by their ability, not by the
way they had carried out the people's will in the past or their willingness to do so in the future.

> because it is knowne that diverse of the magistrates are not like
> to consent to it [repeal of the negative voice], they must there-
> fore be lefte oute . . . and others put in their place . . . dishonor-
> able it would be, to take the power from those whom the Coun-
> trye pickes out, as the most able for public service, and putt it
> into the hands of others, whom they passe by, as the more
> weake.[41]

Winthrop need not have worried. The magistrates of 1642 remained the magistrates of 1643, 1644, and 1645 despite popular dis-
content with their powers.[42] The freemen simply could not bring
themselves to replace the traditional categories of wisdom and virtue

40. Ibid., 140–41.
41. *Winthrop Papers*, 4 : 359–60.
42. For the electoral system in these years see appendix B.

with a willingness to enact their demands. If they could have insisted on the responsibility of the magistrates they would never have needed to contest the negative voice. It appeared dangerous to them only because it put power into the hands of men whose use of power (providing it stayed within the limits of the decalogue) their ideology forbade them to question. They entered every political struggle under the handicap of implicitly accepting the idea of a ruling class.

Consequently, Winthrop made his most convincing points in defense of the veto not in his interpretation of the charter—that remained debatable at best—but in explaining to the freemen that revocation of the negative voice would deprive the magistrates of the very status of ruler which the freemen had given them by election. Massachusetts had passed from a pure aristocracy into a mixed one in 1634 because in that year the people (in the form of their representatives, the deputies) had gained the right to join their rulers, the magistrates, in the making of laws. Using a logic similar to that of the "short treatise," Winthrop argued that without the negative voice a deputy's vote would be equal to a magistrate's, and then the government would be changed from mixed aristocracy to "meere [pure] Democratie." The magistrates (who were also freemen) would cease to be rulers and become exactly like other freemen, casting their votes in General Court in the same manner as all other freemen did. Then the people would have no rulers but themselves, and Massachusetts would indeed be a democracy. True, the magistrate's vote in effect would still be worth many times that of the ordinary freeman because a deputy's vote really contained the votes of all the freemen in his town combined into one, but "the matter lyes not in the number of people Assembled, but in their power." If the freemen desired it they could dispense with the deputies and come and give their votes in person as the magistrates did. For Winthrop the essence of mixed government consisted in the various parts, the rulers and the people, having an absolute check upon each other.[43]

Winthrop's reasoning may not appeal to the twentieth century but the seventeenth found it unanswerable. He observed in his journal that the freemen, carried away with the passion of the moment, had not really understood the issue until he explained it. After their tem-

43. "Defense of the Negative Voice," *Winthrop Papers*, 4 : 382–83.

pers cooled and his arguments had had time to sink in they conceded
the point. On 7 March 1643/44 the General Court voted that hence-
forth magistrates and deputies would sit as two separate houses, no
act of either house having force unless approved by the other.[44]

Winthrop had hardly triumphed in his defense of the magistrates'
rights in the General Court when their authority outside the court as
the colony's executive body received a sharp challenge. Under speaker
William Hawthorne's guidance, the first session of the deputies sitting as a' separate house conceived of a scheme to deprive the magistrates of their power to administer the colony's affairs between meetings of the General Court. In June 1644, the deputies sent up a
commission for the magistrates' approval giving the administrative
power "out of court" to a committee consisting of seven magistrates,
three deputies, and the Rev. Nathaniel Ward of Ipswich.

The magistrates naturally rejected the commission, as the deputies
undoubtedly knew they would. Simply by drawing up the document
the deputies were asserting that no one, not even the magistrates, had
power to govern the country between general courts unless the court
delegated such power to them. The two houses agreed to put the
question off until the next meeting of the court in August and in the
meantime to consult the elders, but to the magistrates' assertion that
they would exercise their traditional powers in the interim, Speaker
Hawthorne replied bluntly, "You will not be obeyed." The magistrates (Saltonstall and Richard Bellingham excepted) countered by
issuing a declaration to the freemen announcing that "by the patent,
and election of the people, they are sett aparte to be the councell of
this common wealth to governe the people in the vacancy of the
General Courte."[45]

The issue proved so serious because magistrates and deputies appealed to two conflicting concepts within a common ideology: the
idea that the ruler's authority came from the people by virtue of the
covenant between governor and governed, and the idea that the ruler's
authority came from God, who ordained the office of governor and

44. *Winthrop Journal*, 2 : 142–44; *Mass. Rec.*, 2 : 58–59.
45. *Winthrop Journal*, 2 : 204–06; *Winthrop Papers*, 4 : 467. Winthrop
thought the whole thing a plot by the Essex deputies to draw off the government
into their country.

merely allowed the people to name the person to fill it. The deputies claimed that no office of government existed unless the General Court as the soverign power of the state created it. The magistrates countered that, while the court could regulate their office, it could not deprive them of it, nor of inherent powers it derived from the terms of the charter and from the nature of the divinely ordained calling of governor. As usual Winthrop stated the point most succinctly:

> to make a man governour over a people, gives him, by necessary consequence, power to govern that people, otherwise there were no power in any case where it might fall out, that there were no positive law declared in.[46]

Fortunately, Hawthorne had gone too far for most freemen, who chose to obey the magistrates when they acted as a council during the period between the May and August general courts. The report of the ministers delivered to the latter body and promptly adopted by it confirmed the magistrates in their claim that by virtue of the charter and their election they were "the standing council for the commonwealth in the vacancy of the general court" and therefore had the power "to act in all cases subject to government according to the said patent and the laws of this jurisdiction." By concentrating on the patent the report neatly side-stepped the question of whether the magistrate's power originated in the people or in God.

> the magistratical power is given to the governour, etc., by the patent. To the People is given by the same patent, to designate the persons to those places of government; and to the general court power is given to make laws, as the rules of their [the magistrates'] administration.[47]

Winthrop had also made use of the summer of 1644 to say something about the judicial powers appropriate to rulers, another subject of prolonged controversy. The magistrates served individually as the chief officials of the inferior quarter courts in their respective counties and also, sitting as a body, as the court of appeals from these

---

46. *Winthrop Journal*, 2 : 204–06.
47. Ibid., 250–56; *Mass. Rec.*, 2 : 91–96. Another act of the General Court formally reconfirmed the magistrates' powers (*Mass. Rec.*, 2 : 125).

lower courts and the court of original jurisdiction for serious civil and criminal cases. All decisions could be appealed in turn to the entire General Court, but even there the magistrates could use the negative voice. Under these circumstances the freemen wanted the magistrates' judicial decisions regulated as closely as possible by positive law.

In his "Discourse on Arbitrary Government" Winthrop advocated leaving the penalties for crimes up to the judges. Aside from claiming that the punishment ought to fit the criminal, he advanced his favorite argument that the powers of "judicature" were reserved exclusively to the calling of ruler. The people had the right in both the old Israel and the new of appointing the best among the tribes to the office of judge, but they had no calling as subjects to exercise that office themselves. If the General Court, which consisted of the people as well as their rulers, attached fixed penalties to its criminal statutes, then the people would have acted as judges and exceeded their calling. In effect, Winthrop claimed that unless rulers and ruled observed the limits of their respective callings there could be no superiority, and so no government.[48]

When the ministers presented their report to the General Court in August 1644, the deputies questioned them about Winthrop's doctrine and received a highly qualified reply. Penalties for certain specific crimes could be found in the word of God; the judge should use his discretion in punishing other crimes in order to take into account the varying circumstances of the offender, but positive law should fix the range of penalties from which he could choose.[49] Deputies and ministers came closest to agreement (and moved farthest from Winthrop) in their common demand for limitation of government by a fixed body of codified statutes. Ultimately the deputies would win this point with the issuance in 1648 of *The Lawes and Liberties of Massachusetts*, which prescribed fixed penalties for many crimes.

In 1644, however, the freemen and deputies had no way of knowing this. Fourteen years of simultaneous application of the doctrines of relative duties and of social covenant to the Massachusetts political system had produced a class of elected rulers with extensive inherent legislative, executive, and judicial powers subject to control only by

48: *Winthrop Papers*, 4 : 468–82.
49. *Mass. Rec.*, 2 : 93–94.

the acts of a bicameral legislature in which they sat as the upper house. Attempting to curtail the powers of the rulers while admitting their unaccountability had failed, had, in fact, only confirmed them with those powers all the more thoroughly. Some of the deputies had finally become desperate enough to forget orthodox Puritan political theory temporarily in order to strike directly at the office of magistrate itself. They would make the magistrates responsible to the General Court as a whole by using a device the English parliament had developed for similar purposes: impeachment.

Technically a judicial process, impeachment of the king's ministers when their policies proved sufficiently objectionable provided an effective means of parliamentary control of government. First employed in 1376 against Edward III's ministers and again in 1386 against Richard II's minister, the Duke of Suffolk, impeachment had passed out of use after 1450, only to be revived with new vigor in the parliament of 1621. At the very time the deputies decided to employ it in Massachusetts, the impeachment process had just produced its greatest prodigies in England by precipitating the fall of Strafford, Laud, Finch, and the ship money judges.[50]

The occasion selected for the attempt arose out of an incident far less trivial than Goody Sherman's suit for her sow. The people of Hingham had replaced an unpopular militia commander with one they found more agreeable, and when the magistrates restored the first officer some of the militia refused to serve under him. The magistrates considered the affair contempt of authority. Winthrop (currently serving as deputy governor) and three other magistrates bound over the Hingham ringleaders for appearance at the next General Court. Such disputes occurred often enough, but this time when the General Court met on 14 May 1645, eighty-one inhabitants of Hingham presented a petition "wherein they complained of their liberties infringed." The petition named Winthrop and Winthrop only, and the deputies insisted he stand trial before the whole court. Winthrop himself, and undoubtedly everyone else in Massachusetts, appreciated the political nature of the trial: he did not stand charged with any specific criminal offense and, although three other magistrates had

50. George Burton Adams, *Constitutional History of England*, 2d ed. (New York, 1962), pp. 207–10, 280–82, 310–12.

joined him in the disputed act, he alone, the chief upholder of magisterial powers, had come under indictment. The prime movers of the business were attempting to establish a degree of responsible government in Massachusetts by borrowing the English technique of using a judicial process to try a magistrate for purely political offenses.[51]

The venture ended in disaster for the deputies. Impeachment of Winthrop obviously went too far for most of the freemen: the managers in the lower house had trouble carrying even a bare majority of the deputies themselves with them on most points. From the first the deputies saw no chance of really punishing Winthrop and held out for a light censure on one minor point, while the upper house insisted on full acquittal and heavy fines for the petitioners. A deadlock resulted until the magistrates moved to call in the clergy as arbitrators. Knowing "that many of these elders [ministers] understood the cause, and were more careful to uphold the honor and power of the magistrates than themselves well liked of" and "finding themselves now at the wall," the deputies capitulated unconditionally. The court imposed heavy fines on the chief instigators of the Hingham petition, including the two deputies from the town, ordered the rest of the petitioners to pay £50 towards the court costs, and declared Winthrop himself "legally acquited of those things that have beene complained of."[52]

Then Winthrop made his famous "little speech" on liberty to the assembled deputies and magistrates. For its eloquence and lucidity the speech deserves all the attention it has received, but it did not contain a single new idea. Even the definition of civil liberty as "a liberty to that only which is good, just and honest" had been heard before.[53] Winthrop simply reiterated the standard propositions of Puritan political theory, but the occasion of the speech carried them home to the deputies with tremendous force. In calling Winthrop to account for an action not clearly wicked, the deputies had violated the law of God

51. *Mass. Rec.*, 2 : 97. Winthrop himself held that the Hingham case climaxed the conflict between magistrates and deputies that had first arisen in 1642 (*Winthrop Journal*, 2 : 282–86).

52. *Mass. Rec.*, 2 : 114; 3 : 19–26; *Winthrop Journal*, 2 : 271–79.

53. Cf. John White to John Winthrop, 16 November 1636, *Winthrop Papers*, 3 : 322.

and they knew it. Winthrop shrewdly began by making this point perfectly clear.

> It is yourselves who have called us to this office, and being called by you, we have our authority from God, in way of an ordinance, such as hath the image of God eminently stamped upon it, the contempt and violation whereof hath been vindicated with examples of divine vengeance.

Then he brought up the covenant theory:

> The covenant between you and us in the oath you have taken of us, which is to this purpose, that we shall govern you and judge your causes by the rules of God's laws and your own, according to our best skill.

But the magistrate as a fallible human being "doth not profess nor undertake to have a sufficient skill for that office, nor can you furnish him with gifts, etc." Called to the office because he possessed wisdom superior to the people's, he could not be resisted or removed merely because he seemed to have done something unwise. The people might call a magistrate to account only when he committed an act with a clearly wicked intent:

> But if he fail in faithfulness, which by his oath he is bound unto, that he must answer for. If it fall out that the case be clear to common apprehension, and the rule clear also, if he transgress here, the error is not in the skill, but in the evil of the will: it must be required of him. But if the case be doubtful, or the rule doubtful to men of such understanding and parts as your magistrates are, if your magistrates should err here, yourselves must bear it.[54]

The deputies were undone. Winthrop reassumed the governorship the next year and held it until his death, the elders apparently assuming it no longer wise to "labour" for rotation in office. Though he died in 1649, for the rest of the century the office of magistrate would retain the powers and definition he had given it: a ruler elected by the people but deriving his authority from God. Thanks to Winthrop the

54. *Winthrop Journal*, 2 : 279–82.

government of Massachusetts was a mixed aristocracy, not a mixed or pure democracy. The bulk of political power, executive, legislative, and judicial, resided in that branch of government not responsible to the people.

> It is so fixed in the Governor and assistants, as (how many soever shalbe joyned to them, as coadjutors or counsellars etc. yet) the maine strengthe of Authoritye (in pointe of dispensation) will rest in them, and can by no lawe be avoided.[55]

Of course, no power, theoretical or actual, required the magistrates to ignore the wishes of the people, who might (and often did) petition the General Court to express their desires. But the petitions had to take the forms of requests or humble advices, not demands or flat statements of the popular will. As a peaceable and humble man, the good ruler should willingly yield to the people's wishes on minor matters in order to maintain social unity; generally, the rulers were so willing, particularly with a moderate and conciliatory individual such as Winthrop in the governorship.[56] No one, however, not even the people, believed that the magistrates had to follow the popular will on any matter, major or minor, or that their tenures of office depended upon it.

By default the magistrates even triumphed on the delicate issue of office for life. The standing council had disappeared in the chaos of 1644, but it was no longer needed in any case. Life tenure for magistrates came into practice after 1645 without help from any statute. Upon Winthrop's death Endicott assumed the governorship and held it (with the exception of two years) until he himself died; the remaining three governors under the old charter also served for life, as did the deputy governors unless they succeeded to the governorship. With only a few exceptions, the assistants also held their posts until death, retirement, or removal to England.

55. *Winthrop Papers*, 4 : 360.
56. For example, the General Court granted an allowance toward maintenance of fortifications on Castle Island on 7 March 1643 even though it thought they would be almost useless, because six of the towns insisted on the fort, and the Court wished "to keep loving correspondency among all the towns" (*Winthrop Jounral*, 2 : 188).

Stability in the magistracy did not settle all the problems of the Bay Colony. Less than a year after the Hingham speech of 1645 Robert Childe and his Remonstrants reminded the General Court that neither the rights of the nonfreemen nor the colony's relationship to England were closed issues. Two years later the Cambridge synod of 1648 turned up ominous doctrinal disputes that would reach their climax in the protracted struggle over the half-way covenant in the latter part of the century. Contention over government policy inevitably raised the question of the status of the governors themselves, while the two houses also continued their sporadic feuding over the negative voice in judicial cases.[57] None of these controversies, however, involved a direct assault on the most essential prerogatives of the ruling class. John Winthrop continued to set the terms of political argument and the limits within which a decision had to be reached long after he was in the grave and his grandsons were making very tawdry good rulers.[58]

Despite obvious inadequacies, the settlement of 1645 provided the inhabitants of Massachusetts with the only political vocabulary they had, and they were obliged to use it for the next forty years even at a heavy cost in divided council and confused policy. Mounting tensions within and without the body of freemen had little effect on the composition of the magistracy; if anything, it was a more stable body after Winthrop's death than before. The freemen saw nothing incongruous in simultaneously electing men of the most diverse opinions to the magistracy. Richard Bellingham, the archprosecutor of Quakers and other religious dissidents, and Francis Willoughby, a strong advocate of toleration, served together as governor and deputy governor respectively for six years without anyone thinking it odd. When the government of Charles II attempted to bring Massachusetts into a more integral relationship with the rest of the British Empire, the freemen still elected the same men magistrates, whether they sup-

57. We now have a very detailed account of these controversies and their effect on the magisterial ideal, in Timothy H. Breen, *The Character of the Good Ruler* (New Haven, 1970), chap. 3. Prof. Breen's work has been very important in the revision of my own thinking on the subject, though some differences in emphasis and interpretation remain.

58. On the declining fortunes of the Winthrop family, see Richard Dunn, *Puritans and Yankees* (Princeton, N.J., 1962).

ported a strongly independent policy for the colony or advocated conciliating the king. Even Joseph Dudley, who actively intrigued against the charter, enjoyed the same right of continuous reelection to the office of assistant. In the climactic year of 1684, Increase Mather led a movement to purge the magistracy of those willing to submit to the royal demands for revocation of the charter, but only three men out of twenty lost their posts, and the chief of them, Dudley, regained his the next year.[59]

For all Increase Mather's efforts the charter fell in 1686. The short-lived "tyranny" of Royal Governor Edmund Andros held sway for the next three years, only to be overthrown by a local variation of the Glorious Revolution in 1689. For another three years the Bay Colony operated in a legal void, following the fallen charter amidst growing complaints of "mob rule," until in 1692 Increase Mather arrived back from England with a new document from William III that restored the legal proprieties and became the colony's instrument of government until the American Revolution.[60]

Edmund Andros in his reign and ruin both had made an important contribution to Massachusetts political life: *anarchy* and *liberty*, *mob* and *despot*, now had all the meaning a compelling experience could give them.[61] They had not been words in Winthrop's lexicon, at least they had not the same significance attached to them, and yet with the restoration of order in 1692, society's official spokesmen, the ministerial class, reverted back to formulations appropriate to 1645. The uncertainties of New England's interregnum probably heightened the appeal of the Good Ruler immune to faction and party, but the new charter presented insidious challenges to the orthodox theory of po-

59. The other two were William Browne and Bartholomew Gedney. Of the four men for whose defeat Increase Mather allegedly called in 1684 (Simon Bradstreet, William Stoughton, Peter Bulkeley, and Joseph Dudley), only Dudley lost his post. *Calendar of State Papers, Colonial Series, America and West Indies, 1681–1685* (London, 1898), p. 607.

60. Despite its obvious biases, the most complete account of the Dominion period and the revolution of 1689 remains Viola F. Barnes, *The Dominion of New England* (New Haven, 1923). Cf. also Michael G. Hall, *Edward Randolph and the American Colonies* (Chapel Hill, N.C., 1960), chaps. 4–5.

61. Again I am heavily indebted to Breen, *The Character of the Good Ruler*, chaps. 4–5, which treat the subject thoroughly, though again differences in interpretation remain.

litical authority—challenges the theory could not entirely meet. Under
the new electoral law a broad property franchise replaced the old requirement of church membership. Although almost all of the new
freemen (and almost everyone else in Massachusetts) continued to
adhere to the Congregational faith, godly rule would have to depend
on others than visible saints.[62] The eighteen assistants and the deputies of the old charter simply became the twenty-six councilors and
the representatives of the new, but the colony also received a royal
governor, appointed by the crown, with power to veto acts of the colonial assembly. Instead of the freemen electing the new councilors
directly, this power now lay with the representatives and the outgoing
council board voting jointly. As a group the representatives were
probably more willing to sacrifice virtue to party considerations in
their choice of councilors than the people at large would have been.
Still, the ministers continued to say the same things to the representatives in their election sermons as they had to the freemen under the
old charter, and up to a point the representatives did as the ministers
said.[63]

Even among the ministry, however, these doctrines had begun to
lose some of their power. Increase Mather had described the royal
governor in 1693 as he "whom God has made captain over his people
in this Wilderness."[64] Fifteen years later, however, both Mathers,
Increase and his son Cotton, had a political falling out with the incumbent governor, Joseph Dudley. Unfortunately, Dudley was a
ruler, and rulers might be criticized only for wickedness, not particular political decisions. The Mathers responded by ignoring the specific items at issue and denounced Dudley roundly for an odd assort-
ment of crimes, small and great: bribery, unrighteous dealing,
scheming against the New Charter, "much hypocrisy and falseness in
the affair of the college," murder, and keeping bad company on the

---

62. Years before, in discussing the proper function of Massachusetts government, John Cotton claimed he was talking only about a system in which most
freemen were church members (*A Discourse About Civil Government in a
New Plantation whose Design is Religion*, pp. 11–13).

63. The councilors under the province charter are in Whitmore, *Massachusetts Civil List*, pp. 46–64. They are almost as stable an elite as their Old
Charter predecessors.

64. *The Great Blessing of Primitive Counsellours*, p. 19.

Sabbath—all improved by appropriate scriptural citations. Cotton
Mather even intimated that the Lord would find Dudley's sins ex-
ceedingly provoking.

> Your *age* and *health*, as well as other circumstances, greatly
> invite you, Sir, to entertain *awful thoughts* of this matter, and
> solicit the divine mercy through the only sacrafice.

Dudley, for his part, had sat through enough election sermons to
know how to reply. He refused to answer any of the Mathers' accu-
sations and told them curtly that the powers that be are ordained by
God.

> I must think you have extremely forgot your own station, as
> well as my character; otherwise it had been impossible to have
> made such an open breach upon all the laws of decency, honour,
> justice and christianity, as you have done in treating me with an
> air of superiority and contempt, which would have been greatly
> culpable towards a christian of the lowest order, and is insuffer-
> ably rude towards one whom divine Providence has honoured
> with the character of your governour.

He advised the Mathers to remember "the Apostles wholesome advice, 1 *Thes*.iv.11."[65]

The Mather-Dudley exchange pointed up the extent to which the
orthodox concept of ruler was ceasing to be meaningful to Massachusetts political life. Both sides simply traded biblical phrases without
ever mentioning the real differences between them. Yet the very fact
that they restricted themselves to traditional forms meant those forms
still exerted a strong hold on the contemporary mentality.

For all that, much of the political theory the inhabitants of
eighteenth-century Massachusetts inherited from the seventeenth
could not have seemed very relevant to the problems of frontier defense, paper currency, or the conflicts between governor and assembly.[66] The ministers continued to preach that God's vicegerents on
earth deserved adequate maintenance but could not show what that

---

65. The entire exchange is in I *Coll. MHS*, 3 : 126–37.
66. Cf. Perry Miller, *The New England Mind from Colony to Province*,
pp. 367–84.

had to do with the Massachusetts royal governor's demands for a fixed salary and control of the colonial treasury. The eighth commandment still forbade a currency that changed in value, but the Massachusetts ministry failed to demonstrate how the decalogue would solve their colony's currency shortage more adequately than paper money. Nor was it the Good Ruler who would solve most of these problems. Traditional thought had neglected the representatives to concentrate on the magistrates, and thereby opened the way for competing doctrines more relevant to an age of increased power for the lower house of the Assembly.[67] Other voices besides those of Winthrop and Cotton began to be heard in the land: the voices of Puffendorf and Locke, of Trenchard and Gordon.[68]

Against all these difficulties the old ideology held out for a surprisingly long time. Seventeenth-century orthodoxy did not evaporate the first time an eighteenth-century minister cribbed a passage from Locke in his election sermon or a Boston newspaper reprinted *Cato's Letters.* Merely putting Locke in his footnotes hardly guaranteed that a New England author would read *The Second Treatise of Government* in the sense in which it was written or in the same way as other authors who included Locke in their footnotes read it. The Rev. Jared Eliot cheerfully recommended "Lock on Government" to readers of his Connecticut election sermon of 1738 and then went on to picture man in the state of nature as Ishmael out of Genesis, a description closer to the ideas of John Winthrop (and Robert Filmer) than to those of John Locke: "*a wild man; his hand being against every man, and every mans hand against him.*"[69] The acceptance, interpretation, and use of eighteenth-century English political theory in New England

67. On the lower house of the assembly in the provincial period, see Pole, *Political Representation in England and the Origins of the American Republic,* pp. 54–75.

68. The best and most succinct account of the entry of Whig ideology into colonial intellectual life is Bernard Bailyn, *The Origins of American Politics* (New York, 1968), chaps. 1, 2. But see also Alice M. Baldwin, *The New England Clergy and the American Revolution,* reprint (New York, 1958).

69. Jared Eliot, *Give Cesar his Due* (New London, Conn., 1738), pp. 27–28, 27n. Cf. Zabadiel Adams, *A Sermon Preached Before His Excellency John Hancock, Esq.* (Boston, 1782), p. 35. Locke explicitly distinguished between the state of nature and the state of war: *Two Treatises of Government,* ed. Peter Laslett (New York: Mentor Paperbacks, 1965), p. 321, par. 19.

owed much to an already well-established native ideology on whose stock it was grafted.

New England's politicians were no more consistent than her intellectuals. Out of conviction or inertia or both, that eminently political body, the Massachusetts House of Representatives, continued to display a traditional aversion to tampering with the bastion of magisterial privilege, the Council. Nor was this because the two bodies were always in harmony. In the years 1719 to 1721 the House, the Council, and the royal governor came into conflict over everything from Indian policy to public notaries, and with such intensity that Thomas Hutchinson thought "the contests and dissensions in the government rose to a greater height than they had done since the religious feuds in the years 1636 to 1637." Indifferent to temptation, the House refrained from making any wholesale changes in the composition of the Council despite frequent and prolonged disagreement between the two bodies. Seventy years and more after Winthrop's death social standing, with its implied attributes of talent and virtue, remained a major qualification for a seat on the Council. In 1731 the Rev. Samuel Fiske could still announce with pardonable pride that "we have also a continual growth of *Families* of Distinction, Education and Substance; which yield an increase of candidates for the Council Board."[70]

Nevertheless, in the face both of rival ideologies and an ever-increasing number of questions for which tradition had no answers, there would ultimately come a time when the endlessly repeated doctrine of the election sermons became just a collection of words. It came in the "land bank house" of 1741. The representatives that year and the men who elected them did not want councilors with wisdom or virtue, they wanted a land bank. The Rev. William Williams, who gave the election sermon, could think of nothing more meaningful to say to the assembled representatives than to recite the standard catalogue of the attributes of a good ruler and repeat the old injunction to

---

70. Hutchinson, *History of Massachusetts*, 2 : 170–96, 200–05. In 1720 the representatives elected nearly the same board as in 1719, while in 1720 they purged only three men out of twenty-six (Nathaniel Payne, Lt. Governor William Dummer, and Jonathan Belcher), all of whom later regained their seats. Whitmore, *Massachusetts Civil List*, pp. 51–52; Samuel Fiske, *The Character of the Candidate, for civil Government, especially for the Council* (Boston, 1731), p. 40.

choose rulers for their ability, not their advocacy of a particular scheme.

> therefore you will not suffer any *particular Party-cause*, or private *Selfish Views*, to influence you, or a regard to Men as *Favourers of such or such a Scheme*, no, tho' your *Principals* may have chosen you very much with such a Design. . . . [do] not, for the sake of any worldly views, neglect to chuse the *best and ablest* Men.[71]

The representatives might have slept through the whole sermon for all the attention they paid to it. Having listened politely, they purged fourteen of the eighteen councilors sitting for the area forming the old colony of Massachusetts Bay and replaced them with land bank advocates so partisan that Governor Jonathan Belcher vetoed thirteen of the nominees. The next day the representatives just had time to give Williams the customary vote of thanks and order that the sermon they had so totally ignored be printed, when Belcher dissolved the assembly as a hopeless case.[72]

By 1741 the traditional theory of authority was certainly bankrupt, but nothing as coherent or compelling had replaced it. Nathaniel Appleton's doctrine in the election sermon the following year was just as orthodox as William's had been and probably had about as much effect.[73] It remains to be proven, however, that any alternative theory had a greater impact on political life. The "triumph" of the land bankers would make a rather odd monument to the dawn of a new era: ten of the fourteen purged councilors regained their seats within a few years, while only two of the thirteen vetoed by Belcher ever gained a council seat at a later date.[74]

71. *God the Strength of Rulers and People, and Making them to be so, to each other mutually* (Boston, 1741), p. 42.

72. Brown, *Middle Class Democracy*, pp. 53–54. Hutchinson, *History of Massachusetts*, 2 : 298–301.

73. *The Great Blessing of Good Rulers, depends upon God's giving his Judgements & his Righteousness to them* (Boston, 1742), pp. 45–48.

74. The ten who regained their positions were William Dudley, John Osborne, Ebenezar Burrill, Benjamin Lynde, Jr., Daniel Russell, Ezekiel Lewis, William Browne, Thomas Burry, Nathaniel Hubbard, and Samuel Welles. The only two land bankers to become councilors were James Minot and John Otis (Whitmore, *Massachusetts Civil List*, pp. 56–58, 65).

Political exigencies undoubtedly account for this peculiar fact and for the subsequent stability of the Council prior to the Stamp Act crisis. Still, one can not help but wonder if Cato was less influential than Winthrop and Cotton had been in their heyday. Innovations in politics, as in every branch of human affairs, do not necessarily require the benefit of moral injunctions, but cumulative development often does. If the land bankers had been able to invoke a positive ideology as universally accepted and widely inculcated as that of their ancestors, their gains might have proven less ephemeral. As it was, the next time a royal governor would feel the need to veto thirteen councilors the year would be 1774, and the General Court would return the compliment by deposing the governor and the king for whom he governed. The ideal of the Good Ruler seems to have had an influence of sorts in the mid-eighteenth century, if a largely negative one. It would take a revolution to change it.

4   Wealth: The Calling, Capitalism, Commerce, and the Problem of Prosperity

Just as the doctrine of social covenant had unlooked-for consequences when applied to political theory, the Puritan economic ethic too contained features subversive of the social order it was designed to support. The Protestant concept of calling and the older doctrine of the stewardship of wealth encouraged a form of economic mobility inconsistent with the ideal of an ordered social hierarchy, and the tension affected every man who seriously attempted to live according to orthodox ethical precepts. The logical consequence of all that was holy in the New England economy was the one thing the American Puritans most despised, Max Weber's "spirit of capitalism."

The spirit in question had its origin in an unlikely place, the doctrine of the "calling." Men received a call from God, a divine command to live a certain kind of life. Most important was the general calling "whereby a man is called out of the world to be a child of God," to be one of his elect and to behave in this life as befitted one whom he had predestined to salvation.[1] But there was also a particular calling, the specific occupation God had designated for each individual as the way in which he should provide his own maintenance and serve the common good. A man could attempt to live in a particular calling without having a general one, without having received saving grace, but then his work, no matter how faithfully executed, amounted at best to "nothing else in God's sight, but a beautiful abomination."[2] Both callings must be exercised together: as a saint practiced his particular calling as a lawyer or husbandman he should simultaneously practice the duties of his general calling as a redeemed Christian. Should the two callings come in conflict, the particular had to give way to the general.[3]

1. William Perkins, *A Treatise of the Vocations or Callings of Men* in *Works*, 1 : 724.
2. Perkins, *The Nature and Practice of Repentance*, *Works*, 1 : 456. Cf. *Treatise of Callings*, *Works*, 1 : 743.
3. *Treatise of Callings*, *Works*, 1 : 733–34, 734–35.

General or particular, a calling was, as Williams Perkins defined it, "a certain kind of life, ordained and imposed on man by God for the common good,"[4] and God understandably wanted it practiced exactly as he had ordained. Christians could not choose any calling for themselves any more than they could choose any man to be their ruler. In both cases they had to agree voluntarily to serve God on the terms he laid down. Since God had instituted callings so that each man might contribute in his own particular way to the common good, a Christian could become anything useful from a swineherd to a prince, but he could not become a mountebank, a fortune-teller, or a gambler. To live dishonestly in a lawful calling was just as bad, and to live without any calling was worst of all. However wealthy and able to live without work men might be, God did not make them members of a commonwealth in order that they might receive its benefits without contributing to its welfare.[5] "If thou beest a man that lives without a calling, though thou has two thousands to spend, yet if thou hast no calling, tending to publique good, thou art an uncleane beast."[6]

Again men must try to see that they entered the calling God had actually designated for them. Because he was efficient as well as omnipotent, the talents and inclinations he had given each individual indicated the calling he had chosen for them. Anyone who entered a calling not suited to his particular skills in effect defied the divine order.[7] "Every man," Thomas Dudley advised his nephew, "ought (as I take it) to serve God in such a way whereto he hath best fitted him by nature, education, or gifts, or graces acquired."[8]

4. Ibid., 727.
5. Ibid., 732-33. Cf. William Ames, *Conscience with the Power and Cases Thereof* in *Works* (London, 1643), p. 248 (3d pagination); John Cotton, *The Way of Life* (London, 1641), pp. 439; Cotton Mather, *The Christian at his Calling* (Boston, 1701) pp. 42-44; Samuel Willard, *A Compleat Body of Divinity,* pp. 691-92.
6. Cotton, *The Way of Life,* p. 449. Cf. Perkins, *Treatise of Callings, Works,* 1 : 733; Richard Sibbes, *Works* (Edinburgh, 1862), 6 : 521.
7. Perkins, *Treatise of Callings, Works,* 1 : 735-36. Cf. Cotton, *The Way of Life,* 439-40; Willard, *Compleat Body of Divinity,* p. 693.
8. Thomas Dudley to John Woodbridge, 28 November 1642, quoted in *Winthrop Journal,* 2 : 309n-10n. Woodbridge took his uncle's advice and entered the ministry, for which Dudley thought him well suited.

44 904

Circumstances by the same logic served as further indications of the appropriate calling.[9] When Governor John Winthrop's son Samuel, sent on a trip to London, instead stopped off at Teneriffe en route and apprenticed himself to a local merchant, he defended his action on the grounds that "I have no fixed calling, not knowing what profession I should embrace," and because "I seem persuaded in this my choice by providences of God concurring in this wise: as if God had purposely provided this position for me at a time when all his [the Teneriffe merchant's] clerks have left him, so that no one is left to attend his business."[10]

Samuel also pointed out with youthful enthusiasm that the position provided a ready opportunity to make money. If his father the governor answered the letter, he probably reminded his son that the primary end of a calling lay in serving God and one's fellow men, not in amassing wealth. At least Thomas Dudley took this firm line with John Woodbridge, his nephew: "Above all commend the case in prayer to God, that you may look before you with a sincere eye, upon his service, not upon filthy lucre."[11] William Perkins had explained it all years before. "All societies of men are bodies, a family is a bodie, and so is every particular church a bodie, and the commonwealth also," within which the members had their assigned parts for the good of the whole. If a man would fulfill his function as a member of the commonwealth, if he would not abuse his calling, then he had to exercise it for the common good, not his own personal advancement.[12]

It followed that whatever men did, they must do it within the limits of their calling (the subject not usurping the functions of the magistrate, nor the magistrate the functions of the minister) and that men might change their callings only for the weightiest reasons. If they would become more serviceable to the public by such a change,

9. Ames, *The Marrow of Sacred Divinity, Works,* p. 327 (paged separately). Ames admitted that the call to a profession through outward circumstances was not as explicit or clear as the call to salvation.

10. Samuel Winthrop to John Winthrop, ca. March 1645/46, 2 *Proc.* MHS, 7 : 14–15. Original in Latin.

11. *Winthrop Journal,* 2 : 309n–10n.

12. Perkins, *Treatise of Callings, Works,* 1 : 728.

Lincoln Christian College

as when a private man received a call to the ministry or to public office, then they had God's warrant, but a change of calling simply to obtain wealth or status manifested a love for God's creatures that interfered with love for God himself. Those of "meene place and calling" would find their consolation in considering "that in serving of men, by performance of poore and base duties they serve God: and therefore that their service is not base in his sight: and though their reward from men be little, yet the reward at Gods hand, shall not be wanting."[13]

Read this way the doctrine of calling provided one more justification for inequality among men, for social stability, and for social hierarchy. God might hold all callings equal in the light of eternity, but during their brief journey through this life men were not obliged to. Though no lawful calling should be despised, those of liberal parts, those with education, wealth, or social standing, should choose liberal and not servile occupations.[14] And certainly if the public welfare lay behind the operation of all callings, then those who contributed most to it deserved more "honor" than those who contributed less. The husbandman did not deserve the same degree of deference, wealth, attire, ornament, or even food as the magistrate, and he should not aspire to it.[15]

In William Perkins's view the whole notion of calling rested on inequality: "Persons are distinguished by order, whereby God hath appointed, that in every society one person should be above or under another, not making all equall . . . And by reason of this distinction of men, partly in respect of gifts, partly in respect of order, come personal callings." God had given men different gifts and consequently different callings; their inability to function without each other made society both possible and necessary, and with it the social hierarchy. Any attempt to leave that calling dictated by God as the best means by which each man could serve society, could not fail to disrupt society:

    13. Ibid., 734.
    14. John Downame, *A Guide to Godlynesse* (London, 1622), pp. 258–59. Cf. Willard, *Compleat Body of Divinity*, p. 615.
    15. Perkins, *Cases of Conscience* in *Works*, 2 : 134–36. *A Commentarie upon the Eleventh Chapter to the Heberewes, Works*, 3 : 41 (2d pagination). Cf. Downame, *Christian Warfare*, pp. 510–13.

Every man must judge that particular calling, in which God hath placed him, to be the best of all callings for him. . . . The practice of this dutie is the stay & foundation of the good estate both of church & common wealth: for it maketh every man to keepe his own standing, & to employ himselfe painfully within his calling. But when we begin to mislike the wise desposition of God, and to thinke other mens callings better for us than our own, then followes confusion and disorder in every societie.[16]

Every man content in his place, devoting himself diligently to the duties appropriate to it, and to it only—hardly a new or uniquely Puritan teaching. Yet the very same doctrine, by encouraging and even demanding that every man unceasingly and systematically pursue his livelihood, virtually forced him to get out of his place, to strive to grow richer, and in time possibly to pursue profit for its own and not the Lord's sake.

That such a change did take place, that continuous work for the glory of God ultimately became an irrational but "rationalized" pursuit of profit without limit, constitutes the basic contention of Max Weber's much criticized *The Protestant Ethic and the Spirit of Capitalism*.[17] Though the question of the real importance of Weber's *Geist der Capitalismus* to modern capitalist development lies beyond the scope of this discussion, much of what Weber theorized does help to explain the development of New England and the true nature of the peculiar tension that inhered in Puritan economic life.

16. Perkins, *Treatise of Callings, Works*, 1 : 731–33.

17. All references to this work are to the Scribners' paperback edition, trans. Talcott Parsons (New York, 1958). The literature dealing with the Weber thesis is very large indeed, and I will not attempt to summarize it. There is a partial bibliography in R. H. Tawney, *Religion and the Rise of Capitalism* (New York, 1963), p. 237. Reference is to the Mentor paperback edition. Tawney gave his own modifications of Weber in ibid., pp. 8–9, 262–63. Among the more notable outright attacks are H. M. Robertson, *Aspects of the Rise of Economic Individualism* (Cambridge, 1933); Winthrop Hudson, "Puritanism and the Spirit of Capitalism," *Church History* 18 (1949): 3–17; Charles G. and Katherine George, *The Protestant Mind of the English Reformation, 1570–1640* (Princeton, N.J., 1961), pp. 144–73; Kurt Samuelsson, *Religion and Economic Action* (New York, 1961); Michael Walzer, *The Revolution of the Saints*, pp. 304–07 and passim.

In restricting themselves to demonstrating that the Puritans held an unremitting hostility to the "spirit of capitalism," Weber's critics have not come to grips with his argument. Granted, Puritan writers had a name for the appetite that craved profit without end or final purpose, and it was covetousness; and a name for economic individualism, and it was pride; and a place for the covetous and the proud, and it was hell. The road to that hell was well paved with the good intentions of certain distinguished casuists.

Certainly John Cotton, no friend of pride and covetousness, would have seconded Weber's association of diligence in one's calling with a predestinarian theology.[18] Cotton answered the question "how shall I know that I have that life, in having of which, I may know I have Christ?" in part with the directive: "looke at thy worldly business, art thou diligent in thy calling, it is well, and you say, *cursed is He that doth the worke of the Lord negligently*, and the work of his calling is, the worke of the Lord."[19]

Diligence in a calling not only gave proof of salvation, it was, as Cotton wrote, the work of the Lord: it glorified God, and this, after all, was the chief end of man. Ascetic Protestantism has given an almost sacramental quality to the affairs of this world.[20] Men who performed them in the right spirit rendered as much service to God this way as when they knelt in prayer or took the sacrament. The Christian life, John Downame explained, involved more than the performance of certain especially holy things:

> if we thus performe the duties of our calling, in love towards God, and in obedience to his commandements, and desire by prayer his blessing upon our labours, and yield him praise when he hath vouchsafed to give it, then shall we therein doe service unto God, though our condition and the workes of our vocation be never so meane and base, as well as in hearing the word, or

18. Weber, *The Protestant Ethic*, pp. 109–15.

19. *Christ the Fountaine of Life* (London, 1651), p. 126.

20. As the Georges point out, English Protestants laid so much stress on the particular calling that it came "very close to becoming the spiritual, salvation-working calling as well as the moral, socially utilitarian vocation" (*Protestant Mind of the English Reformation*, p. 169. Cf., Weber, *The Protestant Ethic*, pp. 108–09).

receiving the sacrament, or in performing the most excellent
duty which he hath commanded, seeing though they differ in the
matter, yet not in respecte of our minde, and the manner of
doing them.[21]

The believer did not buy his way into heaven by accumulating a
sufficient number of individual holy works; he glorified God, showed
his gratitude to Him, and gave evidence of his salvation by the total
pattern of his behavior over a whole lifetime. Downame made it perfectly plain that "we are called to be Gods labourers; and therefore
we must intend our business, that it may prosper in our hand, and not
undoe in one day, that which we have done in another. . . . But we
must in the whole & daily course of our lives, give *all diligence to
make our calling and election sure*, by holding a constant and continual course, in the Christian exercises of a godly life."[22]

Precisely *because* men labored for God and *not* for gold (or status
or honor), they had to continue working in their callings constantly:
material needs or even the desire for riches might be satisified at some
finite point, God never. Downame had no use for "the common practice of the world" that "many may live without any calling at all, or
having one, may onely labour so much as they neede or will stand
with their credit and place. As though there were no other bonds to
tye them unto any paines, but necessity among the poorer sort, increase of riches among those who desire to increase their wealth to an
higher pitch, and honour and authority among those who are in a

21. *Guide to Godlynesse,* p. 248. Cf. Richard Mather, *A Farewell Exhortation* (Cambridge, Mass., 1657), pp. 16–18. Thomas Shepard even wrote that
devout thoughts which disrupted work at a calling had been sent by the devil.
God was more honored by the "mean and base outside of civil affairs" if that
was what he had called the believer to, than by noble thoughts and prayers if he
had not given him a call to that. *Certain Select Cases Resolved* (London, 1648),
pp. 34–35.
22. *Guide to Godlynesse,* pp. 168–69. "Wee must constantly and continually,
in every thing, and at every time, performe service unto God in all our actions
and throughout our whole course and conversation. . . . Neither is God alone
served, when we performe some religious act, as praying, hearing the Word, sing-
ing Psalmes, or some eminent workes of charity and sobriety, but also in the
meanest duties of the basest calling, yea even in our eating and drinking, lawful
sports and recreations, when as wee doe them in faith" (Ibid., p. 164. Cf. Weber,
Protestant Ethic, pp. 115–21).

place of government." The divine injunctions to work at a calling "concerne all men of all estates and conditions, rich and poore, noble and base, so long as they are able to take paines, and are not made unfit by age and impotency, sicknesse and such other infirmities."[23]

Like most Puritans Downame allowed men "due recreation." They must work at their callings most of the time, but not all. That would breed melancholy and weariness, as much "the mother and nurse of waywardness and impatiency" as idleness. Men should take moderate indulgence in "walking in pleasant places, conferences which are delightful without offence, Poetry, Musique, Shooting, and such other allowable Sports as best fit with mens severall dispositions for their comfort and refreshing." But this in turn should serve only as refreshment to make men once more fit for their callings and more efficient in them than if they had taken no rest at all. Another prominent English Puritan, Richard Sibbes, wrote that the goldly should use their recreations "as whettings to be fitter for our callings, and enjoy them as liberties, with thankfullness to God, that allows us these liberties to refresh ourselves."[24]

New England Puritans tended to be even less indulgent toward activity outside a calling than their English predecessors and contemporaries. The Massachusetts General Court early passed and enforced laws against idleness and required parents to bring their children up in a warrantable calling,[25] while the ministers labored so strenuously to promote diligence and industry that they sometimes seemed to lose contact with reality. As early as 1636, when everyone in Massachusetts undoubtedly had quite enough to do just trying to stay alive, the Rev. Hugh Peter was already lamenting that idleness would be the

---

23. *Guide to Godlynesse*, p. 257. By the same logic, the poor also had to remain in their callings (if they could not find new ones), even if they did not earn enough to live on or their occupations involved drudgery, discouragement, and little reward. Ibid., pp. 259–61.

24. Downame, *Christian Warfare*, pp. 969–90. Sibbes, *Works*, 6 : 507.

25. *Mass. Rec.* 1 : 109, 198, 203, 2 : 126, 180, 5 : 373. Instances of enforcement and the laws against idleness are very numerous in both Essex and Suffolk counties. *Essex Cty. Ct. Rec.*, passim. *Suffolk Cty. Ct. Rec.* passim. See the respective indexes under "Crimes, Idleness" and "Idle Persons." Cf. below, chapter 5, pp. 166–67.

26. *Winthrop Journal*, 1 : 222, 249.

ruin of the commonwealth.[26] Even Peter's energy paled by comparison with the leading light of the third generation in New England, Cotton Mather, who urged constant and diligent work as a remedy for everything from economic depression to masturbation.[27] Mather also had nothing against appealing to his readers' self-interest as a spur to industry:

> I tell you with *Diligence* a man may do marvellous things. *Young* man, *Work hard* while you are *Young:* You'll Reap the Effects of it, when you are *Old.* Yea, How can you ordinarily Enjoy any Rest at *Night*, if you have not been well at Work, in the *Day?* Let your *Business* Engross the *most* of your Time. Tis not now and then an Hour at your *Business* that will do. Be stirring about your *Business* as Early as tis Convenient. Keep close to your *Business*, until it be convenient you should leave it off.

As for the negligent, "I will say as the Apostle, *They are dead while They live.* And I will add, probably they have not long to *Live;* and They will Dy not having where with to *Live.*"[28]

Mather also had some strong opinions on efficiency. If men might not do the Lord's work lazily, neither could they do it carelessly. The Christian must not only attend his calling constantly, he must manage it with prudence or he failed the trust the Lord had given him. Mather's *Christian At His Calling* exhorted to double-entry bookkeeping and frequent inventories, all in the name of religion:

> Take this Advice, O Christian; 'Tis a *Sin*, I say, 'Tis ordinarily a *Sin*, and it will at Length be a shame, for a man to *Spend* more than he Gets, or make his *Layings out* more than his *Comings in.* A frequent Inspection into the *State of your Business*, is therefore not among the least *Rules* of *Discretion.* It was among the Maxims of Wisdom given of Old, *Be Thou Dilligent for to know the State of thy Flocks;* That is to say, often Examine the condition of thy Business, to see whether thou go for-

27. Cotton Mather, *Concio ad Populum* (Boston, 1719), pp. 16–17; *A Flying Roll for the House of the Thief* (Boston, 1713), p. 33; *The Pure Nazarite* (Boston, 1723), p. 16.

28. *A Christian at his Calling*, pp. 48–49.

ward or backward, and Learn to Order thy Concerns accordingly.[29]

The status of prudence as a virtue went back at least as far as Aristotle, and a Catholic friar invented double-entry bookkeeping. Protestant, Catholic, or Hindu, whenever men turn their minds to virtue they usually come up with the same dreary catalogue, for sensualists rarely write books of casuistry.[30] The real importance of the injunctions to industry and prudence lies in the general religious scheme within which they function, as Weber realized when he identified the Protestant ethic as *"innerweltliche* askete.*"* Puritanism contributed to *der Geist des Kapitalismus* because it made the standard virtues not merely good things, but religious essentials, as important in their six days of the week as prayer and the sacraments were on the seventh.

There were other ways of looking at the world in the seventeenth century. The moment the railings went up around the communion tables in English churches the Protestant ethic was undermined; for in making altars and prayers especially holy and therefore worthy of special care, the Laudians made plows and shop counters less holy, less significant as means of glorifying God and working out salvation. Merely to admit *adiaphora* (things indifferent) began a retreat from the Protestant ethic that found its climax in "the beauty of holyness" and its ultimate end in Nicholas Ferrar and the "Arminian Nunnery" of Little Gidding. If the Little Gidding community took up bookbinding as a way to avoid idleness, that merely underscores the fallacy of identifying Puritan and non-Puritan social thought by a simpleminded comparison of their ethical maxims. The Ferrars withdrew from a wicked world in the name of personal purity, and the asceticism they practiced was distinctly not of the *innerweltliche* variety.[31]

By contrast Puritans really did see ordinary routine activities as significant works of religion and evidences of sanctification (and there-

29. Ibid., pp. 53–54, Cf. Richard Steele, *The Trades-Man's Calling* (London, 1684), pp. 62–63.

30. In terms of injunctions to work and wealth, the writings of the supporters of the existing settlement of the Church of England are indistinguishable from those of its opponents. Cf. Timothy Hall Breen, "The Non-Existent Controversy: Puritan and Anglican Attitudes on Work and Wealth, 1600–1640," *Church History* 35 (1966) : 273–87.

31. See "Nicholas Ferrar," *The Dictionary of National Biography.*

WEALTH 109

fore salvation). For them a well-kept ledger was as much of a monument to God as a stained-glass window was to the Ferrars. When the grasping but devout Boston merchant Robert Keayne came to write his lengthy will/apologia in 1653, he devoted nine full pages to his bookkeeping. Keayne's career had been marred by charges of covetousness in 1639 and 1642 and of drunkenness later in his life. Now, for his defense he pointed to his account books. There, he wrote, lay the record of his virtue, there lay the proof that he had "redeemed his time" and lived his life by the Lord's precepts:

> if all these [account books] should be of no other use, yet they will testify to the world on my behalf that I have not lived an idle, lazy, or dronish life, nor spent my time wantonly, fruitelessly or in company-keeping as some have been too ready to asperse me, or that I have had my whole time either in Old England or New many spare hours to spend unprofitably away or to refresh myself with recreation. . . . Rather I have studied and endeavored to redeem my time as a thing most dear and precious to me and have often denied myself in such refreshings that otherwise I might lawfully have made use of.

Unknowingly parodying Cardinal Wolsey, Keayne concluded his apologia with the plaintive lament that, had he kept the books "of that spiritual estate between God and my own soul" as carefully as those of his material estate, he would not now be naked to the aspersions of his enemies.[32]

If a man would obey the Lord personal expenses demanded the same careful attention. William Ames, foremost of casuists in New England eyes, required a Christian "frugality" and "parsimony" of his readers as their duty under the eighth commandment. Luxury and wastefulness, he pointed out, were not the ways of a godly man. No one had ever maintained that they were, but then no one had ever brought household and business economy directly under the eye of an omnipotent and somewhat vengeful god before either. The Lord sent men their wealth as well as their callings, and they were to use both for the same purpose, to glorify him and to serve society. No man

---

32. Bernard Bailyn, ed., *The Apologia of Robert Keayne, Publ.* CSM (Boston, 1964), 43 : 316–22.

really owned his estate; he received it in trust and administered it as a faithful steward would, for his master's appointed ends.[33] As God's stewards we must "beware wee doe not idly lavish those things, which can bee employed either in profitable or honest causes" and that "wee looke, that no considerable thing of those, which may bee useful bee lost." This care Ames defined as "honest parsimony." "Honest frugality" required "that wee do not lay out our money upon vaine, and unprofitable things" or excessive pleasures, but rather "wee imploy our money in those things, which have a real use."[34]

Ames was not trying to idealize the tight-fisted bourgeois shop-keeper—he required an honest liberality too. Resources were to be carefully husbanded in order that they might be spent on "real uses": an appropriate maintenance for self and family and the support of the poor, the church, and the commonwealth. Nevertheless, his instructions properly followed by those anxious to follow the Lord's will could hardly fail to increase the estate of at least some of them, a development Ames sanctioned so long as it did "not proceed from the love of riches; but out of conscience towards God, whose benefits wee ought not to abuse." He carefully noted that "not every desire of riches is covetousnesse, but onely the inordinate love of them; and that love is inordinate which is repugnant to the love, which wee owe to God, or ouer Neighbour."[35]

Since wealthy pious men would prove more serviceable to their neighbors and the commonwealth than poor ones, most Puritan writers not only permitted but commanded men to increase their estate by virtue of their stewardship and the "positive" duties of the eighth commandment. The ruthlessly consistent Perkins did not think even a desire to help the poor legitimated the search for wealth,[36] but as early as 1616 John Downame was announcing that "because the

33. "Noe man is made more honourable than another or more wealthy etc. out of any perticuler and singular respect to himselfe but for the glory of his creator and the common good of the Creature, Man; Therefore God still reserves the property of these guifts to himselfe." (John Winthrop, *A Modell of Christian Charity, Winthrop Papers,* 2 : 283).

34. *Cases of Conscience, Works,* pp. 254–55 (3d pagination).

35. Ibid., pp. 235, 260–61 (3d pagination).

36. Perkins, *Cases of Conscience, Works,* 2 : 126. Not to be confused with Ames's work of a similar title.

Scriptures require, that we should be bountiful and plentiful in good works, this should increase our care and diligence in preserving and increasing of our estates, by all lawful meanes, in acquisition and getting by our honest and painefull labours in our callings, and by our frugall husbanding and thriftie spending of our goods, that so having greater plentie we may be the richer in good workes." Anyone who could not give to charity because he had failed to increase his estate stood condemned for sloth, negligence, wastefulness, and ill husbandry.[37]

Downame's contemporaries and successors reiterated the same doctrine throughout the seventeenth century. [38] A hundred years after the *Plea for the Poore*, Samuel Willard's *Compleat Body of Divinity* made the identical point:

> It is not sufficient to take heed that nothing be wasted, but we must husband our Estates to *Advantage:* It is not enough to *get* an Estate, but there is a Duty to endeavour that it may prosper by good Husbandry of it, in the best way. *Prosperity* is a Blessing to be desired, (tho' not insatiably to be grasped after, which is a Temptation to Sin,) . . . *Riches* are consistent with *Godliness*, and the more a Man hath the more Advantage he hath to do Good with it, if God give him an Heart to it.[39]

Riches were not evil, nor was an advance in social status, but only covetousness and ambition, the desire for these things for their own sake rather than for the glory of God. If a man did not seek riches as the end of his calling, according to John Preston, the master of Emmanuel College, Cambridge, he would most likely find them as God's reward for diligent service. "*God* calls not a man to trust in himselfe to make riches his ayme and end, to seeke excess, superfluity and aboundance . . . our ayme must bee GODS glory and the publique good, and then GOD will cast riches upon us as our wages."[40]

37. *The Plea of the Poore. Or a Treatise of Benificence and Almes-Deads* (London, 1616), p. 23.
38. Cf. Arthur Hildersham. *CVII Lectures Upon the Fourth of John*, 2d ed., rev. (London, 1632), pp. 238–39, and Richard Baxter's much quoted Dictum 9, *A Christian Directory* (London, 1673), p. 450.
39. P. 709.
40. John Preston, *A Remedy against Covetousnesse* in *Four Godly and Learned Treatises* (London, 1633), pp. 43–45 (1st pagination).

It all came down to a matter of motives. Preston understood the difference between the Protestant ethic and the spirit of capitalism with a subtlety and exactness that would have delighted Weber: "God makes us rich, by being diligent in our callings, using it to his glory and more good, he doth cast Riches on us. Man makes himselfe rich, when as he makes riches the end of his calling, and doth not expect them as a reward that comes from God."[41]

Since Preston died in 1628, his thought can hardly be labeled the product of a Puritanism gone soft and forced to compromise with the material interests of its most important backers. Some change naturally occurred in Puritan social thought in the course of the seventeenth century, some of it significant, but the basic elements of the economic ethic remained largely intact. Certainly, Cotton Mather saw the cosmos differently from William Perkins: a whole century of intellectual upheaval lay between them. Perkins died while Queen Elizabeth still reigned; Mather came to his maturity after God had said let Newton be, and there was not only light but a new concept of order in his world. God in the whirlwind gave way in part to God in the machine.[42] Instead of exhorting men to work in their calling *so as* to further the public good, Mather tended to assume that anyone who did work in a lawful manner automatically furthered it. In his definition of calling, God's instrumentality seemed more remote than in Perkin's writings, and he placed a new emphasis on equity and utility:

> Every Christian hath also a *Personal Calling;* or, a certain *Particular Employment,* by which his Usefulness in his Neighbourhood, is distinguished. God hath made man a *Sociable* Creature. We expect Benefits from *Humane Society.* It is but equal,

41. Ibid., p. 42.

42. "It is now plain from the most *evident Principles,* that the Great GOD not only has the Springs of this immense *Machine,* and all the several Parts of it, in his own Hand, and is the *first Mover;* but that without His *continual Influence* the whole Movement would soon fall to pieces." Mather added, true to a part of his heritage, "Yet besides this, He has reserved to Himself the power of *dispensing* with these laws, whenever He pleases." *The Christian Philosopher* (London, 1721), p. 88.

that *Humane Society* should Receive Benefits from Us. We are Beneficial to *Humane* Society by the Works of that Special *Occupation*, in which we are to be employ'd according to the order of God.[43]

The same difference in attitudes appeared in Mather's discussion of personal expenses. Perkins sent the perplexed believer to some hypothetical wise man, who would objectively determine his social status and tell him how much of his income he should spend to maintain himself in the station to which God had appointed him and how much was "superfluity" to be devoted to "pious uses."[44] Cotton Mather would have sent the same believer to an account book with the injunction not to spend more than he earned; as for charity, he advised a minimum of ten percent of income, more when possible.[45]

Mather's passion for utility led him to advise Protestant propagandists to use the "Argument ab utili" to persuade "the European Powers to shake off the chains of popery"—"One showes, That the Abolishing of Popery in England, is worth at least Eight Millions of Pounds yearly to the Nation."[46] Still, in a mechanically efficient universe the categories of "useful" and "good" probably would coincide. Mather may have come fairly close to Benjamin Franklin and even to Adam Smith on some points, but he stayed well within the essential Protestant tradition most of the time. The categories of "necessity" and "superfluity" went back to the Schoolmen[47]: there was nothing particularly Puritan or even Protestant about them, and if Mather exchanged them for a simple accounting system he did not thereby

43. *A Christian at his Calling*, p. 37.
44. *Cases of Conscience, Works*, 2 : 125. Cf. Downame, *Christian Warfare*, pp. 448–51.
45. On income and expenses see above pp. 138–39. Cf. Samuel Moodey, *The Debtors Monitor* (Boston, 1715), pp. 17–18. On charity cf. Cotton Mather, *Bonifacius* (Boston, 1710), p. 140. Richard Baxter and Thomas Gouge seem to have accomplished the change from superfluity to a minimum of ten percent of income in the 1670s. Cf. *The Christian Directory*, pp. 192–99 (2d pagination).
46. *Bonifacius*, p. 180.
47. Tawney, *Religion and the Rise of Capitalism*, p. 38.

introduce anything new into the orthodox concept of calling, however hysterically he may have stated some of its features.[48]

Long before Mather, in its earliest and most rigorous form, the Puritan doctrine of calling enjoined a properly motivated individual to increase his estate and gave him specific instructions on how to do it. The same ethic that assigned a calling according to some objectively determined social order made the calling an instrument for the continuous disruption of established order. The Puritans never could find an answer to this problem. Their descendants would solve it (after much of the sense of human inability and divine omnipotence that lay at the root of Puritanism had dissipated) by doing away with the notion of order altogether, converting the Protestant ethic into a straightforward idealization of frugality and industry for their own sakes.

Given these ambiguities and the peculiar economic needs of New England, the Puritan society established in the New World had no quarrel with either commerce or mobility. Somehow individuals who amassed large fortunes in trade fell into a very different category from simple workmen who grubbed together some petty sum. Neither John Winthrop nor New Englanders in general had much use for the laborer who accumulated £25 by taking extortionate wages and then returned to England "with his prey," presumably in search of extravagant pleasures and a higher social station. Jehovah being just, the laborer lost all his money in the mother country and had to return to Massachusetts and his former humble calling, much to Winthrop's

48. William Ames broke with his teacher William Perkins on the subject of social mobility and tacitly legitimated it. Perkins had implied (though he never actually stated) that all superfluity should be given away, and he read 1 Corinthians 7:20, "Let every man abide in the same calling wherein he was called," to mean just that. Ames refused to give a specific answer to the question "how much must be bestowed in almes," contenting himself with "much more on pious uses" than on pleasures. And though he kept the distinctions of necessity and superfluity, concepts which varied with a man's social standing, he never read 1 Corinthians 7:20 to mean that this standing could not be changed: "neither doth he [St. Paul] there command that every one abide in that state in which he was called: for he permits a servant to aspire to freedome, verse 21. But teacheth that here is no difference of a free man and a servant in respect of Christ and Christian (general) calling, Verse 22" (Ames, *The Marrow of Sacred Divinity* in *Works,* p. 328; *Cases of Conscience* in *Works,* pp. 255-58, 3d pagination).

satisfaction.[49] The death of John Hull in 1683 was another matter
entirely, a cause to consider *The High Esteem which God hath of the
Death of his Saints*. Though he had risen from modest beginnings to
become one of Boston's leading merchants and a magistrate, Hull had
used his money soberly, remembering that it was God and not his
own ability that determined his commercial fortunes. He built himself a mansion house, as befited his new rank, but he also gave liber-
ally of his acquired wealth for the support of the poor and the commonwealth. It redounded only to his credit, in the orthodox view,
that "providence had given him a prosperous and Fluorishing Portion
of the Worlds Goods," because he knew what to do with it.[50]

New England could not afford an old-fashioned suspicion of commerce as unproductive or as more exposed to temptation than occupations which had less to do with money.[51] No one in Massachusetts
would have condemned trade on the grounds that it did not produce
anything—the whole of the colony's economic life too obviously depended on transatlantic commerce. John Oxenbridge, though he
warned that magistracy was not a "merchandising business," still
held in his election sermon of 1671 that a good magistrate would
encourage the development of staple commodities "which may command supplies from abroad."[52]

Governor William Bradford of New Plymouth did remark sourly
in his history, "*put not your trust in Princes* (much less in mar-
chants),"[53] but Plymouth was a poor farming community dependent
on grasping and dishonest English merchants who took the settlers
for all they were worth and more. Massachusetts Bay's mercantile
community, home grown and fully integrated into Puritan society,
could legitimately claim a major role in bringing prosperity to the
Bay Colony.

No society has ever totally escaped some degree of friction among

49. *Winthrop Journal*, 2 : 119.
50. Samuel Willard, *The High Esteem Which God Hath of the Death of His
Saints* (Boston, 1683), pp. 16–17.
51. For this attitude toward trade and commerce, see Tawney, *Religion and
the Rise of Capitalism*, pp. 36–39; George O'Brien, *An Essay on Medieval Economic Teaching* (London, 1920), pp. 136–54.
52. *New Englands Freeman Warmed and Warned* (Cambridge, Mass., 1673),
p. 41.

its constituent parts, and occasionally Massachusetts merchants, like members of other groups, came into conflict with the community as a whole. During the first decade of settlement the economic life of the colony was particularly tenuous, particularly dependent even for necessities on imports from England, and the colonists resented the sizable profits some men made out of this trade. In 1639 the General Court singled out the Boston merchant Robert Keayne[54] for punishment as an example to the rest of the merchant community, fining him £200 for taking fifty to one hundred percent profit on his transactions.[55] Keayne also had to appear before the Boston Church, of which he was a member, to answer charges of covetousness. In his defense, Keayne argued that he had mistakenly thought "that if a man lost in one commodity, he might 'help himself in the price of another" and that "if, through want of skill or other occasion, the commodity cost him more than the price of the market in England, he might sell it for more than the price of the market in New England." John Cotton responded by reading him the doctrine of the just price in a form that would easily have satisfied St. Thomas Aquinas:

> A man may not sell above the current price, i.e., such a price as is *usual in the time and place, and as another (who knows the worth of the commodity) would give for it*, if he had occasion to use it, as this is called current money, which every man will take, etc.[56]

Keayne "did with tears, acknowledge and bewail his covetous and corrupt heart," and the church let him off with an admonition, while the General Court remitted the larger part of his fine. [57] It would be

53. *History of Plymouth Plantation*, 1 : 258.

54. Bernard Bailyn has handled the Keayne incident in detail in "The *Apologia* of Robert Keayne," *William and Mary Quarterly*, 3rd ser., 7 (1950) : 568–87 and in his introduction to Keayne's will, *Publ. CSM*, 42 : 243–48. The discussion above should indicate that I dissent from Bailyn's interpretation.

55. Keayne "was charged with many particulars; in some, for taking above six-pence in the shilling profit; in some above eight pence, and in some small things, above two for one" (*Mass. Rec.*, 1 : 281; *Winthrop Journal*, 1 : 377–80).

56. *Winthrop Journal*, 1 : 380–82. Cf. William Perkins, *A Golden Chaine*, *Works*, 1 : 65–66; William Ames *Cases of Conscience*, *Works*, 236–39 (3d pagination).

easy to develop from this case an irrepressible conflict between the "medieval" oligarchy of magistrates and ministers, who prized piety, stability, and order, and a "modern" class of merchant capitalists, who valued mobility and material acquisition. It would, in fact, be much too easy.

John Cotton's version of the just price did not entail any use of the price system to enforce some sort of preexisting social hierarchy, and aside from the atypical speculations of the fifteenth-century schoolman Henry of Langenstein, it does not seem that the just price ever involved that concept. [58] Cotton's just price amounted to nothing more than the going market price of a product free from monopoly, misrepresentation, or coercion but fully subject to the ordinary fluctuations of supply and demand.[59] This was scarcely a very restrictive notion, whatever its medieval heritage.

Cotton had invoked the just price because of its suitability to an economy far more backward than that of the Europe of Aquinas. The just price was intended to protect consumers under conditions of imperfect competition: its real beneficiaries were the country areas away from the market towns; but in 1639 virtually the whole colony outside Boston was one vast hinterland in just this situation. After nine years of continuous immigration, Massachusetts had changed from an empty, howling wilderness into a howling wilderness with ten thousand ill-equipped people in it who relied on imports from abroad for everything vital to life above the bare subsistence level.

Robert Keayne became obnoxious neither because he was rich nor because he was a merchant, but because he was a Boston merchant

57. *Winthrop Journal,* 1 : 380; *The Records of the First Church of Boston, Publ.* CSM, 39 : 25, 29.

58. On the just price in general and Henry of Langenstein in particular, see Raymond de Roover, "The Concept of Just Price: Theory and Economic Policy," *Journal of Economic History* 18 (1958) : 418–34, with discussion on pp. 435–38.

59. Aquinas's concept of just price probably amounted to no more than this; certainly the just price came down to that by the sixteenth century (Ibid., pp. 422–24). Cotton specifically stated that "where there is a scarcity of the commodity, there men may raise their price; for now it is a hand of God upon the commodity, and not the person" (*Winthrop Journal,* 1 : 381). Cf. Ames: "that price is just, if the thing bee sold for so much as it can bee sold for: that is, as it can bee sold for commonly, not out of any affection, or for the profit of this or that man" (*Cases of Conscience, Works,* pp. 236–37, 3d pagination).

taking advantage of the complete dependence of the country towns on the colony's one major port. The Rev. Ezekiel Rogers of the country town of Rowley grew so excited about the "oppression" of the Boston merchants that, at the opening of the Keayne case, he advocated "a Law to hang up some [of the merchants] before the Lord, they deserve it, and it would to him be a sacrifice most acceptable. Shall the already persecuted and impoverished members of Christ be made a pray to Cormorants?"[60] But seven years later in 1646 Rogers warmly welcomed a direct trade link between Rowley and the Yorkshire merchant William Sykes if it would break the Boston monopoly:

> Boston men at the other end of the Country are in a way of Trading for all things. We at this ende of the Country, who are neerer to the Fishing places, timber etc. than they have hitherto bought all of them. but we growe weary of it And being now in a deepe consultation (upon prayer) what way to take for some way of Trading out of Englande, yor Lettere were brought to us, as by a Speciall hand of Providence, which did not a little affect us.[61]

As the economy of the coastal regions improved, the "just price" retreated westward. Willard's *Compleat Body of Divinity*, the product of a Boston minister of the early eighteenth century, denied that commodities had an "Intrinsical Value" and held the common market price to be the fair one, providing there was no monopoly of goods.[62] At the same time Solomon Stoddard of the western town of Northampton continued the old thunder against "oppresion," applying the doctrine exclusively to country areas, where poor transportation and inadequate market and credit facilities allowed retail supply merchants to take advantage of the rural buyer's ignorance and special necessity by charging him well above the going price at the market town:

60. Rogers to John Winthrop, 3 November 1639, *Winthrop Papers*, 4 : 150–51.
61. Rogers to Sykes, 2 December 1646, British Museum, Add. MS. 4276, fol. 105, quoted in Amos E. and Emily Jewett, *Rowley, Massachusetts* (Rowley, 1946), pp. 33–34 and verified against the original. The venture failed because of Sykes's financial difficulties. Rogers to Sykes, 24 January 1648/49, Add. MS. 4276, fol. 108.
62. Pp. 704–08.

When there is a general Scarcity, the Market-price will in-
avoidably rise; but where there is no Market, particular persons
may be in great necessity; there be few in Town that can supply
them. If they go to another Town to buy, the charge will be considerable; the man is also in a strait because strangers will not
trust him, and the Seller takes that advantage to oppress him.[63]

The last stronghold of "medieval" economics seems to have been the
American frontier.

Economic backwardness, not economic progress, had caused the
Keayne case; it represented no more than an example of inevitable
social friction in the early days of a pioneer community, not the first
stage of a nascent conflict between a medieval, aristocratic order and
a rising class of bourgeois merchants. The cure for the problem lay
in more merchants, more markets, better roads, and fewer shortages
—in brief, in economic growth. In the course of the seventeenth century, price and wage regulations relaxed[64] and social divisions be-

63. *An Answer to some Cases of Conscience* (Boston, 1722), pp. 1–2.
64. Though a law against demanding exorbitant wages or charging excessive
prices remained on the books from 1635 on, instances of its enforcement against
men selling goods they had not produced themselves (as opposed to artisans taking too high a price for articles they had also manufactured) occur very infre-
quently. Aside from Keayne, the General Court also admonished the Boston
merchant Robert Sedgwick in 1639 and the Assistants Court fined two individuals for "extortion" the same year (though they may not have been merchants). Further enforcement seems to have been left up to the county courts,
which prosecuted rarely if at all. The Essex County court records for a fifty-year
period contain only four definite convictions, three of them within six months
of each other in 1658. Though the General Court strengthened the law against
oppression during King Philip's War, allegedly increased vigilance produced
exactly one individual indicted for extortionate prices in Suffolk County for the
whole period 1670 to 1680, and none at all in Essex County. *Mass. Rec.,*
1 : 159–60, 279; *The Lawes and Liberties of Massachusetts,* ed. Max Farrand
(Cambridge, Mass., 1929), p. 43; John F. Noble and J. F .Cronin eds., *Records
of the Court of Assistants of the Colony of the Massachusetts Bay* (Boston,
1901–28), 1 : 283; *Essex Cty. Ct. Records,* 1 : 34, 2 : 69, 100, 118; *Suffolk
Cty. Ct. Records,* 2 : 632. Indictments for taking excessive wages occur more
frequently, especially in the first decade of settlement, both in the colony records
and those of the individual counties, but their total number is relatively small
too. Richard B. Morris and Jonathan Grossman have treated this subject in "The
Regulation of Wages in Early Massachusetts," *New England Quarterly* 11
(1938) : 470–500.

tween magistrates, ministers, and merchants grew smaller.[65] Long before the old charter fell many if not most of the Massachusetts magistrates were merchants. The men who originally filled the offices of governor and assistants had mainly acquired their wealth as members of the English landed aristocracy or as prominent lawyers, but once in New England William Pynchon, Simon Bradstreet, and John Winthrop, Jr., among other magistrates, turned to trading as well as farming. Before long men primarily engaged in mercantile activity, such as Francis Willoughby and Edward Gibbons, also joined the magistracy, so that by 1673 the governor (John Leverett) and at least half of the remaining twelve magistrates were either merchants or deeply involved in mercantile ventures. The merchants as a class could not have opposed the magistrates without opposing themselves.

In addition, merchants such as Samuel Sewall, Anthony Stoddard, and Thomas Brattle sent their sons into the ministry, while the ministers reciprocated by marrying their daughters to merchants and making merchants of their own sons. So, far from being at odds, merchants, magistrates, and ministers, through family connections and intermarriage, formed one integral community.[66] Indeed, the merchants occupied so central a position in their society's upper stratum, that Massachusetts seems more analogous in this respect to contemporary Venice or Ragusa than to England, where the landed gentry still predominated and would continue to do so for another century and more. But unlike the ruling classes of the southern European trading states, the Massachusetts merchants occupied the seats of power in a community where the vast majority of the population engaged in agriculture. In this one sense, at least, seventeenth-century Massachusetts was as unique as its inhabitants claimed.

The real flaw in Puritan economic teachings lay, not in setting medieval farmers against modern merchants, but in setting every man against himself if he sincerely tried to follow the impossible command to immerse himself in the things of this world and still not set his affections upon them. A man did not have to have Robert Keayne's margin of profit to consider himself covetous; he could take no profit at all and still sin if he delighted in material goods in themselves.

65. This subject is treated at greater length in appendix C.
66. See appendix D.

Covetousness was the mother sin, an idolatry deserving eternal death, yet it came terribly close to resembling the most virtuous possible pattern of life, at least as John Cotton described that life:

> For a man to *rise early, and goe to bed late,* and eate the bread of carefullnesse, not a sinful, but a provident care, and to avoid idleness, cannot indure to spend any idle time, takes all opportunities to be doing something, early and late and looseth no opportunity, go anyway and bestir himselfe for profit, this will he doe most diligently in his calling: And yet bee a man deadhearted to the world.

Cotton admitted that the work of two men in their callings might appear externally identical and yet the one might be a worldling and the other a redeemed saint because the first made earthly things his chief goal while the second, as a true Christian, improved his talent according to God's law and set his heart and mind on heaven. This curious combination of labor "morning and evening, early and late" with "dead-heartedness" to the world Cotton conceded to be "such a mystery as none can read, but they that know it."[67]

Men should grow rich and New England prosper, saith the preacher —but in the next breath he added that riches and public prosperity would likely lead to pride, willfulness, vain and idolatrous trust in wealth, luxury, "and the following of every affection with contempt of God."[68] Writing of Plymouth Colony, Cotton Mather concluded: "Religion begat prosperity and the daughter devoured the mother." Michael Wigglesworth put it still more tersely: "when creatures smile god is under valew'd."[69]

Men might allowably take some joy in the creatures, but only of a very special sort: "Yee may joy in it with a remisse joy, and ye may also sorrow for it with a remisse sorrow; yee may joy in it as if *yee*

67. *Christ the Fountaine of Life,* pp. 119–20.

68. Ames, *Cases of Conscience, Works,* pp. 253–54 (3d pagination). Cf. Downame, *Christian Warfare,* p. 376; Richard Sibbes, *Works,* 6 : 237–38.

69. Mather, *Magnalia Christi Americana* (Hartford, Conn., 1853), 1 : 63. Edmund S. Morgan, ed., *The Diary of Michael Wigglesworth, Publ.* CSM (Boston, 1951), 35 : 326. Mather called covetousness "the SIN of the LAND; A sin which threatens My Own Countrey, as much as any one sin that can be mentioned" (*A Very Needful Caution* [Boston, 1707], p. 50).

joyed not, and sorrow in it as if yee sorrowed not."[70] A forceful paradox, but one man's paradox is another's contradiction. If Christians had been under orders to die daily for sixteen hundred years before a European ever set foot in New England, at least they had not always been told to pursue their mundane affairs with a truly holy violence in the process. Just how could a man live actively in the world and still not "live to" it? It all depended on his attitude,[71] but he had to judge his attitude by a standard which almost always required him to bring in a verdict of guilty. It was not that the Puritan economic ethic somehow "unleashed" covetousness, that it aroused an impulse that went berserk, but rather that when it came to translating the subtle distinctions of the treatises into a working guide for actual conduct, the difference between covetous affection and diligent zeal could be grasped only by a mental contortionist. The more a man sincerely tried to fulfill the ideal, the more he would be forced into self-denunciation.

A remarkable individual like John Winthrop might bring it off; he was, as Israel Stoughton said, "indeed a man of men." More often the tensions within Puritan teachings led to the tortured and insufferably repetitious self-recriminations of a Michael Wigglesworth. That worthy filled his diary with one long lamentation for his sins without ever achieving any actual misconduct. He dwelt instead entirely on his frame of mind, accusing himself of pride, sensuality, and above all "whoorish desertions of my heart from God to the creatures."[72] Wigglesworth spent so much time excoriating himself, he may have actually believed he really was (as he called himself) "the chief of sinners." In point of fact he was only the dullest.

Each individual could keep a diary like Wigglesworth's, while the ministry arraigned New England as a whole for the same sins. Urian Oakes called worldliness "an *Epidemical* disease of New England"

70. John Preston, *A Remedy Against Covetousness* in *Foure Godly and Learned Treaties*, p. 23. The italicized phrase is an allusion to 1 Corinthians 7 : 29–31.

71. Merely using lawful means to procure wealth did not exonerate men from covetousness—"The love of wealth for the satisfying of the flesh is unlawful, whatever the means be." Indeed, a man could be a worldling and yet be content only with what he had if he "overloved" it (Richard Baxter, *A Christian Directory*, p. 256).

72. *Wigglesworth Diary*, p. 336.

in 1673; two years before, Samuel Danforth had cried that "Pride, Contention, Worldliness, Covetousness, Luxury, Drunkenness and Uncleannesse breaks in like a flood upon us, and good Men grow cold in their love to God and to ane another." Danforth was sure he saw calamity approaching because "inordinate worldly cares, predominant Lusts, and malignant Passions and Distempers stifle and choak the Word, and quench our affections to the Kingdom of God."[73]

The second and third generations of New Englanders liked to flatter themselves by thinking that they had degenerated from the irreproachable behavior of the founders, but that group of individuals had not considered themselves exempt from the standard catalogue of Puritan sins. John Cotton, who had seen the *Arbella* off in 1630 with the observation that material as well as spiritual prosperity showed God's blessings, some years later wrote of "this countrey, wherein men that have left all to enjoy the Gospel now (as if they had for gotten the end for which they come hither) are ready to leave the gospel for outward things." As early as 13 March 1638/39, the Massachusetts General Court declared a day of humiliation because of the prevalence of "novelties, oppression, atheisme, excesse, superfluity, idleness, contempt of authority."[74]

73. Urian Oakes, *New England Pleaded With* (Cambridge, Mass., 1674), p. 33; Samuel Danforth, *A Brief Recognition of New-England's Errand into the Wilderness* (Cambridge, Mass., 1671), pp. 10–16. Perry Miller anatomized this type of literature, the "Jeremiad" as he named it, in *The New England Mind, From Colony to Province* (Boston, 1961), pp. 27–39 and in the title essay of *Errand into the Wilderness* (New York, 1964), pp. 1–15.

74. Cotton, *Gods Promise to His Plantations* (London, 1630), reprinted in *Old South Leaflets*, no. 53, pp. 11–13; *A Briefe Exposition with Practical Observations Upon the Whole Book of Ecclesiastes* (London, 1654), p. 1; *Mass. Rec.*, 1 : 253. Earlier, in *New England's First Fruits* (London, 1643), New England's prosperity had been cited as a sign of God's approval of the colony. Reprinted in Samuel Eliot Morison, *The Founding of Harvard College* (Cambridge, Mass., 1935), pp. 440–46. On the "degeneration" of the first generation cf. also Charles Chauncy, *Gods Mercy Showed To his People in Giving Them A Faithful Ministry and Schools of Learning for the Continual Supplyes Thereof* (Cambridge, Mass., 1655), pp. 18–21; Thomas Shepard, *Wine for Gospel Wantons* (Boston, 1668), p. 13. The latter was a sermon delivered in 1645. It would be almost as easy to write a history of seventeenth-century New England in terms of the "declension" of the first generation as in terms of the apostacy of the second and third (as is usually done). Indeed, Darrett B. Rutman has recently done just that, in *Winthrop's Boston*.

The same men who saw themselves preoccupied with worldly goods and alienated from God also relished "affliction" because it returned their affections to the proper place. When men doted on the creatures the Lord showed them the frailty and transitoriness of earthly things. He sent them every variety of financial reverses, natural disasters, mortalities, plagues, famines, Indian wars, and other horrors—all to restore New England and individual New Englanders to their senses. "Prosperity" as Samuel Sewall confided to a friend, "is too fullsom a diet for any man . . . unless seasoned with some grains of adversity."[75] Much earlier, John Winthrop made a point of entering into his journal the cautionary tale of "a godly woman" of Boston who doted overmuch on her fine linen. A providential accident destroyed it, "but it pleased God that the loss of the linen did her much good, both in taking off her heart from worldly comforts, and in preparing her for a far greater affliction by the untimely death of her husband."[76]

Again and again Puritans used the metaphor of a purging or purifying fire to describe (and welcome) affliction: "I consider affliction is Gods furnace, it shall purge away filth, so that I shall be fitter either to live better, or dy happier, having a weightier crown of glory."[77] Though God's people might initially resent his chastisements, according to Urian Oakes, they soon realized that they were proofs of his particular love to them: "When they come to themselves and see how righteous it is with God, how profitable to themselves, they recover themselves, and say, it is good for them to be afflicted,

75. Samuel Sewall to Daniel Gookin, 16 March 1671/72, *Sewall Papers,* 6 *Coll. MHS,* 1 : 17.

76. *Winthrop Journal,* 2 : 36. Cf. William Pynchon to John Winthrop, 4 November 1645, *Winthrop Papers,* 5 : 50. In 1629 Winthrop answered those who objected that emigrants from England would leave "a fruitful lande with peace and plenty of all thinges" by replying: "Onely this is the advantage of a meane condition, that it is at more freedom to dye and the lesse comfort any hathe in the things of this world, the more liberty and desire he may have to laye up treasure in heaven" ("General observations for the Plantation of New England," ibid., 2 : 116).

77. *Wigglesworth Diary,* p. 407. Cf. George Fenwick to John Winthrop, 17 March 1646/47, *Winthrop Papers,* 5 : 142.

because thereby they are reduced from their strayings, into the way of obedience."[78]

Self-accusation and the love of affliction became for most New Englanders the only possible resolution for the mass of conflicting imperatives that comprised Puritanism. Historians for some reason have often taken their pronouncements of declining times at face value and so have written either enthusiastically, or occasionally tragically, of the decline of the wilderness Zion and the subsidence of piety in greed and worldliness. But except by the Puritans' own impossible and contradictory standards this is not necessarily a true judgment, any more than Michael Wigglesworth's description of himself as the "chief of sinners" is an accurate statement of fact. No man could fulfill the Puritan economic ideal and still retain a favorable opinion of himself because the definition of sin came so close to the ideal of virtue that fallible men would invariably pass back and forth from one to the other. Even contemporaries realized this much. Men were supposed to condemn themselves, and they sinned all the more if they did not:

> [Those] that are not sick of themselves and their aversness and indisposition to Gods service, are doubtless weary of God. For experience shews that the best of Gods People have their weary fits, much of what we have spoken of, weariness of God and His service, may be applyed to the sincere faithfull servants of God at sometimes, and in some pangs of temptation. . . . But then they do not allow themselves in it, but judge and condemn themselves for it.[79]

As long as New Englanders continued to denounce themselves, as long as they were sure they had deserted their ideal, they were faithful to it. When they *stopped* bemoaning their worldliness and no longer felt a sense of guilt, at least one part of the Protestant ethic had finally given way to the spirit of capitalism.

78. Urian Oakes, *A Seasonable Discourse Wherein Sincerity & Delight in the Service of God is earnestly pressed upon Professors of Religion* (Cambridge, Mass., 1682), p. 21.

79. Ibid. pp. 26–28.

In a real sense New England was founded so that it might decline. From the first it was to be a New Israel, and the story of the twelve tribes, new or old, would be incomplete without a concluding tale of the falling away from God, of the wrath of Jehovah, of temporary revivals, and finally of ultimate failure. No part of the Bible was dearer to the Puritan heart than the first half of the Book of Jeremiah. New Englanders loved the majestic rhythms of the prophet's towering rages, the solemn and awful cadences in which he arraigned Israel's sin and declension. From Jeremiah the ministers of the second and third generations derived the literary form that served as the Puritan equivalent of the confessional, a ritual chastisement of the self told as the story of the congregation's apostacy from the ways of their ancestors. They had not really fallen away, they only suffered from paradoxes inherited from their fathers, but that did not matter then. The jeremiads offered purification not history. Still, it might have been better for them—and for us—if they had abandoned Jeremiah now and then to take their texts from Ecclesiastes: "Say not thou, What is *the cause* that the former days were better than these? For thou dost not inquire wisely concerning this" (7:10).

5 Poverty: Affliction, Poor Relief, and Charity

THE COMFORTABLE BENEFIT OF AFFLICTIONS

Though the New England preacher's advice sometimes resembled Iago's "put money in your purse," anyone who knew the uncertainties of life in the seventeenth century knew that the Lord sent affliction as well as prosperity, that he made men poor as well as rich. Puritans had much to say about poverty but, certain modern writers to the contrary, they knew better than to teach that the godly would invariably prosper and that the poor were innately vicious.[1] If a just god

1. The theory that Puritanism identified poverty with evil, that "like the friends of Job, it saw in misfortune, not the chastisement of love, but the punishment of sin," usually calls up the name of Max Weber, although as a matter of fact he never maintained this proposition. Weber noticed and made use of the passages in Puritan and Calvinist writers which maintained that "God probably allows so many people to remain poor because He knows that they would not be able to withstand the temptations that go with wealth." The closest he came to the doctrine for which he has suffered considerable criticism was an ambiguous footnote: "The analogy between the unjust (according to human standards) predestination of only a few and the equally unjust, but equally divinely ordained, distribution of wealth, was too obvious to be escaped. . . . Furthermore, as for Baxter . . . poverty is very often a symptom of sinful slothfulness." That passage does not necessarily mean that the states of reprobation and poverty were identical, but only that apparently arbitray poverty—like apparently arbitrary damnation—actually conformed to a mysterious but deliberate divine plan, the purpose of which was known only by God himself. This, in fact, was the only point made by the section of Weber's text to which the passage just cited was a footnote. Weber came closer to arguing that Calvinists identified virtue and financial success, but even here he realized that they considered riches full of temptations; he only pointed out that, while they distrusted the *state* of wealth, they sanctified the *process* of money-making. (*The Protestant Ethic*, 156–57, 163, 172, 174, 177–78, 281 nn 102, 103).

The passage cited at the beginning of this note comes from R. H. Tawney (*Religion and the Rise of Capitalism*, p. 219), who did write that Puritanism had the effect of making poverty synonymous with sin and riches with virtue (his full discussion comes in the section entitled "The New Medicine for

ruled the world, since the Fall no man dared ask for justice alone, and
R. H. Tawney's version of the Puritan Jehovah did not always conform to the Rev. Samuel Willard's: "as Riches are not Evidences of
God's *Love*, so neither is *Poverty* of His Anger or *Hatred*; being such
things as in themselves make Men neither better nor *worse*; and are
equally improvable for Eternal Salvation."[2] Willard merely reiterated
a doctrinal commonplace in a particularly concise and lucid way. In
the first half of the seventeenth century, John Cotton had been just
as categorical. "No man can certainly discern the love or hatred of
God to himself or others, by their outward events or estates," he

---

Poverty," pp. 210–26). Margaret James attempted to prove a similar case in
Social Problems and Policy During the Puritan Revolution 1640–1660 (London, 1930), pp. 15–22, 241–302. Tawney and James came up, however, with
nothing more than contemporary denunciations of idle beggars. As it happens,
Puritan writers did make explicit statements in profusion that absolutely denied
any necessary correlation between adversity and sin. The indirect evidence, the
contention that the poor laws and private charity collapsed during and after
the Interregnum, is not accurate. The poor rates actually brought in more
money during the Civil War and Protectorate than before, and charitable giving,
though it fell off between 1640 and 1650, remained substantial and began to
recover its former magnitude in the decade 1650 to 1660. See Wilbur K. Jordan,
Philanthropy in England 1480–1660 (London, 1959), pp. 137–39, 245, 369
(table); A. L. Beier, "Poor Relief in Warwickshire 1630–1660," *Past and
Present 35* (December 1966): 77–100. Christopher Hill, however, attempts
to reconstruct the Tawney-James thesis in modified form, in "William Perkins
and the Poor," *Puritanism and Revolution* (London, 1958), pp. 215–38; "The
Poor and the Parish," *Society and Puritanism in Pre-Revolutionary England*
(London, 1964), pp. 259–97.
        Finally, lest I be accused of committing the same mistake for which I
criticized Weber's opponents in the previous chapter, I must admit that it is
conceivable that Puritanism could foster an attitude at the same time that it
explicitly condemned it. When Puritan theorists denounced "covetousness,"
however, they simultaneously advocated an activity which they admitted to
be externally identical to it, differing only in its motivation. There is no analogy
in Puritan thinking on affliction: most writers not only denied that the afflicted
were by definition sinful, they went on to describe how *profitable* the elect would
find their sufferings.
        2. *Compleat Body of Divinity*, p. 708.

wrote in an exposition on Ecclesiastes, and proceeded to fill a page
with biblical examples to prove it.³

William Ames had set down the orthodox position on poverty
with admirable precision at about the same time. To pray for
poverty or give away all to live on alms Ames considered "a madnesse
to bee condemned," not to say a popish abomination, but involuntary
poverty he considered neither shameful nor unlawful for those who
suffered it. Like all estates, poverty had its peculiar temptations. The
devil might prompt a poor man to despair, to murmur against God's
providence, to use unlawful means to relieve his misery, or to envy
others, but once these were overcome, poverty, with the grace of God,
could prove just as good a path to salvation as prosperity.⁴

The Puritan thought of poverty the same way he thought of all
affliction, as heaven sent but neutral. A man judged his spiritual
estate not by the afflictions that befell him but by the use he put them
to. "Tis true, that all kinds of crosses fall alike to all, sicnesse, poverty,
& c. upon the godly and the wicked; the difference is onely in the
issue. . . . Consider therefore whether thy afflictions brings [sic] thee
home to the Lord, or whether it drives thee from the Lord upon the
rockes."⁵ Afflictions came to try a man's faith, to wean him from vain
and empty creatures, or even to punish him for his sins, but whatever
the cause the elect would find them profitable and, in John Cotton's
words, "the fruits of Gods Fatherly love." A man under affliction had
to follow a simple but demanding rule of behavior: "be carefull to
come better out of affliction then you went in; what proud, impatient,

3. *A Brief Exposition on Ecclesiastes*, pp. 96–97. Other instances of the
same position occur regularly in both the seventeenth and eighteenth centuries.
Cf. Perkins, *A Commentarie or Exposition upon the Five First Chapters of the
Epistle to the Galatians, Works*, 2 : 313; Arthur Hildersham, *Lectures upon
the Fourth of John*, pp. 394–97; Thomas Hooker, *The Christians Two Chiefe
Lessons, Viz Selfe-Deniall, And Selfe-Tryall* (London, 1640), p. 65; Samuel
Moodey, *The Debtor's Monitor*, pp. 24–25; William Hubbard, *The Benefit of
a Well-Ordered Conversation*, pp. 16–17.
4. *Cases of Conscience*, pp. 251–53.
5. John Preston, *The Golden Sceptor Held Forth to the Humble* (London,
1638), pp. 288–89. A sinner who did *not* suffer affliction could only conclude
that the Lord had abandoned him to destruction (Ibid., p. 290). On the
neutrality of afflictions, cf. Downame, *The Christian Warfare*, pp. 858–60.

and covetous when you went in, and come sow out? God forbid, desire God rather never to leave you, till you get some good by the
afflictions you undergo."[6]

John Preston did write that, though God sent some afflictions for
trial, "yet for the most part they come from sinne"; but his readers
understood that no man escaped sin and that, since all men stood in
need of purification, punishment itself when properly used became a
blessing. Preston's contemporary, John Downame, pointed out that
even the regenerate received only justice no matter what blows God
rained on them, for before grace they too shared fully in the universal
human corruption and even in their gracious state they had to pay for
their former sins. Affliction fell on the just and the unjust alike, coming to the one in fatherly chastisement and to the other in vengeance.
Only the afflicted himself, through examination of his response, could
tell to which group he belonged. Downame had charity enough to
caution his readers not to judge themselves reprobate merely because
they did not seem to profit by their reverses and used "inconsiderate
speeches" in their suffering: A man had to evaluate his spiritual state
and its improvement after his affliction ceased, just as he determined
his bodily strength only in times of health and not of disease.[7]

Having vigorously repudiated the Catholic tenet of the holy nature
of poverty, the Puritans indirectly revived it again in preaching "the
comfortable benefit of afflictions." Obliged to distrust prosperity at
the same time he was enjoined to seek it, the believer could only welcome anything that disturbed his enjoyment of the creatures as with-
drawing "that which is the fuel of sin."[8] Poverty held temptations,
and severe ones, but prosperity held many more. Hooker did not feel
the least bit popish in declaring that "Adversity is a *safer condition*
for a *Christian* man, than Prosperity," any more than Thomas Shepard
thought himself cynical in writing in his diary that "men are better
generally under the Rod, than under mercy. We see what an Admir-

6. Cotton, *The Way of Life*, pp. 471, 479.
7. *The Golden Sceptor*, pp. 290–91; *Christian Warfare*, pp. 94–95, 841.
8. Richard Sibbes, *The Churches Complaint and Confidence, Works*, 6 : 184.
This sermon originally appeared in 1639. Cf. Downame, *Christian Warfare*,
pp. 913–14.

able Spirit there is under sore afflictions, which Men cannot attain to or keep, but then."[9] By direct consequence, in Richard Sibbes's words, "the state of God's church and children in the world, for the most part, is to be afflicted and poor in their outward condition,"[10] so that nation which considered itself the godliest in the world could hardly avoid taking pride in its underdeveloped economy—when it was not invoking the fact that it had an economy at all as witness to its contention that God had given his blessing to the New England Way. John Eliot, the "Apostle to the Indians," told a wiseacre brave who wanted to know why if the New Englanders were so godly they were not rich, "that God knows it is better for his children to be good than to be rich; he knows withal, that if some of them had riches they would abuse them, and wax proud and wanton, etc., therefore he gives them no more riches than may be needful for them, that they may be kept from pride, etc., to depend upon him."[11]

Abject poverty, the inability to maintain oneself on one's own income, New Englanders feared as much as any men, but a very moderate financial competence punctuated by periodic reverses had a curious attraction for them.[12] Ezekiel Cheever, Boston's great schoolmaster, had lived ninety-four years, most of them in New England, when on his deathbed in 1708 he gave Samuel Sewall a farewell exhortation that summarized the whole of the Puritan colonies' experience: "The Afflictions of God's people, God by them did as a Goldsmith, Knock, Knock, Knock, Knock, Knock, Knock, to finish the

---

9. Hooker, *A Treatise of Self-Denyall*, p. 70; Shepard, *Three Valuable Pieces* (Boston, 1747), p. 12. Downame also thought adversity "farre lesse dangerous" than prosperity *Christian Warfare*, p. 90).

10. *The Rich Poverty: or the Poore Mans Riches*, in *Works*, 6 : 237–38. The sermon was first issued in 1638.

11. *Winthrop Journal*, 2 : 370–71.

12. Thus Cotton Mather prayed in 1686, at the age of twenty-four, that "I might have a comfortable *Habitation* provided for mee, and that the Lord, my glorious Master would afford mee, all Conveniences, without the Distresses and Temptations, which *Poverty* does expose unto." He admitted, however, in good Puritan fashion, "that I count myself *unworthy* of the least Bitt of Bread; that I must own, I have given way to the lusts whereof *Penury* is the just punishment" (*Mather Diary*, 1 : 124).

plate: It was to perfect them not to punish them." Two days later he was dead.[13]

Cheever's attitude was not restricted to superannuated school-teachers and apostles to the Indians. William Coddington, a merchant, early New England magistrate, and founder of Newport, knew the meaning of the destruction of his farm buildings and livestock during the severe winter of 1644 as well as any writer of treatises: "the Lord hath begunne to let me see by experience that a mans comfort doth not depend in the multetude of those things he doth possese."[14] Financial loss hurt as much then as now, but men interpreted their pain differently.

When individual hardship multiplied whoesale, be it in plague, famine, or depression, the same theory of affliction was invoked on a massive scale. God improved whole countries as well as single inhabitants; that people he most loved could expect the greatest amount of his fatherly correction. "To turn Blessings into Idols, is the way to have them clap'd under a Blast: If the Lord loves his People, he will deliver those Weapons out of their hands, that they are obstinately resolved to fight Him with. . . . Better is it that *Israel* be saved and Prosperity lost, than that Prosperity be Saved and *Israel* lost."[15]

More concerned with promoting morality than commerce, Puritan economic thought often seems incomprehensible today. Cotton Mather's *Concio ad Populum*, a lecture sermon delivered to the Massachu-

---

13. *Sewall Diary*, 2 : 230. The habit of relishing afflictions extended beyond New England and survived the seventeenth century by a long period. Richard Henry Lee of Virginia wrote Samuel Adams on 2 February 1776 concerning "our ill fortune in Canada": "Those who sail gently down the smooth stream of prosperity, are very apt to loose that energetic virtue so necessary to true happiness. It seems that discipline, and pretty severe discipline too, is necessary for the depraved heart of man, nor have we any right to expect security in the enjoyment of the greatest human blessings until we have learnt wisdom and moderation in the school of adversity." James Curtis Ballagh, ed., *The Letters of Richard Henry Lee* (New York, 1911), 1 : 167–68.

14. William Coddington to John Winthrop, 5 August 1644, *Winthrop Papers*, 4 : 489–90. Cf. Anne Gibson to John Winthrop, 19 April 1629, *Winthrop Papers*, 2 : 81; the merchant William Pierce to Governor Bradford of New Plymouth, 25 December 1632, *History of Plymouth Plantation*, 2 : 155–56.

15. John Danforth, *The Vile Prophanations of Prosperity by the Degenerate Among the People of God* (Boston, 1704), p. 9.

setts General Court in 1719, claimed that hard times were caused by
New Englanders living *too* well, overindulging in luxuries. By way
of remedy, "the GRAND EXPEDIENT, is, *Frugality*," "a discrete, a
Righteous, a needful FRUGALITY, in our Domestick Expenses: more
particularly a Frugality in our Habits." Though Mather demanded
that the rich should lead the colony into frugality by their example,
he reserved his strongest admonitions for the poor, those living *beyond* their means: "It is to be demanded of the *Poor*, that they do not
indulge in an Affectation of making themselves in all things appear
equal with the *Rich*: But patiently submit unto the *Difference*, which
the *Maker of you Both*, has put between you." At the same time he
closed his discourse with the traditional rejoicing in New England's
lack of affluence, giving thanks that "in *Our Time*, such is the Constitution of the Country, that many *Great Estates* must not soon be
raised in it." Great estates would produce only a vanity so immense
as to proclaim to all the Lord's children, "*Depart, For this is not your
Rest: It is Polluted.*" But contentment with a decent estate and frugality and industry would together cure the depression and lead to
"good manners," "moral honesty," and a favorable balance of
trade."[16]

Mather had simply reiterated the old distrust of the creatures under
the guise of macroeconomics, the kind of approach that appealed to a
country whose elected legislature four years later banned "extravagant" expenditures on funerals "when the circumstances of the
province so loudly calls [*sic*] for all sorts of frugality."[17] Debate over
the issuing of paper money in inflationary quantities often involved
the same hostility to creature comforts and the same esteem for frugality. In 1726 the author of "A Speech without-doors touching the
Morality of Emitting more Paper Bills," a secular tract, not a sermon,
argued against further issues mainly under the banner of frugality.

16. *Concio ad Populum* (Boston, 1719), pp. 10–14, 27. Cf. *The Present
Melancholy Circumstances of the Province Considered* (Boston, 1719) in
Andrew M. Davis, ed., *Colonial Currency Reprints, Publications of the Prince
Society* (Boston, 1910–11), 1 : 351–63 and the various replies to Jonathan
Coleman's *The Distressed State of the Town of Boston, & C. Considered* (Bos-
ton, 1723) in Ibid., 1 and 2, passim.

17. *Acts and Resolves*, 2 : 229–30. The act was renewed in 1724 and
strengthened in 1742 (Ibid., 2 : 336, 1086).

His pamphlet claimed that the inevitable result of fiat money was that "the Affectation and use of Gayety, Costly Building, "[Dis]Stilled and other Strong Liquors, Palatable though Unhealthy Diet, Rageth with great Impetuosity, and in (its to be feared) in [*sic*] all orders and Degrees of Men."[18] A modern might consider a state in which all classes could indulge in "gayety" and costly buildings prosperity; seventeenth- and early eighteenth-century New Englanders labeled it luxury and considered it vice.

Poor Relief and Private Charity[19]

For all their ambivalence toward prosperity, New Englanders had no love for chronic poverty or the dependent poor. As Puritans they did not consider the desperately poor necessarily sinful or reprobate, yet as taxpayers they did fiercely resent contributing to their support. Somewhat grudgingly, but effectively, they adopted the English system of poor relief with certain peculiar variations, the product of the changed conditions of the New World and of the Puritanism of its inhabitants.

The laws of New England followed those of the mother country in distinguishing between the worthy poor, who could not earn enough to live on, and the idle poor, individuals able to work but unwilling

---

18. *Sewall Papers, 6 Coll.* MHS 2 : 235–39. The author of the piece may have been still another Mather, Warham of New Hampshire. Cf. *A Letter from One in the Country to his Friend in Boston* (Boston, 1720) in Davis, ed., *Colonial Currency Reprints,* 1 : 415–42. This pamphlet is attributed to the Rev. Edward Wigglesworth. Another minister, Thomas Paine, reversed the argument by claiming that paper money would cure extravagance and introduce industry and prudence. *A Discourse Shewing that the real first Cause of the Straits and Difficulties of this Province of the Massachusetts Bay, is its Extravagancy, & Not Paper Money* (Boston, 1721), in ibid., 2 : 280–300.

19. Some aspects of this subject have received detailed treatment elsewhere, and I will not repeat material that others have covered except in summary or where I differ from or wish to supplement a previous work. Citations to these sources will be given at the appropriate places in the text. The most detailed treatment of New England's system of poor relief in print is Robert W. Kelso, *The History of Public Poor Relief in Massachusetts 1620–1920* (Boston, 1922), which provides an adequate outline of the mechanisms of public welfare in colonial Massachusetts and little else.

to.[20] The second class presented some problems in law enforcement but none in ethics. "As for your *Common Beggar* 'tis usually an Injury and a Dishonour unto the Country, for them to be countenanced; as for those that Indulge themselves in *Idleness*, the Express Command of God unto us, is *That you should Let them Starve.*"[21] Idlers should be forced to work and the recalcitrant punished, sent to the house of correction, or even deported. The proper authorities were quite prepared to enforce the laws ruthlessly, to the discomfort of any number of idle New Englanders. In 1672 Steven Hoppine of Dorchester, living idly and singly, learned the cost of trifling with his town selectmen. Ordered to find employment, he put the selectmen off with evasions and outright lies until they lost their patience and had him sent to Suffolk County House of Correction to be kept at hard labor until "he bee orderly settled in some convenient service according to Law."[22] Eleven years later another Suffolk County idler, William Batt of Boston, proved even more incorrigible, resisting every effort of the Boston selectmen to set him to work, until they applied for and received power to ship him off to the West Indies.[23]

New England justice was particularly savage toward vagabonds, idle persons who wandered from town to town, "thereby drawing away children, servants and other persons both younger and elder,

20. *Mass. Rec.*, 1 : 264; 2 : 180, 199; 4 : pt. 1, 230, 365; pt. 2, 43; *Acts and Resolves*, 1 : 67–68, 378–81, 452–53, 538–39; *The General Laws and Liberties of New-Plymouth Colony* (Cambridge, Mass., 1672), pp. 27, 29–30; *The Book of the General Laws for the People within the Jurisdiction of Connecticut* (Cambridge, Mass., 1673), pp. 31, 57; *Acts and Laws, of His Majesties Colony of Connecticut in New-England* (New London, 1715), pp. 54, 94; *Acts and Laws of His Majesties Colony of Rhode-Island and Providence-Plantations in America*, p. 10.

21. Cotton Mather, *Durable Riches* (Boston, 1695), p. 20. Cf. Perkins, *Cases of Conscience, Works*, 2 : 144–45; Downame, *The Plea of the Poore*, pp. 38–39.

22. *Boston Rec.*, 4 : 158, 176, 177; *Suffolk Cty. Ct. Rec.*, 1 : 89. For other instances of individuals sent to the house of correction or "disposed to service" as punishment for idleness, see *Town Records of Salem* 1 : 124, 140, 142, 150; *Suffolk Cty. Ct. Rec.*, 1 : 231, 258; *Essex Cty. Ct. Rec.*, 2 : 57; *Inferiour Court of Pleas*, pp. 108, 132.

23. *Boston Rec.*, 7 : 162. John Smith was similarly expelled from the colony in 1677 (*Suffolk Cty. Ct. Rec.*, 1 : 871).

from their lawfull callings and imployments, and hardening the
hearts of one another against all subjection to the rules of Gods holy
word and the established lawes of all this colony." The Essex County
Court, for example, having adjudged Simond Foster and his wife
wandering persons in 1679, ordered them conveyed out of the colony
by being whipped from town to town at the back of a cartail.[24]

Cartails and bridewells would do for the unworthy poor, criminals
who could support themselves and would not, but that still left some
people whose misfortune was not of their own making. The New
England colonies considered these people entitled to public assistance
from the towns in which they legally resided if they qualified as "im-
potent" poor: orphans, widows, unwed mothers, and men incapacitated by sickness, age, lunacy, or the like. The third class of poor
recognized by the English laws, willing, able-bodied paupers who
could not find work and who were to be put to public employment,
had no place in the New England legislative system or the New England mentality.[25] The conditions that caused poverty in seventeenth-
century England had no equivalent on the other side of the Atlantic,
where the Puritan colonies suffered from a chronic and intense labor
shortage. Connecticut Governor William Leete's answer to a Board
of Trade query about poverty in 1680 might just as well have applied
to the whole of New England of his time: "Every town maintains its
own poor: But there is seldom any want, because labour is dear . . .
[and] because provisions are cheap."[26] No statutes provided for local
officials to set the willing poor at work making hemp, and no person
presented for idleness or living without a calling dared to defend himself by claiming he could not find employment.[27] The town selectmen

24. *Mass. Rec.*, 4 : pt. 2, 43; *Essex Cty. Ct. Rec.*, 7 : 328.

25. English Puritans did recognize that an able-bodied man could need
relief. "But the poore upon whom the godly and blessed man doth exercise his
benificence, is the honest laborer and the poore householder, who either through
the greatnesse of their charge, or badnesse of their trade, crosses, losses, sicnesse,
suretiship, or other casualties being brought behinde hand, are not able in the
sweate of their face to earne their bread" (Downame, *Plea of the Poor*,
pp. 39–40).

26. 1 *Coll. MHS*, 4 : 222.

27. The selectmen of Watertown had only to look at the way Samuel
Benjamine was dressed in 1653 to conclude that he was an idler: "Samuel
Benjamine was presented before us for Idleness . . . which Did two evidently

would have had no trouble in supplying the want. "If the Poor will but *Work*," wrote Cotton Mather, "they would make a better hand of it in this country, than in almost any under the Cope of Heaven. What a pity it is, that such an *Hive* should have any Drones in it."[28]

Thanks to dear labor, cheap provisions, and plentiful land, a people that prided itself on its poverty had few actual paupers in its ranks. Watertown was paying £26 for its poor in 1671 and £70 in 1736, Salem less than £25 in 1657, Charlestown £10 in 1655 and £35 in 1711, Dorchester no more than £8.1.2 in 1662 and only £17 in 1674, while Springfield had less than a £70 bill for the poor as late as 1730. The numbers of paupers involved were obviously not large since even a healthy poor person needed at least £5 and generally £10 to £12 a year for his maintenance, while medical bills might drive that figure considerably higher: one invalid accounted for a full £28 of Watertown's £70 expense in 1736. Even Boston, which later developed a serious relief problem, laid out only £53 for welfare in 1654, £26 of it in tax abatements. No baby was left abandoned on a Boston doorstep until 4 November 1685.[29]

A small number of actual paupers must have brought little consolation to New England taxpayers, who found the figures for the cost of maintenance (and the loss in revenue through tax abatements) quite large enough. Like the contemporary English ratepayers, the New Englanders had little liking for paying even small public charges. Unlike their English contemporaries, however, they did pay. The colonists came from an English background where the primary responsibility for care of the poor fell on private charity, principally the income from charitable trusts established by the legacies of individual philanthropists. The state had enforced the elaborate mechanisms of the Tudor and Stuart poor laws only to supplement these private bequests, and when it tried to do more, as in the decade be-

---

apeare by his ragged clothes" (*Watertown Records* [Watertown, Conn., 1894–1939], 1 : 33). Any able-bodied man willing to work could have afforded better dress.

28. *Concio ad Populum*, p. 15.

29. *Watertown Records*, 1 : 108–09; 3 : 135, 146–48; *Salem Records*, 1 : 204; Frothingham, *History of Charlestown*, pp. 149–50, 246; *Boston Rec.*, 4 : 115–16, 202, 205; *Springfield Records*, 2 : 459–63; Rutman, *Winthrop's Boston*, pp. 218–220. *Sewall Diary*, 1 : 103.

fore the calling of the Long Parliament, the ratepayers resisted strenuously and with effect.[30] In New England, by contrast, private charity only supplemented the local rates, voted and paid for by the fellow townsmen of the individual needing relief. Like idleness and illiteracy, poverty was regarded as an essentially public evil, remediable at public expense.

Though some New Englanders did leave money as capital bequests rather than for outright distribution, the nature of the colonial economy made charitable trusts neither necessary nor very practical: the trustees found few safe investments yielding a good return.[31] Massachusetts waited until 1671 before passing a law corresponding to the Elizabethan Statute of Charitable Uses and enacted very little legislation on trusts in general during the colonial period, as opposed to the extremely complicated body of charity law that developed at the same time in England.[32] While New Englanders gave considerable amounts to charity during their lifetimes, particularly through church collections, they left relatively little in their wills for the relief of poverty or any other benevolent purpose. In the ten-year period 1651–60, a decade when many leading members of the first generation of settlers died and when the New England economy attained some degree of stability, the citizens of Essex County left the unimpressive total

30. Jordan, *Philanthropy in England*, pp. 126–42, 240–63.

31. When Major John Richards left a legacy "to be improved for the poor" in 1694, the selectmen of Boston could think of no better way to invest it than to use it to refinish the upstairs of a local store as a chamber for rent (*Boston Rec.*, 7 : 226). Leaving land was equally bad: New England land titles were so confused that the heirs often inherited nothing more than a lawsuit, and even if they had clear title they had trouble renting land while freeholds were available at little cost. Samuel Eliot Morison, *The Founding of Harvard College*, pp. 322–24. A recent student has found few instances of capital bequests in a massive survey of over three thousand New England wills for the periods 1650–70, 1705–15, and 1758–62 (Kenneth A. Lockridge, "The Charitable Impulse in Old and New England: An Enquiry into the Origins of the American Character," p. 11. The author has kindly allowed me to read his study in manuscript).

32. *Mass. Rec.*, 4 : pt. 2, 488. On English charity law see Jordan, *Philanthropy in England*, pp. 109–25; David Owen, *English Philanthropy 1660–1960* (Cambridge, Mass., 1964), pp. 70–71.

sum of £5 for the benefit of the poor.[33] Suffolk County, which included Boston, did rather better with just over £238, but two individuals, the merchants Robert Keayne and Henry Webb, accounted for £225 of this amount between them.[34] Keayne and Webb only reflected the tradition of their native London, where they had learned that a merchant died disgraced unless he left substantial benefactions in his will.[35] Such pious and substantial men as the Rev. John Cotton, Major General Daniel Dennison, and Deputy Governor Samuel Symonds, whose estates totaled £1,000, £2,000 and £2,500 respectively, left nothing at all to charity, while Governor Thomas Dudley contributed only five marks (£3.6.8) for the poor out of an estate of £1,500. Governors Endecott and Winthrop died poor, and Governor Richard Bellingham, who left enough to charity to provide the basis for a lawsuit lasting over a century, designated the whole amount for the maintenance of the ministry.[36]

Since secular charitable trusts were relatively unimportant in New England, the center for private charity remained the church. The Eng-

33. This has been determined by a survey of *The Probate Records of Essex County Massachusetts* (Salem, 1916–20) for the appropriative years. The only legacies for the poor are in 1 : 216, 223. Total gifts for charity amounted to £12.80, an annuity for Harvard of unspecified amount, and a cow (Ibid., 1 : 128, 141, 207, 235). Secondary legacies have not been counted in these or other figures if they were conditional on the extinction of the line of the primary heir. Just after the period considered, the Rev. Ezekiel Rogers did leave the bulk of his estate of £1,535 to the church of Rowley, or to the town, for the maintenance of the ministry of the church (Ibid., 1 : 333–34).

34. *NEH&GR*, 5 (1851): 296; 8 (1854): 356; 10 (1856): 179–80; Keayne, *Apologia*, pp. 265–70. Other causes received £567 in cash, a £5 annuity and four grants of land, at least one of them substantial. In addition to the citations given, cf. *NEH&GR*, 4 (1850): 53, 54; 5 : 301, 302, 443; 8 : 281; 9 (1855): 36; 10 : 86, 265.

35. Keayne and Webb accounted for £470 of the cash bequests for other causes and the largest grant of land as well. While in England Keayne had adopted the interesting system of putting aside one penny out of every shilling he earned and assigning it to the poor. He kept it up for forty years (*Apologia*, pp. 268–69). On the munificence of the London mercantile community, see Jordan, *Philanthropy in England*, pp. 348–51.

36. *NEH&GR*, 5 : 241; 7 : 23–24, 128v; *Essex Probate Records*, 3 : 263–71; *NEH&GR*, 5 : 296; *Sewall Papers*, 2 : 9–10. Lockridge's much more extensive sampling of wills confirms the infrequency of any kind of charitable bequest ("The Charitable Impulse in Old and New England," pp. 8–11 and passim).

lish "brief," a letter from the king as head of the Church of England authorizing the collection of charity in the churches of a given county for a stated cause, obviously violated Puritan sensibilities and had no New England equivalent, although the device remained in use in England until 1828.[37] But abandoning the brief did not mean abandoning the poor, and it would be incorrect to assert that the churches ignored their duty in this area. As early as 1642 a receipt of the First Church of Boston referred to a deceased member "who in the tyme of his sicness was maintained at the churches charge a longe season."[38] Throughout the century the Boston churches received occasional legacies for the poor (including half of Robert Keayne's £120) and sometimes shared with the town the costs of keeping a poor member or administered the town's grant to him.[39] Boston considered the deacons of its First Church sufficiently expert on poverty to appoint them to supervise the construction of the public alms house in 1660.[40] All the churches of the town aided the poor of their own congregations and elsewhere by special collections, and in addition the First voted a regular monthly contribution for its poor in 1688.[41] Scattered evidence indicates that churches of other towns aided the

37. On the brief, see Jordan, *Philanthropy in England*, pp. 149–50, 353, 362–63; Owen, *English Philanthropy*, p. 84. A complaint against briefs is included in the list of "common grievances" presented to the Parliament of 1624 in the *Winthrop Papers*: the petitioners objected that charitable collections should be left to the discretion of the localities—"None so fitt to releeve the poore as the county which may easily enquire of the certeyntie of the losse of the poverty and liyfe of the partie whither fitt to be releeved" (1 : 302–03).

38. *Winthrop Papers*, 4 : 354.

39. In addition to Keayne's bequest, the First Church received £4 from Mary Ward in 1667 and £230 from Anne Mills in 1725, and there are probably other bequests for which the records have been lost or are not readily available (*Suffolk Cty. Ct. Rec.*, 2 : 1032; *Boston First Church Rec.*, 2 : 469). For instances of the churches sharing the expenses of their poor members with the town, see *Boston Rec.*, 7 : 114, 147, 149.

40. *Boston Rec.*, 7 : 7.

41. *Boston First Church Rec.*, 1 : 119. In 1650 the First Church raised a special contribution to help the suffering Congregational church of the Bermudas, and in 1711 the Second Church raised £260 to aid victims of the great Boston fire of that year, to give only two examples. *First Church Rec.*, 1 : 50–51; Carl Bridenbaugh, *Cities in the Wilderness* (New York, 1955), p. 235.

poor as well,[42] but the general rule both in Boston and elsewhere remained as the First Church voted in 1691: "the poor beinge poore of Towne so under their care, and only as church members to have some addition."[43]

When the church refused to contest for primary responsibility for the poor, the trust devolved on the towns, which in their turn pursued a policy combining a genuinely charitable impulse with an overriding passion for keeping taxes low and a ruthless zeal for order. Dorchester could raise contributions for the family of the minister of Braintree and the relief of the fleet in the Caribbean in 1667, and five years later order out of town the daughter of an inhabitant, despite her advanced state of pregnancy, because she had married a Beverly man who had not properly provided for her. The selectmen regarded her continued residence in Dorchester as "contrary to good order, and to the hazarding of a charge upon the towne."[44] Precisely because the towns acknowledged that they had to support their own needy inhabitants, they often went to extravagant lengths to make sure they admitted no one as a resident who might someday need support. Most towns passed ordinances forbidding residents to entertain strangers without permission and required bond of perspective inhabitants guaranteeing that they would not cost the town anything during their residence. Town selectmen also made sure to

42. Thomas Dudley left his five marks for the poor to the deacons of the church of Roxbury, for example, and by 1654 at the latest, the deacons of the church of Dorchester had begun to disperse stock and funds for the poor and distressed of their own and other towns. For Dudley's will, see the last citation in note 36 above. For the activities of the deacons of Dorchester between 1654 and 1689, see *Boston Rec.*, 4 : 112; *Records of the First Church of Dorchester, in New England, 1636–1734* (Boston, 1891), pp. 8–9, 53, 56, 83, 90, 91–92, 93–94, 96, 100, and the references in the index under "church benevolences." Cf. also *Salem Records*, 3 : 20.

43. *Boston First Church Rec.*, 1 : 120.

44. *Boston Rec.*, 4 : 141, 147, 185. They may not have been very successful in getting her to leave, since the selectmen had to repeat the order twice in the next two years (Ibid., pp. 192, 199). Towns could appeal to the county courts when recalcitrants refused to obey their orders to leave. See *Essex Cty. Ct. Rec.*, 3 : 62, 65, 95, 218; 4 : 397; 6 : 192; 7 : 179, 271; 8 : 22, 45, 186, 292.

"warn out" anyone who was not a legal inhabitant and who seemed to need aid.[45]

The selectmens' vigilance, shared by all who had to pay taxes, sometimes resulted in unseemly jurisdictional disputes. Newbury warned out Evan Morice in 1682, because he had become a public charge in his old age, and sent him back to Topsfield, from which he had moved five years previously. Topsfield retaliated by warning Morice back to Newbury even though he had been one of the earliest settlers of the town and had "born lot and scot" in all town charges for over thirty years. Both towns appealed to the Essex County Court, which assigned Morice to Newbury but required Topsfield to pay one-third of his charge.[46]

Warnings out became common occurrences in many areas in the eighteenth century. Not surprisingly, urban Boston had a large number (over five hundred warned out between 1721 and 1742), but even the towns of rural Worcester County issued thirty-four separate warrants ordering single persons, couples, and sometimes entire families to depart from their jurisdiction in the years 1733–37 alone.[47] By this period the order had lost its original purpose because of changes in the Massachusetts residency laws. For the most part the selectmen were no longer trying to have the objectionable parties removed— they would have had to pay for removal—but only serving formal notice that the town would not be responsible for their support if they became indigent.[48] At the end of the century some towns took to

---

45. These practices, the law governing them, and instances of their enforcement are treated in detail for all the New England colonies in Josiah Henry Benton, *Warning Out in New England* (Boston, 1911).

46. *Essex Cty. Ct. Rec.*, 8 : 291–92. For other instances in which the county courts assigned paupers to particular towns see *Suffffolk Cty. Ct. Rec.*, 1 : 89, 429, 605; 2 : 1061; *Inferiour Court of Pleas*, pp. 148, 149, 154.

47. Bridenbaugh, *Cities in the Wilderness*, p. 392; "Records of the Court of General Sessions of the Peace," *Proceedings of the Worcester Society of Antiquity*, pp. 82, 92, 104, 109, 122, 126, 129, 132, 138, 146, 148, 151, 154, 155, 165, 166, 175, 177, 182.

48. Under an act passed in 1659, any person or his family resident in a town for three months automatically became a legal inhabitant unless the selectmen not only warned him out, but actually forced him to leave by petitioning the county court, "and the same prosecuted to effect." A poor person

warning out their entire population so that they might avoid com-
pulsory poor rates entirely. This practice and similar abuses brought
the whole warning-out system into disrepute, and it was abolished by
statute in Massachusetts in 1793.[49]

Most towns did not reach the point of giving notice of eviction to
every resident, but they all tried to cut the costs of poor relief by
binding out orphans, bastards, and children of indigent families as
apprentices or servants.[50] Inhumane as the practice may seem, it owed
as much to a concern for morality as for economy. In the sober judgment of the town, those children who needed poor relief also needed
close regulation because their parents were either dead, disabled,
missing, or unmarried. When the selectmen made their inspections
of literacy and family order, the children who could not read their
catechisms, who were not trained in some lawful calling, and who
lacked discipline usually turned out to be the children of the indigent.
The selectmen of Watertown bound out Edward Sanderson's two children in 1671 because the town would find it hard to support them,
but also because even if it could, "yet it would not tend to the good
of the children for their good education and bringing up soe as they

---

belonging to no town under the terms of the act could be settled in any town
of the county, to be maintained at the charge of the county (*Mass. Rec.*, 4 : pt. 1,
365). This act fell with the old charter, and when the legislature passed a new
act in 1692 it kept the three-month residence requirement but only required the
town to register its warning out with the county court in order to be freed of all
charges for poor relief that might arise in the future. The town, in addition,
could secure a warrant from any justice of the peace to remove the person warned
out if it wished, but in that case it would have to pay for the cost of his
transportation back to his legal residence. In the cases from the Worcester
County Court cited in the previous note, the court only approved of the towns'
warnings out; it did not take steps to see that they were effectually prosecuted
(*Acts and Resolves*, 1 : 67–68).

49. Benton, *Warning Out in New England*, pp. 1–3, 52, 116.

50. This practice is discussed in Lawrence Towner, *A Good Master Well
Served: A Social History of Servitude in Massachusetts 1620–1750* (Ph.D. diss.,
Northwestern University, 1955), pp. 84–104. For instances of children being
placed out (besides those in Watertown cited below) cf. *Suffolk Cty. Ct. Rec.*,
2 : 647, 915; *Inferiour Court of Pleas*, p. 160; *Dedham Records*, 4 : 203; 5 : 8,
50; *Boston Rec.*, 4 : 150, 212.

may be usefull in the common weall or themselves to live comfortable and use fully in time to come."[51]

In their own view the Watertown selectmen had done the Sanderson children a service. The selectmen of Andover were of the same mind in 1675 in requesting permission to place out the children of Samuel Hutchenson in order "to deliver them from much suffering" after their father was indicted for improvidence.[52] The Puritans broke up the families of the poor out of respect for the institution of the family itself, seeing it not so much as kinship unit but as the primary means for transmission of education and discipline.

URBAN POVERTY: BOSTON

Boston stands as at least a partial exception to much of what has just been said about the nature of New England poor relief. The town's size, its urban character, its status as a resort for the poor and displaced of the whole of New England, and the vulnerability of its working force to commercial depression produced a larger problem and also one of a different sort.[53]

Boston's position as the center of commerce and the main port of New England, as well as the intermittent Indian wars that plagued the inland between 1675 and 1722, brought streams of the indigent and the uprooted into the town, to the great discomfort of the selectmen and inhabitants. In 1679 a town meeting declared, in what be-

51. *Watertown Records*, 1 : 105. The town's action took place in the context of regular surveys to see that children were being properly educated. In 1727 the selectmen observed once again that families "That are under very Neady and Suffering Circumstances" often had children able to work and also to go to school and attend public worship, but that "through the willfulness Negligence & Indulgence of their parents they are brought up in Idleness, Ignorance and Ereligion, and are more Likely to prove a trouble and Charge, then blessings in their Day and Generation if not timely prevented." They prevented it by breaking up a poor family the next month (Ibid., 1 : 114, 122, 135–36, 137; 2 : 340–41).

52. *Essex Cty. Ct. Rec.*, 6 : 26, 425.

53. Boston's problem and the methods used to combat it have received ample treatment in Bridenbaugh, *Cities in the Wilderness*, pp. 81–83, 233–35, 392–94. The General Court admitted in 1735 that the poor laws in force were "not so suitable to the circumstances of the said town, which are different from those of the other towns in the province" (*Acts and Resolves*, 2 : 756).

came an annual litany, that the selectmen needed the power to reject strangers without having to appeal to the county court for a warrant, because "the towne is fild with poor idle and profane persons" and refugees "that come hither for shelter and releife in time of warr," and because "the constitution of the Towne of Bostone is such in respect of the continuall resort of all sorts of persons from all partes both by sea and land, more than any other towne in the collony." The town did not get the power it wanted until 1735, and by then it could do little good.[54] The General Court also helped out with occasional grants of money, generally for the relief of war refugees, but with the exception of a generous allotment of £1,000 during the small pox epidemic of 1721, this aid never proved substantial.[55]

Boston developed all the problems of urban communities. Usually its difficulties seemed to be small-scale versions of those that beset seventeenth-century London, though occasionally they had a more modern sound. In 1734 the town complained of a dwindling tax base ("And it is observable that many Inhabitants of good Circumstances are gone out from us, And many indigent Poor have fill'd the Vacancy, and encreas'd our Polls"), and in 1738 it protested against the establishment of Rumney Marsh as a separate jurisdiction—one hesitates to say suburb—on the grounds that the inhabitants derived their wealth from Boston and ought to pay its taxes.[56]

Whatever the analogies, Boston's inhabitants did pay large sums for the relief of the poor. The town was complaining in 1686 when the bill still stood at less than £200 a year; twenty-one years later, in 1700, it had doubled to £400, and another £500 had to be added that year for a "Stock to set the poor on work." Thereafter the annual charge rose more slowly, reaching £940 in 1728 and 1729, but then suddenly jumping to £2,069 by 1734, and in 1737 doubling once

---

54. *Boston Rec.*, 7 : 135. Cf. ibid., 2 : 152; 7 : 241; *Acts and Resolves*, 2 : 756–58. The town charges for the poor rose steeply all the same: even with twelve overseers there were still too many poor inhabitants for the town to supervise them carefully.

55. *Boston Rec.*, 7 : 107, 111–12; *Acts and Resolves*, 8 : 43, 106, 256; 9 : 47, 109, 226, 298, 474; 10 : 123.

56. *Boston Rec.*, 12 : 122, 207.

more to £4,000.[57] The population had just about tripled between 1686 and 1737; the cost of poor relief had multiplied over twenty times.[58]

57. Ibid., 7 : 187; 8 : 3; 12 : 121–22, 178; *Sewall Diary*, 2 : 8. These figures differ slightly from some of those given by Bridenbaugh because he uses the total amounts voted to defray the costs of the poor *and* other necessary charges. The statistics for 1728 to 1737 come from petitions for tax abatements, ordinarily highly unreliable documents. However, the *total* charges for poor and other expenses voted by the town did rise by the appropriate amounts. Moreover, a town meeting complained to the overseers of the poor about the same increase in poor rates noted in its petition of 1735, and other figures given in the petition—notably the claim to have spent £1,200 on the town watch—are confirmed by other entries in the town records that were not intended for outside circulation (*Boston Rec.*, 12 : 6, 86, 108, 140, 173).

58. Inflation places considerable difficulties in the way of accurate comparisons of the different figures for the cost of poor relief. In particular, the Boston records do not indicate which of the several currencies then in circulation was used in raising a poor rate. Assuming that the selectmen employed the same currency in fixing the assize of bread as in setting the town rate, comparison of wheat prices will give some indication of changes in the actual burden of poor relief. Estimating the town population at 6,000 in 1686, 6,700 in 1700, 13,000 in 1728 and 1729, and 15,000 in 1734 and 1737, and the price of a bushel of wheat in these years as 4.0s., 5.5s., 9.0s., 10.25s., 12.08s., and 14.75s. respectively, the per capita cost of poor relief in Boston amounted to .17 bushels of wheat in 1686, .22 in 1700, .16 in 1728, .14 in 1729, .22 in 1734, and .36 in 1737. A 1685 wheat price has been used for 1686 and a 1700 one for 1701, and in any case all these figures are very rough.

Nevertheless, the cost of poor relief had obviously increased considerably by 1737, after a brief decline in the 1720s. Moreover, a rise in the proportion devoted to the poor out of the total town tax bill also indicates that Boston spent more and more of its public resources on the relief of poverty as the years passed. In 1728 the poor cost £940 out of a total public expenditure on all charges of £4,700; in 1734 £2,000 out of a total of £6,700; and, in 1737 £4,000 out of £8,000. The grain prices come from George F. Dow, ed., *An Inventory of the Contents of the Shop and House of Captain George Corwin of Salem* (Salem, Mass., 1910), p. 18; Arthur H. Cole, et al., *Wholesale Commodity Prices in the United States, 1700–1861* (Cambridge, Mass., 1930), 1 : 117. The Cole study in turn derived its figures by averaging the monthly assizes of grain for each year from 1701 on, as reported in *Boston Rec.*, vols. 11, 13, and 14, passim. Estimates of the population are based on those in Lemuel Shattuck, *Report to the Committee of the City Council Appointed to Obtain the Census of Boston for the Year 1845* (Boston, 1846), p. 5 (table). For the citation for the annual town budgets see the previous note.

This kind of massive poverty and the peculiar mercantile economy of the town brought about the local reappearance of a phenomenon the colonists thought they had left behind in England: the "willing poor" unable to find work. John Hull had jotted down in his diary in 1656 that "Twenty persons, or about such a number, did agree to raise a stock to procure a house and materials to improve the youth of the town of Boston (which wont employment) in several manufactureres," and the town meeting of 18 December 1682 revived the old Elizabethan division of the poor into *three* classes. It talked of "those that are sick, aged and incapacitated for labor," those "that mispend their time in idleness and typlinge with grate neglect of theire callings," and also of "many persons that would worke but have not where with all to imploy themselves." The meeting consequently proposed a combination almshouse-workhouse to replace the simple almshouse that had burned down in the great fire that year. Unfortunately, the project never worked properly because Suffolk County used the new building for its house of correction, which prevented "many Honest Poor Peoples going there for the designed Reliefe and Support."[59]

Though the town made other sporadic attempts "for setting the poor to work," it did not build a workhouse devoted solely to the "willing poor" until 1735, when a town meeting adopted an elaborate scheme to make the poor all but self-supporting in a new structure where they could both reside and earn money picking oakum.[60] Workhouses had held little appeal for English philanthropists, but in Boston a better combination of the virtues of frugality and industry combined with a tax savings could not have been imagined, and the overseers of the poor had little difficulty raising £3,600 by private subscription from 121 donors to pay for the project. When that amount turned out to be insufficient, another £729 came in by way of contributions, and the town raised a rate of £377 to complete the building.[61]

59. *Hull Diary*, p. 178; *Boston Rec.*, 2 : 129; 7 : 157; 8 : 93.

60. *Mather Diary*, 1 : 422; *Boston Rec.*, 7 : 241; 8 : 23, 9 : 20; 12 : 111, 235-40.

61. Jordan, *Philanthropy in England*, pp. 270-72; *Boston Rec.*, 12 : 181-83, 248.

This workhouse was a financial success, but it could not have gone very far toward solving the problems of Boston's poor. In 1741 it held a total of fifty-five persons, only ten of them adult males. In fact, all of Boston's public relief, large as it was, could have met only a part of the burden of its indigent by the second quarter of the eighteenth century. In 1737, when the town paid £4,000 in poor relief, it had been forced to vote £859 in tax abatements to individuals on its book of polls, "most of it whole Rates of poor People not able to pay." Since at least some of these individuals had families, the abatements figure alone indicates the existence of at least several hundred poor people. Still another 270 persons, some of them also presumably heads of families, had not been rated because of their poverty, "besides many Hundreds for [the] same Reason not Entered in those Books at all." Yet in 1735, two years earlier, the almshouse had only eighty-eight people in it. Many individuals undoubtedly received public aid although resident in private homes, and some of the people who received abatements probably could support themselves without direct aid, while the town may also have been exaggerating its plight; but even with these qualifications neither the poor rate nor the existing public institutions seem adequate to have maintained all the indigent in Boston. Private charity must have had to relieve many of them if they were relieved at all.[62]

A municipality that could raise £4,300 in voluntary contributions for a workhouse obviously did have considerable charitable resources. The churches in particular contributed heavily through both regular and special collections: on just two sabbaths during the severe winter of 1741 they managed to collect £1,240 between them for the relief of the poor. Individual donors helped too, often handsomely. John Hull, the richest Boston man of his generation, contributed enough at various times for Samuel Willard to declare at his death in 1682 that the poor had lost "a liberal and Merciful friend," and others stood ready to take up where Hull left off. Madame Dorothy Saltonstall left £200 to be distributed among the poor in 1738, and thirteen

62. *Boston Rec.*, 12 : 122, 178, 273.

years earlier another widow, Anne Mills, willed £560 to the First and Second Churches for the support of the poor of their congregations.[63] Best of all, Boston had Cotton Mather. The man who wrote "G.D." before each daily entry in his diary, that "Good Deeds" might be repeated 365 times a year, made one of his major functions in life providing for the poor. As he was careful to point out in the diary he prepared for the edification of his descendants, "no little Part of my Life is taken up in promoting Intentions of Charity."[64] Mather gave much of his own salary to the poor, he administered the gifts of others, and above all by written word and oral exhortation he promoted good works in the people of Boston. Orthodox Puritan theory had always held that men ought to give to the poor in obedience to God's explicit commands and in fulfillment of their role as his stewards, as well as because such behavior confirmed their justification and demonstrated that they shared in the bonds of love.[65] Many divines had even admitted, somewhat inconsistently, that the charitable man might expect both temporal and spiritual blessings as

63. Bridenbaugh, *Cities in the Wilderness*, pp. 393–94; Samuel Willard, *The High Esteem which God hath of the Death of his Saints*, p. 16; *Boston Rec.*, 12 : 217–18; *First Church of Boston Records*, 2 : 469. Mrs. Mills left an equal amount to the churches of Watertown.

64. *Mather Diary*, 1 : 529. Mather wrote at one point in 1713 that "the distressed Families of the Poor to which I dispense, or procure needful Releefs, are now so many, and of such Daily Occurrence, that it is needless for me here to mention them" (Ibid., 2 : 260). Mention them he did, however, with such regularity that a full list of the references to his charitable activities in his diary would take up the better part of a page (the index does not indicate more than a fraction of them under "poor" or related headings). Barely a month went by in the first two decades of the eighteenth century when he did not put several entries into his diary on the order of "Several very poor in the Flock, are objects for my further cares" or "Several New Objects, full of Poverty and Misery, offer themselves into my Cares" (Ibid., 525, 546). He also kept lists of the poor, both for his own benefactions and to aid others (Ibid., 1 : 271, 2 : 152.).

65. Giving alms would not get a man into heaven but it would confirm the fact that God had predestined him to go there. Cf. Perkins, *Cases of Conscience, Works*, 2 : 146–48; Downame, *The Plea of the Poore*, p. 189. For a brief summary of the reasons for almsgiving see this last work, pp. 47–50. The general Protestant theory of charity is summarized at some length in Jordan, *Philanthropy in England*, pp. 155–215.

his reward.[66] Mather, therefore, was being perfectly orthodox but perhaps a bit insidious when he wrote that, "I could mind you of poor little Tradesmen that have come to Live upon their Rents, by the secret Blessings of God upon their callings, when they have conscientously Laid aside a certain part of their Income, for the Lord." Conversely, he warned that those who withheld a part of their estates from pious uses stood in the greatest danger of forfeiting the whole. He must had his effect, particularly when he "insinuated" in all his visits to "Persons of Capacity" his "Exhortations to a liberal consideration of the Poor."[67]

Using his own and others' funds, Mather engaged in all kinds of projects for aiding the poor: he gave to them outright, he organized charity schools, he promoted "hospitals," he even tried to get "two poor persons, objects of my care" to marry, presumably on the theory that two could be relieved as cheaply as one. In giving and in soliciting gifts Mather did good to all men, those of the household of faith and those not.[68] Orthodox ministers and a "Froward Anabaptist Minister," the godly and the ungodly, sober men and drunkards, the

66. John Downame, for example, had admitted that charity had rewards not only in the next world but in this one. God, he wrote, "payeth us with our owne money also, even with the coyne of worldly blessings which is so current among us. . . . So that if we sow the seeds of our beneficence it will returne unto us a double harvest; the crop of temporall benefits in this life, and of everlasting blessedness in the life to come" (*The Plea of the Poore*, pp. 211-13). Cf. Thomas Gouge, *The Surest Way of Thriving* (London, 1676), p. 10.

67. *Durable Riches*, p. 24; *Mather Diary*, 1 : 529. Men who fail to give to charity "bring a *Confiscation* upon the Rest of their Estates; they bring all under a *Forfeiture.*" *Pascentius* (Boston, 1714), pp. 21-22.

68. For Mather's promotion of charity schools and "hospitals" (places of hospitality) for the poor, see his *Diary*, 1 : 530; 2 : 179, 180. His plans to marry two poor people are in ibid., 2 : 445. For instances of Mather aiding individuals he considered ungodly, atheistical, or wicked, and also of his charity to individuals of other religious persuasions or even other races, see Ibid., 1 : 209, 580-81; 2 : 67, 96, 141, 151, 240, 335, 457, 556, 581, 769. For a "drone" he tried to find not only relief but employment (Ibid., 2 : 336). In 1711 he had so many poor people on his lists that he was reduced to casting lots to see which ones he should relieve out of his own limited funds, and in 1712 he boasted that "Not one Day has passed me, without Expending some Little Portion of my Revenues on Pious Uses." Ibid., 2 : 67; William R. Mannierre, II, ed., *The Diary of Cotton Mather, D.D., F.R.S. for the Year 1712* (Charlottesville, N.C., 1964), p. 124.

diligent and the idle, Negroes and whites all benefited from his bounty, though the ungodly may possibly have resented his accompanying the money with books and words of admonition and his advice to other donors to do the same: "Can't you contrive, to intermix a *Spiritual Charity*, with your *Temporal?* Perhaps you may Discourse with them about the *State of their Souls*, and obtain from them, which you now have a Singular Advantage to do, some Declared *Resolutions* to Do what they ought to do."[69]

Mather's frenetic energy joined to its private and public resources may have earned Boston Carl Bridenbaugh's judgment that "no town in Europe or America showed so much concern for its unfortunates as did Boston."[70] Yet the periodic unemployment of able-bodied and willing poor in the city, temporary as it may have been in an expanding economy, revealed a potentially dangerous aspect of the colonial attitude toward the poor. Poverty in itself might either punish or perfect, but when it came to dealing with sinners the Puritan God tried to make the punishment fit the crime, and for certain sins, including idleness and intemperance, he thought poverty an especially fitting reward.[71] When Joseph Belcher complained in the Massachusetts election sermon of 1703 that idleness and drink were "the Parent of a great deal of the Poverty and Beggery, which is to be seen upon many,"[72] he may have been stating little more than empirical fact in a land of a labor shortage and a basically agricultural economy, but the temptation would remain to identify *all* the able-bodied poor as idle and vicious fellows, whatever the circumstances, as one striking instance illustrates.

A scarcity of grain in 1710, aggravated by profiteers who exported part of the little stock available, produced steep bread prices in Boston and caused a near riot among its poor. Judge Samuel Sewall,

69. *Bonifacious*, p. 146.
70. *Cities in the Wilderness*, p. 394.
71. "Some sins are Impoverishing. As uncleannes . . . Intemperance . . . Injustice is also Impoverishing. . . . So is Idleness . . . The like may also be said of Keeping bad company." William Burnham, *Gods Providence in Placing Men in their Respective Stations & Conditions Asserted & Shewed* (New London, Conn., 1722), pp. 11–12.
72. *The Singular Happiness of Such Heads or Rulers As Are able to Choose Out their Peoples Way, and Will Also Endeavour their Peoples Comfort* (Boston, 1701), p. 42.

whose name was a byword for conservatism, had little sympathy for either the lawless or the profiteers; but he understood the former's distress, and to his pastor, the Rev. Ebenezar Pemberton, he made the sympathetic but traditional observation that "God's people . . . though they brought themselves into straits by their own fault, yet God pitied and help'd them." Pemberton's reply left Sewall "stricken": "They were not Gods people but the Devil's people that wanted Corn. There was Corn to be had; if they had not impoverish'd themselves by Rum, they might buy Corn." Sewall was the more orthodox of the two and the minister promptly lost his invitation to dine at the judge's table, while the selectmen of Boston, their sense of charity sharpened by a dislike of bread riots, took care of the profiteers by maintaining public granaries and by securing a law that banned the export of grain.[73] Still, Pemberton was as learned and godly a minister as any produced by New England, and was considered a doctrinal "liberal." The opportunity to think as he did would increase in years not far in the future, when more and more of the Massachusetts economy resembled Boston's and Boston itself had gone on to develop depths of poverty undreamed of in 1710[74]

It is, of course, unfair to condemn a social theory for not anticipating developments that occur a century or more after its formulation. In the context of their time, the Puritans' view of poverty can be criticized only on the same grounds as their concept of wealth: neither gave a man much peace. Never satisfied, the believer mistrusted both poverty and riches and, indeed, all states of *being*, putting his faith only in becoming. The word *security* the Puritans used mainly in reproach. To be really happy they would have had to discover a way of earning money without ending up rich or of losing it without growing poor.

---

73. *Sewall Diary*, 2 : 281. During a similar dearth three years later, Cotton Mather busied himself soliciting gifts of bread for the poor (*Mather Diary*, 2 : 336). For the ban on exports see *See Records*, 8 : 84; *Acts and Resolves*, 1 : 724–25. The town officials laid up grain in advance and sold it in times of scarcity at reasonable rates. *Boston Records*, 8 : 101, 104, 111, 127, 133, 220.

74. On the increase in the New England poor in the middle and late eighteenth century cf. Lockridge, "Land, Population and the Evolution of New England Society," pp. 71–74.

PART THREE

Potentials

Like all heirs we are less interested in the careers of our ancestors than in their legacies. Never mind what they did, what did they leave us? The contribution of American Puritanism to the present, however, resists simple definition in just the same way as Puritanism itself does. A diverse movement, full of contradictions, it could take many forms under the pressure of events. Perhaps Americans owe democracy or capitalism or even quantum mechanics to the fact that some Englishmen were Puritans; still, neither the English nor the American Puritans were deliberately democrats, capitalists, or physicists. Theirs was ultimately an ambiguous ethic, and examination of it ends most appropriately with a discussion of its most fateful ambiguity.

6 Puritanism and Democracy: A Mixed Legacy

By seventeenth-century standards Puritan society had little chance of surviving in the New World. Lacking most of the traditional means through which Europeans ordinarily established social cohesion and maintained order, the New England colonies should, in theory, have quickly disintegrated from internal disunion or collapsed at the first blow from a foreign or savage enemy. Stability would have to wait on the development of a landed aristocracy approximating the familiar upper stratum of European societies: a class of men who combined in the same hands economic, social, and political power, monopolized all pretensions of education, and claimed public service as their exclusive right and duty.

The early history of the Chesapeake region confirmed this gloomy prediction: peace and order could come only in the eighteenth century with the multiplication of large plantations and the great planters who owned them. Seventeenth-century New England, suffering from the same defects as its neighbors to the south with a few disabilities of its own making thrown in, should have fared even worse; instead, it enjoyed what unsympathetic contemporaries must have regarded as an unseemly success. Facing a bleak environment and the necessity of instituting unprecedented ways of life, New Englanders still managed to preserve a high degree of unity and a respectable capacity for resisting external pressure. Potentially explosive issues like the Antinomian crisis passed without too much breach of the peace, and even the massive mortality and economic dislocation following King Philip's War left the New England colonies still in one piece, while a much milder Indian threat in Virginia at the same time precipitated Bacon's Rebellion and the virtual collapse of that colony's governing institutions.

Safety in early America seemed to lie in being Puritan. The organization of the New England town and the clearly articulated goals of the Puritan experiment made for a tighter, more homogeneous society that knew what it was and where it was going and had a host of devices, from public schools to printed sermons, to remind it of that fact. Most important of all, the terms of the Puritan experiment demanded that every morally capable adult give his positive and knowing assent to the imperatives issued by pulpit and press. Though it sounds strange to say it, few societies in Western culture have ever depended more thoroughly or more self-consciously on the consent of their members than the allegedly repressive "theocracies" of early New England.

The state's last resort, force, rested in the hands of a militia embracing all able-bodied males, and every aspect of public life in New England demanded the formal assent of the public. Church members elected their ministers, town meetings their selectmen, freemen their deputies and magistrates, and militiamen their officers. Not even full membership in the visible church came automatically: only those explicitly willing to could sign the church covenant and take communion. The temptation to find the genesis of modern democracy in New England or Puritanism or both seems irresistable; indeed, there have been many unable to resist it from the time of the founding of New England to the present day.[1]

1. The literature on the relationship between Puritanism and democracy rivals that on the Weber thesis in bulk, and I have neither space nor inclination to recapitulate it. The latest historiographical article on the subject at the time this note was written was Leo F. Solt, "Puritanism, Capitalism, Democracy, and the New Science," *American Historical Review*, 73 (October 1967): 18–29. But see also the highly critical comments in C.H. George, "Puritanism as History and Historiography," *Past and Present* 41 (December 1968): 97–100. To my mind the briefest, most lucid argument for the Puritan as protodemocrat remains A. S. P. Woodhouse, *Puritanism and Liberty* (London, 1938). More diffuse, more complex, more tentative, William Haller's *Liberty and Reformation in the Puritan Revolution* (New York, 1955) still stands (in my estimation) far above any of the other discussions of the subject.

Among the most recent works to take up the matter, directly or indirectly, are Michael Walzer's *The Revolution of the Saints* and Alan Heimert, *Religion and the American Mind From the Great Awakening to the Revolution* (Cambridge, Mass., 1966). American Puritanism has attracted rather fewer seekers after democracy than the English variety, but B. Katherine Brown has made

American Puritanism did substitute a radical voluntarism for most
of the customary engines of social coercion of early modern Europe.
In the place of a hereditary monarch, a titled nobility, a church hierarchy, and a landlord class stood the characteristic Puritan covenants, written and unwritten, that legitimated the civil and ecclesiastical politics of New England. And yet the leader of the Puritan
colonies hoped to achieve through this least traditional and most
"modern" of means, the most traditional and ancient of ends: peace,
order, unity, and love. God was not glorified by division, by diversity,
by social conflict, by all that is the strength and weakness of liberal,
pluralistic democracy. Holiness as much as statecraft called for every
man in his place, bound to every other by the rights and obligations
appropriate to his position in an organic social hierarchy. But holiness
as much as statecraft also demanded that every man actively and repeatedly consent to his own inequality, that by covenant and ballot
he confirm his adherence to the Lord's unitary truth and the small
group of laymen and clergy who were its executors. Such a formula
would have struck any prudent European as quixotic if not subversive; but, considering the stormy history of seventeenth-century
Europe, the New England states did obtain far more unity and order
than most European governments with similar goals and (in traditional terms) much more formidable instruments for achieving them.

Present-day sensibilities, conditioned by three centuries of contrary
experience, find it difficult to understand subordination by consent of
the subordinated. It is easier to identify the voluntaristic elements in
Puritan society with more modern aspirations or to seize on every instance of lawbreaking as proof positive that so ridiculous an ethic did
not influence anyone aside from a few callow writers of sermons. Be-
lieving in no one way ourselves, we forget that men who did could
cast their votes, less as an expression of their individual preferences
than as a sign of their collective union with the established interpreters and custodians of God's eternal law. Winthrop's "civil liberty,"

---

an interesting case for the democratic nature of New England political life
in "A Note on the Puritan Concept of Aristocracy," cited earlier, and in two
other articles: "Puritan Democracy: A Case Study," *Mississippi Valley Historical Review* 50 (December 1963): 377–96; "Puritan Democracy in Dedham,
Massachusetts: Another Case Study," *William and Mary Quarterly*, 3d ser.,
24 (July 1967): 378–96.

the "liberty to that only which is good, just and honest," accurately embodied the ideals of an age that understood freedom only as a voluntary acquiescence in a divinely ordained system of authority and deference. Annual elections failed to convince Winthrop that he owed an accounting of the ordinary course of his government to anyone but God. He told the electorate as much in his Hingham militia speech of 1645—and, justly rebuked, they promptly reelected him governor once a year every year for the rest of his life.

"Civil liberty" may have been a Puritan peculiarity, but it received powerful reinforcement from social assumptions that New Englanders held in common with the rest of Western civilization. Hierarchy seemed natural, equality glaringly abnormal. The deputies, the most representative part of the Bay Colony's polity, represented their constituents by repeatedly voting for sumptuary laws that would deny to a large portion of the men who elected them the finery deemed suitable only to richer and more honorable citizens.[2] The God of order, graded social order, did not deprive himself of his basic nature in endowing his people with the ballot.

For all their penchant for voting, New Englanders seemed unable to pass over so much as a list of names without arranging them in an order of precedence. Every Sunday morning a fair number of Puritan congregations came face to face with their God decently and in order, taking seats in the meeting house assigned according to formulas based on arcane combinations of age, wealth, and social standing. Ranking of students at Harvard and Yale according to the status of their parents testified to the same faith in inequality, as did the assorted honorifics from "esquire" down to "goodman" affected by men of local prominence.[3]

2. The Essex and Suffolk county court records reveal only a very sparse history of enforcement for any of these laws. The question at issue for the moment, however, is not achievement but aspiration, and here the very fact of the passage of such legislation is important. See above, chap. 1, (p. 28).

3. The church of Watertown, for example, gave as its rules for seating in 1656: "1. office 2. age 3. [e]state 4. gifts" (*Watertown Records*, 1 : 37, 59, 81; 3 : 211). For other seating plans and the altercations they produced see Ola Winslow, *Meetinghouse Hill* (New York, 1952), pp. 142–49; *Dedham Town Records*, 5 : 20, 21; Sylvester Judd, *History of Hadley* (Springfield, Mass., 1905), p. 312; *Town Records of Topsfield, Massachusetts* (Topsfield,

Inconsistency in the use of titles was the rule, while the noisy protests of churchgoers and college students slighted by assignments below their dignity became a depressingly regular feature of ecclesiatical and academic life. Outside of a rigid caste system social distinctions always tend to blur, but such imprecision hardly constitutes a creeping egalitarianism. The violence and frequency of protests over inaccurate assignments in themselves demonstrate that New Englanders took the existence of hierarchy seriously even if they could not agree over their respective places within it. A New England freeholder of middling size might quarrel with his neighbor over a seat in the meeting house, and his town clerk might give him a "goodman" on one tax list and no distinction at all on another, yet freeholder, neighbor, and clerk all knew where they stood in relation to a Winthrop or a Bradstreet.[4]

Admittedly, for every instance of respect cited, a counterinstance of disrespect could probably also be adduced. The sumptuary laws, like all legislation, may be taken as a sign of the weakness of social ideals as well as of their strength, and a criminal brought to justice serves at one and the same time to show that standards were flouted and that they were enforced. Even the absence of criminal prosecutions can be made to show either that laws were obeyed or that they were ignored. The double edge on every bit of evidence makes it im-

1917–20), 1 : 349; 2 : 200; Samuel Sewall, *The History of Woburn* (Boston, 1868), pp. 184–86; Mather Diary, 2 : 53, 194, 353, 360; *The Diary of Cotton Mather . . . for . . . 1712*, p. 9. The definitive study on placing in the seventeenth century is Samuel Eliot Morison, "Precedence at Harvard College in the Seventeenth Century," *Proceedings of the American Antiguarian Society*, n.s., 42 (October 1932): 371–431. For eighteenth-century Harvard see Clifford K. Shipton, "Ye Mystery of Ye Ages Solved," *Harvard Alumni Bulletin*, 57 (December 1954), 258–63. New England titles and their promiscuous use are discussed by Norman H. Dawes, "Titles as Symbols of Prestige in Seventeenth-Century New England," *William and Mary Quarterly*, 3d ser. 6 (January 1949): 69–83.

4. If anything, the better sort seemed to take the idea of rank more casually than the lesser. Cf. The Rev. Ebenezar Pemberton's classic misuse of the word *gentleman* in 1707, and Cotton Mather's difficulties with his distant kinsmen of inferior social rank in 1712 (*Sewall Diary*, 2 : 195–96; *The Diary of Cotton Mather . . . for . . . 1712*, pp. 102–03).

possible to prove that New Englanders or anyone else habitually deferred to their superiors; laws, court cases, and all the rest establish only what the American Puritans thought they *ought* to do, whether they actually did it or not.

If *ought* is a subtler prison then *is*, it is nonetheless a prison. To defy Puritan norms was merely to continue to take them as a point of reference; they could be escaped only by being completely replaced. But any new set of imperatives would need more of a foundation than apathy and defiance, and despite extensive male suffrage and a relatively equal distribution of wealth, despite town meetings and a public school system, seventeenth-century New Englanders had no positive ideological justification for egalitarianism. The *"Levelling Spirit"* that the ministers like to flay was not a coherent social philosophy but the sporadic, directionless, and doomed spirit of revolt that prompted some men more desperate than most to defy values they themselves really felt to be true. New England's levellers were not Lieutenant-Colonel John Lilburne and Colonel Thomas Rainborough, they were the servant who justified bashing in his master's head by claiming to be as good a man as he, and Peter Bussaker, who hoped to meet some of the members of the church in hell and did not question but that he should. The servant died on the gallows, and Bussaker was more drunkard than democrat.

It is difficult to connect the men who punished Bussaker for contempt of authority with the Englishmen of the same religious persuasion who beheaded Charles I in the name of contractual government and fundamental law. New England not only had no John Lilburne, it lacked even a John Milton, who would have at least imposed some sort of equality among the saints even if he had little interest in the rights of the unregenerate. After his triumphant Hingham militia speech of 1645, John Winthrop would probably have choked on Milton's assertion of 1649 that the people might remove their magistrates whenever they chose, with or without cause:

> It follows lastly—that since the King or Magistrate holds his authoritie of the people, both originally and naturally for their good in the first place, and not his owne, then may the people as oft as they shall judge it for the best, either choose him or reject

him, retaine him or depose him though no Tyrant, meerly by the
libertie and right of free born men, to be govern'd as seems to
them best.[5]

For a moment one can almost forget that Winthrop owed his magistracy to annual elections in which a majority of the Bay Colony's
adult males could participate, while Milton's great protagonist, Oliver
Cromwell, could claim his power only by the exercise of naked force.
Apparently Puritans had to be in a minority before they could come
out with anything resembling a doctrine of popular rights. When
they enjoyed majority support, as in America, they had no need to
grow revolutionary; they never had anything to revolt against,

Political radicalism, democratic or otherwise, appeared mainly in
Puritanism Militant, not Puritanism Triumphant. In New England
for the first and last time Puritans engaged in legitimating a new and
unprecedented order rather than in tearing down an old and traditional one. Their chief spokesmen not surprisingly had much to say
about the duties of obedience and submission that would have
sounded odd to their comrades on the bullet-torn fields of Naseby and
Marston Moor. But such emphasis on the lack of "democratic" elements in the New Englanders' thought obscures their real relationship with the English Independents and the extent to which they
actually put into practice the Independents' most visionary and apparently unachievable goals. Insistence on the rule of the saints, on
government of and by the regenerate, ultimately poisoned the concept
of liberty held by men like Milton and turned their beloved commonwealth into Paradise Lost, but Massachusetts managed to base its
franchise successfully on just such a basis for half a century. In their
election of magistrates New Englanders even achieved what the foremost cynic of the seventeenth century, Thomas Hobbes, declared to be

5. John Milton, *The Tenure of Kings and Magistrates* (London, 1649),
pp. 8–9, 14–15. Cf. John Cooke, *King Charls his Case* (London, 1649), p. 22;
Henry Parker, *Observations Upon Some of His Majesties Late Answers and
Expresses*, 2d ed. (n.p.; 1642), pp. 1–8, in William Haller, ed., *Tracts on
Liberty in the Puritan Revolution* (New York, 1934), 2 : 167–75; *A Remon-
strance of Many Thousand Citizens, and other Freeborn People of England
to their owne House of Commons* (London, 1646), p. 13 in ibid., 3 : 363.

impossible, the voluntary submission of the majority of the people to a small minority considered the wise and the virtuous.[6]

Milton's and Cromwell's insoluble dilemma, the reconciliation of the twin goals of reformation and liberty, never existed for their New World brethren because New Englanders did use their liberty to achieve reformation in a way contemporary Englishmen would not. America was really a kind of intellectual Australia, where ideas long extinct elsewhere lived on far beyond their allotted time, sheltered in their isolation from the cataclysms that transformed the same species on the mainland into completely new forms. The main settlement of New England occurred prior to the English Civil War, and Puritan social theory in the New World remained for a century and more much as it had been in the England of the 1630s, the England of the Great Migration, long after the strains of war, the Interregnum, and the Restoration had fragmented and radicalized the parent faith. Lilburne and Prynne had stood together in 1638 and they stood so symbolically ever after, for those of their coreligionists who left England before the great falling out.

American Puritanism nevertheless shared in revolutionary potentials common to reformed Protestantism in general. Everywhere except in a few out-of-the-way corners like New England the radical wing of the Protestant cause found itself in the opposition; and under those circumstances principle and necessity together combined to force it to appeal, over the heads of the powers that were, to the individual consciences of the true believers.

As early as the 1550s the Marian exiles John Ponet and Christopher Goodman had gone far beyond any of the contemporary Protestant writers of the Continent by assigning the duty of overthrowing an ungodly monarch to the "multitude," collectively or even indi-

6. For the twin ideals of rule by the saints and rule by the best in Cromwell's England, see Arthur Barker, *Milton and the Puritan Dilemma* ([Toronto]; 1942), chaps. 11 and 12 and passim. Hobbes gave his low opinion of the possibility of a natural aristocracy in *Leviathan* (London, 1651), p. 77. The Independents were a diverse group, and not all thought these ideals practical or even desirable. Many, however, did see New England as New England wanted to be seen, that is, as a model for any potential English reformation—and many former New Englanders played prominent parts in the Independent cause during the Civil War and Interregnum.

vidually. The law of nature was plain enough, and the duty of enforcing it general enough, for every man who failed to stop the execution of an unjust law to share in the sin of those who had made it. Goodman had no comfort for any who would excuse themselves on the grounds that they were private persons unconnected with affairs of state:

> But they will peradventure excuse theselves, as thogh God had no thing to do with them, because they be not Apostels; nor Prophets. Nevertheless they may be assured, they shall be as they ever have bene, subjects to his plages and punishmentes: and so Will he have a do with them, thogh they would have nought to do with hym.[7]

The special standard of behavior the Lord required of New Englanders only increased the vital material interest each member of the covenanted community had in the conduct of every other member, for a breach of the natural law in Roxbury or a sin left unpunished in Watertown would also bring fire and brimstone to Dedham. When one Tryal Pore confessed to the sin of fornication before the Middlesex County Court, in 1656, she admitted that "by this sinn I have not only donn what I can to Poull doune Judgmente from the lord on my selve but allso apon the place where I live."[8] Public misconduct by the Bay Colony's government would hardly have been less provoking than Tryal Pore's periodic misdemeanors.

Nor could exposition of the fundamental law always remain the exclusive vocation of authorized interpreters acting without reference to the ignorant multitude while the authorities openly disagreed with each other and appealed to the public as a whole. The Marian exiles had fallen back on the people so much sooner that other European Protestants in part because they had no one else to fall back upon— no pope, no provincial parliaments, no *Untere Obrigkeit*. "We must

---

7. Christopher Goodman, *How Superior Powers Oght to be Obeyed* (Geneva, 1558), pp. 73–74, 180–81. Cf. John Ponet, *A Short Treatise of Politike Power* ([London], 1556), reprinted in Winthrop S. Hudson, *John Ponet (1516–1556), Advocate of Limited Monarchy* (Chicago, 1942), pp. 7, 33, 107–08, 173–83 (2d pagination).

8. Quoted by Edmund S. Morgan in his introduction to *The Diary of Michael Wigglesworth*, p. 317.

obey the preachers onely when they bring Gods word," Goodman informed his readers, assuming they had sense enough to realize that
their preachers currently were bringing nothing of the sort.[9] Whatever the prerogatives of the educated and the highly placed, when it
came time to draw swords each individual would have to decide for
himself whom to follow, Bishop Ponet or Bishop Gardiner, John
Milton or Sir Robert Filmer.

For a time the early unity of the New England colonists did enable
their ministry to reassert the rights of the privileged few: "if it be in
matters of Religion, there is the Priest; if in matters civil, there is the
Magistrate."[10] Yet when the Rev. John Norton made that statement
he conveniently overlooked that fact that he was not a priest of the
Holy Roman Catholic Church but of the single most disorganized
and anarchic ecclesiastical organization in Christendom. The issue
which prompted his declaration, the dispute over the half-way covenant, indicated clearly enough that even in the New World the teach-
ers of God's word might occasionally preach against each other, just
as the magistrates could not always keep from airing their disputes in
public, in effect referring them to the freemen for decision at the next
election.[11]

Three thousand miles of Atlantic Ocean did not deprive the inhabitants of New England of all similarities with their English counterparts. There was more than a little foretaste of the Banqueting Hall
on that January day of 1649 in Thomas Shepard's warning of 1638
that if the bramble should reign over Massachusetts, the freemen had
best arm themselves with hatchets to cut it down.[12] There was more

9. *How Superior Powers Oght to be Obeyed*, p. 33 (marginal note).

10. John Norton, *Sion, the Out-Cast Healed of her Wounds*, pp. 8–10.

11. On the difficulties of maintaining the prestige of the magistracy in the
face of public disputes between individual magistrates, cf. *Winthrop Journal*,
1 : 211–14; *Winthrop Papers*, 4 : 403.

12. *NEH&GR*, 24 (1870): 336. On the rare occasions when they addressed
themselves to the point, the first generation of New England ministers generally
did justify the overthrow of wicked rulers and rulers who endangered the
commonwealth. Cf. John Cotton, *A Brief Exposition on the Whole of Ecclesiastes*, p. 108; *The Keyes of the Kingdom of Heaven* (London, 1644), p. 52;
John Eliot, *The Christian Commonwealth* (London, n.d.), reprinted in 3
Coll. MHS, 9 : 133; John Norton (?), "A Small Treatise," *Proc. MHS*,
46 (1912–13): 284.

than a little reminder of John Hampden in Samuel Symond's decision of 1657 declaring void and unenforceable any positive statute violating the "fundamental law of mine and thine."[13] Had there been a bit more interference from England in the 1630s, the New World Puritans too might have discovered, like John Bradshaw, that resistance to tyranny was obedience to God. But Bradshaw's declaration fell short of another one: that all men are created equal and endowed by their creator with certain unalienable rights. Revolution was acceptable to Puritans only because their state existed to enforce a positive pattern of virtue laid down by revealed and natural law. A ruler who diverted the state from that end might be overthrown by an expression of the popular will—a popular will conceived of as the unanimous voice of all right-thinking men, not the sum of the particular opinions of the majority. The question of majorities did not arise in an ideology which presumed that all uncorrupted intellects agreed on the same basic truths. As for minorities, American Puritans consigned them to Rhode Island in this world and the devil in the next. "I dare take upon me, to be the Haerauld of *New-England*, so farre, as to proclaime to the world, in the name of our Colony, that all Familist, Antinomians, Anabaptists and other Enthusiasts, shall have free Liberty to keep away from us, and such as will come to be gone as fast as they can, the sooner the better."[14]

In its original form radical Protestantism all too easily passed over into a millenarianism that led to the dictatorship of the regenerate. The Marian exiles would not have balked at a Protestant minority overthrowing a Catholic majority in the name of the law of nature, nor did Milton see anything wrong in asserting that only those whose natural capabilities had been in some part restored by grace could claim their natural liberties. Only they could read the law of nature written on the hearts of all but obscured by sin for most. If Milton made much of reason, it was right reason, reason illuminated by grace.

If men within themselves would be govern'd by reason, and not generally give up their understanding to a double tyrannie,

13. Thomas Hutchinson, ed., *A Collection of Original Papers Relative to the History of the Colony of Massachusetts-Bay* Publications, of the Prince Society, vols. 2–3 (Albany, N.Y., 1865), 2 : 4–6.

14. Nathaniel Ward, *The Simple Cobler of Aggawam in America*, 4th ed. (London, 1647), p. 3.

of Custom from without, and blind affections within, they would discerne better, what it is to favour and uphold the Tyrant of a Nation. But being slaves within doors, no wonder they strive so much to have the public state conformably govern'd to the inward vitious rule by which they govern themselves. For indeed none can love freedom heartilie, but good men; the rest love not freedom, but license; which never hath more scope or more indulgence than under Tyrants.[15]

Before *The Tenure of Kings and Magistrates* became *The Declaration of Independence* Puritans would have to stop distinguishing between regenerate and unregenerate for political purposes, which meant abandoning many of the central assumptions on which New England politics was based. Seventeenth-century doctrine could be made to yield eighteenth-century republicanism only by a very selective accentuation of individual elements within it, without regard to the logic that bound together the whole.

The components of the original synthesis were disparate enough to begin with. Puritans had painted a black picture of what was largely because they had such a high ideal of what ought to be: natural man's will and intellect seemed so depraved because unfallen man's faculties had been so magnificent. The rub came in deciding just how many of these former powers grace actually restored. On the one hand, a regenerate people could establish a "popular state" in both their civil and ecclesiatical polity; that is, they could elect their governors, lay and clerical. On the other hand, they were not quite regenerate enough to govern themselves, but must elect only the wise and virtuous and leave government up to them. Yet even the wise and virtuous had enough of the Old Man in them to require frequent elections, carefully prescribed bounds to governmental power, and a deliberately fragmented polity.

John Cotton's defense of the New England church system was

---

15. Milton, *Tenure of Kings and Magistrates*, p. 1. Cf. Goodman, *How Superior Powers Oght to be Obeyed*, pp. 198–99. In his indictment of Charles I John Cooke did not deny that the king had great intellect and learning but argued that "his wit and knowledge proved like a sword in a mad-mans hand; he was a stranger to the work of grace and the spirit of God" (*King Charls his Case*, p. 35).

especially ambiguous, and consequently especially pregnant with implication for the future. Critics found the Congregational Way "democratical" and therefore anarchic. Cotton replied by denying it was any such thing, pointing out that while the multitude might elect the church officers they still did not rule themselves, but "are governed by the Elders so long as they rule a right, to wit, while they hold forth the word and voyce of Christ, which the sheep of Christ are want to heare." All well and good, except that he could not stop with that assertion. He had to go on and argue that, even if the churches *were* "democratical," nevertheless the membership, all regenerate, could follow God's laws by itself:

> Though the government were democraticall (as it is not) yet here is no tumultuous disordere, where not the *will* of each man beareth the sway, but the *voyce of Christ* alone is heard, who is the Head and Monarch of the Church.[16]

The seventeenth century found New England's church polity more interesting than its civil government, but New Englanders never denied that as the scriptures guided church affairs, so an equally clear law of nature determined civil concerns. Unfallen man had always been able to follow this law, and to the extent that eighteenth-century writers began (in John Wise's phrase) to "wave the Consideration of Mans Moral Turpitude," that is, to consider all men as unfallen, to that extent they began to lay the basis for a democratic ideology. By 1794 a president of Yale, Ezra Stiles, could digress from an apology for the judges of Charles I long enough to announce that the common people could govern themselves according to the rules of reason, and still think himself the legitimate intellectual heir of the regicides he defended:

> The charm and unintelligible mysteries wrapt up in the name of a King being done away, the way would be open for all nations to a rational government and policy, on such plain and obvious general principles, as would be intelligible to the plainest rustic, to the substantial yeomanry, or men of landed estates,

16. John Cotton, *The Way of the Churches of Christ in New England* (London, 1645), p. 100.

which ought to be the body of the population. Every one could understand it plain as a Locke or a Camden. And whatever the Filmers and Acherlys may say, the common people are abundantly capable and susceptible of such a polity.[17]

Generalizing the rights of the elect by identifying the regenerate intellect with the rational faculties common to all men still might produce a kind of majority authoritarianism. If the truth were all that obvious, then all men of good will should agree on it, and any dissent from their consensus would have to come from men of very ill will indeed. The elective dictatorship of the wise and virtuous could give way to the still more formidable dictatorship of the many. Stiles himself was saved from these consequences by his steadfast faith in the ability of the public as a whole to recognize the truth when it was presented. Error in a popular state generally sprang from misinformation, not the incompetence of the people. "The common people will generally judge right, when duly informed. The general liberty is safe and secure in their hands. It is not from deficiency of abilities to judge, but from want of information, if they at any time as a body go wrong." The best way to keep them well informed was to allow the circulation of the widest possible variety of opinions. "Factionary societies," even those begun "with the primary and direct desire of overthrowing the government," ought to be tolerated, for they could ultimately do a popular state little harm and might do it much good, encouraging "extensive discussions which enlighten the public; defeat insidious and partial cunning, and bring forward an open and firm support of good and acceptable government."[18]

Substitution of natural reason for grace provided only one route from Puritanism to equality. A diametrically opposite process could yield almost the same result: instead of universalizing grace, the heirs of the Puritan tradition could also deny it altogether and democratize depravity. From the very founding of the Puritan colonies most New Englanders preferred to put their faith in written laws and detailed limitations on government rather than in men, however wise or gra-

17. Ezra Stiles, *A History of Three of the Judges of King Charles I* (Hartford, Conn., 1794), p. 262.
    18. Ibid., pp. 240–42, 272–76.

cious. John Cotton spoke for Puritans generally in his often quoted remarks on human nature and power:

> There is a straine in a mans heart that will sometime or other runne out to excess, unlesse the Lord restraine it, but it is not good to venture it: It is necessary therefore, that all power that is on earth be limited, Church-power or other: If there be power given to speak great things, then look for great blasphemies, look for a licentious abuse of it.[19]

A preoccupation with internal corruption has come down to modern times as the Puritans' least agreeable attribute, though oddly enough it had much to do with creating those features of the Bay Colony's government now considered most democratic. Because even magistrates, the most saintly of the saints, had a sizable residue of natural lust left in them, their power had to be limited by a codified body of laws, frequent elections, and the popular element in the "mixt' polity. These devices originally functioned only as emergency safeguards against the occasional aberrations of usually trustworthy rulers, but the moment New Englanders admitted that no man could read the law of nature aright, that all men were equally corrupt, that no faith could be placed in internal self-discipline (call it grace or virtue, piety or learning), then bills of rights and fragmented polity became the sum and substance of sound politics.[20]

In a world without clear and uncorrupted minds the only safety lay in numbers. Delivering the Massachusetts election sermon in that

---

19. *An Exposition upon the thirteenth Chapter of the Revelation* (London, 1656), pp. 71–73.

20. I do not want to make John Adams into a democrat—he was hardly that—but as the work of the most profound political thinker of Revolutionary New England, his theories are a graphic and significant illustration of the loss of faith in internal restraints. Adams was far more interested in devising ingenious mechanisms to keep the power of the wise and able in check than he was in finding ways to get them into governing positions. Cf. *A Defense of the Constitutions of Government of the United States of America, The Works of John Adams*, ed. Charles Francis Adams (Boston, 1850–1856), 4 : 290–91; *Discourses on Davila*, in ibid., 6 : 393–99. Lacking any confidence in the efficacy of saving grace, Adams regarded all talent as John Cooke regarded Charles I's intellect, as a potential sword in a madman's hands.

most significant of years, 1776, the Rev. Samuel West denied that since the Fall any man could understand the law of nature. "We have a law in our members, which is constantly warring against the law of the mind," he announced, neglecting to exempt saints and cultivated gentlemen. But if no special group could claim access to the truth, if there was no grace on which to found dominion, then ultimate authority had to rest with the people as a whole. Given the universal prevalence of self-interest and "the strong propensities of our animal nature" only the consent of the whole of society would guarantee a disinterested decision.

> It is true that the publick may be imposed upon by a misrepresentation of facts; but this may be said of the publick, which can't always be said of individuals, viz. that the publick is always willing to be rightly informed, and when it has proper matter of conviction laid before it, it's judgment is always right.[21]

Belief in a law of nature did not necessarily guarantee a liberal or egalitarian society. In seventeenth-century New England natural law had provided a good part of that one unalterable way that the votes of the freemen could only assent to, never shape, and that could be interpreted only by the learned few versed in the esoteric skills essential to statecraft. John Winthrop had left the determination of what was good, just, and honest to a small body of magistrates and ministers relying on the "light of nature (especially where the image of God in man is in parte renewed by Christ)." For Winthrop, "the best part is always the least, and of the best part the wiser part is always the lesser. The old law was choose ye out judges, etc., and thou shalt bring the matter to the judge, etc."[22]

21. Samuel West, *A Sermon Preached before the Honorable Council and the Honorable House of Representatives of the Colony of the Massachusetts-Bay* (Boston, 1776), pp. 13–14, 27. For similar invocations of majority rule as a check on individual self-interest, cf. Zabadiel Adams, *A Sermon Preached Before His Excellency, John Hancock, Esq.*, pp. 16–17, 34–35; Samuel Adams, *The Writings of Samuel Adams*, ed. Harry Alonzo Cusing (New York, 1908), 4 : 306*n*. By contrast, John Adams did not think even majorities were safe, because most men value security above liberty (Letter to Samuel Adams, 18 October 1790, *Works*, 6 : 418).

22. *Winthrop Papers*, 4 : 487; *Winthrop Journal*, 2 : 428.

Winthrop's more wary contemporaries insisted on laying down the rule for the judges to judge by and on tempering their authority with some participation by the people, but they left the preponderant power with the wisest and best. A positive ideal of majority rule could come only on the day when even the judges lost faith in wisdom and virtue, when even the chief ideologue of the Essex Junto, Theophilus Parsons, could declare that the "morals of all people in all ages, have been shockingly corrupted" and answer negatively his own query, "shall we alone boast an exemption from the general fate of mankind?" Sharing Winthrop's low estimate of human nature without Winthrop's exceptions, Parsons declined to define civil liberty, liberty under government, as the right to follow certain eternal principles. Liberty was nothing more than "the right every man in the state has, to do whatever is not prohibited by laws, TO WHICH HE HAS GIVEN HIS CONSENT."[23]

Comparisons of this sort indicate how far men like Parsons and Stiles had come from the ethic of Cotton and Winthrop as much as the substantial debt they owed to it. It takes a peculiar measure of desperation to make the first New Englanders into democrats: one must be either an unsympathetic seventeenth-century controversialist or a very sympathetic twentieth-century historian. American Puritanism in its heyday was neither democratic nor undemocratic as moderns understand the term; it was sui generis. If it must be assimilated to a twentieth-century model, it could quite plausibly be to one of our postdemocratic political nightmares. In retrospect Puritan voluntarism seems almost plebiscitarian, and its ideal of civil liberty comes horribly close to "democratic centrism."[24]

Any such analogy, of course, would do violence to the intellectual universe of another time; it would seem safer to draw no modern analogies at all. The witches' brew that went under the name of Puritan social thought could have spawned almost anything. Abolishing the law of nature might have led to the Leviathan state; universalizing

23. *The Essex Result* in Theophilus Parsons, Jr., *Memoir of Theophilus Parsons* (Boston, 1859), pp. 365–67, 378.
24. After I wrote this section I recalled that there actually have been at least two attempts to make very similar comparisons: Walzer's *The Revolution of the Saints* and Sir John Neale's *The Age of Catherine de Medici* (London, 1943).

grace might have only substituted the majority for the elect as the executors of God's unchanging decrees. There was nothing inevitable about the transformation the original doctrine would undergo in America, either in 1630 or 1760 or at any point in between. A whole range of individuals from John Locke to Lord North had each his contribution to make before John Winthrop's colony became the Massachusetts of Samuel Adams, let alone the America of George Bancroft.

Seventeenth-century New Englanders would not have found our search for modern facsimiles for their institutions very relevant or very meaningful. Their minds set on other things, they went their way apparently oblivious to the tensions inherent in the tightly knit set of paradoxes that would be their legacy to the future. Professing a faith that preached subordination by consent, ruled by the superiors in a land where physical conditions permitted relatively little material superiority, they dedicated themselves to the establishment of a model society for the reformation of a humanity they considered hopelessly corrupt. Their social ethic stands as a monument to the proposition that the contradictory is not the irreconcilable.

APPENDIX A

The Massachusetts Franchise in the
Seventeenth Century

Studies of the Massachusetts franchise have begun to appear with alarming frequency in recent years. So much has been written already that an attempt at synthesis is extremely appealing. So much more undoubtedly will be written in the near future that any such synthesis is in acute danger of becoming out of date before it ever sees print.[1] Only the broadest generalizations are possible, and even these are liable to contradiction in the next issue of some scholarly journal.

One general statement, however, is not likely to be challenged: specificity should not be confused with accuracy. Early records are often incorrect and/or incomplete, while even the best sets contain inherent deficiencies that make precise calculations difficult. "Seventy three point nine percent" has all the charm that concreteness may provide in an otherwise uncertain world, but it really means only "a large proportion, probably more than half but certainly less than the whole." No one can say exactly what proportion of the free white adult male population became freemen, for the simple reason that the freemen's records are demonstrably incomplete and the population

---

1. The literature on the subject includes: B. Katherine Brown, "Freemanship in Puritan Massachusetts," *American Historical Review* 59 (July 1954): 865–83; idem, "Puritan Democracy: A Case Study"; idem, "Puritan Democracy in Dedham, Massachusetts: Another Case Study"; Samuel Eliot Morison, *Builders of the Bay Colony* (Boston, 1930), appendix; Richard C. Simmons, "Freemanship in Early Massachusetts: Some Suggestions and a Case Study," *William and Mary Quarterly*, 3d ser., 19 (1962): 422–28; idem, "Godliness, Property and the Franchise in Puritan Massachusetts: an Interpretation," *Journal of American History* 55 (1968–69): 495–511; Stephen Foster, "The Massachusetts Franchise in the Seventeenth Century," *William and Mary Quarterly*, 3d ser., 24 (1967): 613–23; Robert Emmet Wall, Jr., "The Massachusetts Bay Colony Franchise in 1647," *William and Mary Quarterly*, 3d ser., 27 (1970): 136–44.

statistics are reasonable estimates at best.[2] In particular, the individual tax lists, land surveys, and so forth used to determine the members of inhabitants of various towns in some "case studies" are not actually anything like accurate population profiles: they contain the names of minors, of nonresidents, and even sometimes of deceased persons, and generally exclude some portion of the adult males actually in residence for good measure.[3]

Elaborate cautions having been made, it still remains possible to say a qualified something about who could vote in seventeenth-century Massachusetts. Recent work by Professor Robert Wall utilizing all the available records (and not just some one set) has established the populations of most of the Bay Colony towns in 1647 within reasonable margins of error. Comparing his lists of inhabitants with all the existing lists of freemen, Professor Wall arrives at the following table:[4]

Adding the county totals, at a minimum 1,210 men (47.6%) out of an estimated total free adult male population of 2,543 were freemen in 1647. This percentage is, however, only a minimum. The population statistics are about as definite as skill and caution are likely to make them, but the number of men legally qualified to vote is certainly greater than these figures reveal. While the General Court initially reserved for itself the exclusive right to create new freemen, in 1642 it also gave this power to the quarterly courts in each county. Enough of the court records of Essex County survive to indicate that the county courts did use their authority between 1642 and 1647, but some of the Essex records and all the records for the county courts of Suffolk and Middlesex have disappeared, leaving no trace of the men made free at their sessions.[5]

Nor should we assume that every adult male church member bothered to become a freeman. The General Court repeatedly complained in the 1640s that qualified church members were deliberately abstaining from taking the freeman's oath in order to remain exempt from

2. I have already discussed this subject in my article, "The Massachusetts Franchise in the Seventeenth Century."

3. Ibid., pp. 622–23.

4. Wall, "Massachusetts Bay Colony Franchise in 1647," pp. 137–40. Reprinted by courtesy of the *William and Mary Quarterly*.

5. Foster, "Massachusetts Franchise in the Seventeenth Century," pp. 614–15.

TABLE 1

Adult Male Population (21 and over) and Freemen in 1647

County	Town	Adult Male Population in 1647	Number of Freemen	Percentage
Suffolk	Boston	389	208	53
	Dedham	107	64	60
	Dorchester	103	65	63
	Roxbury	94	59	62
	Braintree	87	37	43
	Hingham	79	32	41
	Weymouth	68	37	54
	Hull	9	5	56
Totals		936	507	54
Middlesex	Watertown	150	62	41
	Charlestown	129	84	65
	Cambridge	121	68	56
	Sudbury	61	30	50
	Concord	55	36	65
	Woburn	55	27	49
	Reading	28	9	32
Totals		599	316	53
Essex	Salem	246	104	42
	Ipswich	277	67	29
	Newbury	115	51	44
	Rowley	77	42	56
	Gloucester	58	15	26
	Wenham	30	16	53
	Andover	20	9	45
	Manchester	15	5	33
Totals		788	309	38
Norfolk	Hampton	73	25	34
	Salisbury	68	30	44
	Haverhill	36	16	44
Totals		177	71	40
	Springfield	43	7	16

the expensive nuisance of public service.[6] In addition, the residents of the more remote towns probably found it inconvenient to travel to either the General Court at Boston or the local session of the county court to take the oath. Professor Wall has noted that the proportion of recorded freemen in any given town tends to fall as the distance from Boston increases and suggests, plausibly enough, that local authorities in the distant towns may have been rather casual in enforcing the legal requirement for voting and holding office.[7] Since successful criminals by definition leave few traces of their crime, illegal voting is not an easy thing to measure, but without even considering this tangled question it seems apparent that more adult males than not could have qualified for the franchise in the first two decades of the colony's existence.

Massachusetts at a latter date presents a very different picture. Extending his calculations to 1664, Professor Wall finds that the proportion of recorded freemen fell off sharply to well under fifty percent in almost every town.[8] Part of this decline can arguably be attributed to faculty records, part to increased apathy among qualified church members. As the colony expanded geographically, the difficulties in getting to court to take the oath presumably increased proportionately: at the very end of the old charter period the deputies explicitly complained of this problem.[9] But the body of men potentially eligible for the freemanship, as well as the proportion of recorded freemen, was obviously also shrinking in the period after 1650. Until 1664 church membership remained the only qualification for the freemanship; after that date the General Court added a steep property franchise as an alternate qualification, but this was set so high it could not have had a substantial effect on the number of eligible voters.[10] At any time during the life of the old charter most voters

6. *Winthrop Papers*, 4 : 190; *Mass. Rec.*, 2 : 38, 208.

7. Wall, pp. 142–44.

8. By Professor Wall's calculations, the freemen in 1666 amounted to only twenty-nine percent of the Bay Colony's adult male population. Professor Wall has kindly allowed me to see the results of his most recent work in manuscript; his figures exclude Boston and Salem.

9. Massachusetts Archives, 106 : 507, State House, Boston.

10. *Mass. Rec.*, vol. 4, pt. 1, p. 118; Foster, "Massachusetts Franchise in the Seventeenth Century," pp. 617–19; Simmons, "Godliness, Property and the Franchise," pp. 509–11.

would have had to come from the ranks of the church members, and
their proportion of the total population was also falling off markedly
in the later years of settlement. Professor Richard Simmons's calculations show the following decline in male members admitted to full
communtion in the Bay Colony's churches:[11]

TABLE 2
Known Admissions of Males to Massachusetts Churches

	1630s	1640s	1650s	1660s	1671–86
Beverly, 1667–86	–	–	–	39	22
Boston First, 1630–86	265	121	31	75	60
Boston Second, 1650–86	–	–	18	20	79
Boston Third, 1669–86	–	–	–	36	54
Cambridge, ca. 1636–67	52	27	14	18	–
Charlestown, 1632–86	98	42	26	24	39
Dedham, 1637–67	38	43	7	11	–
Dorchester, 1636–86	66	27	24	14	47
Roxbury, ca. 1630–86	112	31	21	15	49
Rowley, 1665–86	–	–	–	36	30
Salem, ca. 1630–50, 1660–69	111	82	–	32	–

The drop in admissions in the 1640s is to be expected. The Bay
Colony's churches were mainly gathered in the first decade of settlement, and the small numbers admitted immediately thereafter probably only reflect a situation where the majority of adult males had
already joined some church. Admissions in subsequent decades, however, are also comparatively low despite the fourfold increase in the
colony's population between 1640 and 1680. By the latter date in any
case, most of the members admitted in the 1630s and 1640s presumably had died, and the slight increase in admissions in some churches
in the last two decades of the period would hardly have compensated
for their loss. By the fall of the Old Charter in 1686, individuals

11. Simmons, p. 501. Table 2 is reprinted by courtesy of the *Journal of
American History* and the Organization of American Historians.

legally qualified for the franchise in the Bay Colony would have constituted a distinct minority of the adult male population.[12]

Both sets of calculations under discussion are liable to errors, but
the large electorate of 1647 and the general downward trend after
that date seem clear enough. For the first two decades of the Bay
Colony's history, perhaps for the first three, half or more of the free
white adult males in most towns probably had the right to vote or
could get it if they would make the effort of taking the freeman's
oath. By the end of the old charter period, on the other hand, the
proportion had apparently dropped to well under fifty percent. Since
the entire experiment of the old charter only lasted fifty-five years,

12. Recent work by Professor Robert Pope has filled in many of the details
of this very general picture and, incidentally, effectively challenged the accepted version of the development of New England religious life. In particular,
Professor Pope has shown that the decline in male admissions to full communion
probably reached its low point about 1660 and that admissions picked up
sharply again after 1676 (Robert Pope, *The Half-Way Covenant* [Princeton,
N.J., 1969], chap. 8 and appendix). Pope's statistics, however, do not contradict
the thesis presented here: the *absolute* increase in new admissions after 1676
is simply too small to offset the decline in the *proportion* of the adult male
population in full communion, which fell steeply after 1650 because of the
increase in total population and the death of the earlier church members.

Even in terms of absolute numbers the post-1676 "revival" is something less
than spectacular. Pope shows that in three of the oldest churches in the Bay
the average number of new admissions per year in the 1680s equalled or
surpassed the comparable figures for the 1640s. But the 1640s in their turn
were a decade of abnormally low admissions because of the unusually small size
of the pool of potential converts, the free white adult males not yet church
members. This group had been seriously depleted by the massive admissions of
the 1630s, when the three churches were founded; it could be replenished only
as males under twenty-one in 1639 attained their majority after that date and
as new adult immigrants arrived in the colony. Since the migration from
England virtually stopped after 1642, the Massachusetts churches must have
depended almost exclusively on natural increase for new recruits in the 1640s,
so that even if every previously unchurched adult had decided to join a church
in that decade the number of admissions per year would not have been very
large—it would not have taken much of a revival among the much larger
unchurched adult population of the 1680s to equal or surpass the admissions
figures for the 1640s. In the long view the revival of 1677–90 is really a
partial arrest in the gradual *relative* decline in full church membership that
took place throughout the latter half of the seventeenth century.

during perhaps half of which more adult men than not could vote, and since the electoral laws under the new charter of 1692 once again enfranchised a majority, the period during which only a minority of the adult males in Massachusetts had the franchise must have been a short one.

The Nomination of Massachusetts Magistrates under the Old Charter

The complexities of the electoral system employed in early Massachusetts have caused enough confusion to lead historians to assert that the laws insured the automatic reelection of incumbents or prevented new candidates from standing for office. The laws actually did neither.

Under an act of May 1640, renewed with variations from time to time until 1649, the freemen in the fall of each year voted for nominees for magistrates and sent the results to the General Court. That body in turn selected the twenty individuals having the highest total votes and sent their names back to the freemen for acceptance or rejection at the time of the Court of Elections the following spring. No new candidates could be proposed after the fall nominations.[1]

Although the wording of the law does not mention it explicitly, the evidence indicates that the incumbent board of magistrates was automatically renominated, and that the court submitted to the towns only enough new names to make a total of twenty when combined with the old magistrates. In October 1640, when the magistrates consisted of the governor, the deputy governor, and eight assistants, the court sent ten additional nominees to the freemen for a total of twenty, and the freemen chose to elect only the incumbents, rejecting all the new nominees. The next year, in December of 1641, the court sent only six additional names to the freemen, and they elected two new magistrates from these six as well as returning the entire incumbent board once again.[2]

In June of 1641 the court did *propose* a new system to do away with the nominations by having every ten freemen elect one of their

1. Mass. Rec., 1 : 293; 2 : 21, 37.
2. Ibid., 1 : 308, 345.

number "to bee sent to the Court, with the power to make election for all the rest." This was only a suggestion, however, which the deputies were to carry to their constituents for approval or rejection. They must have rejected it for the court employed the regular nominating system in December.[3]

Finally, in 1649 the court did change the procedure slightly by eliminating the automatic renomination of incumbents. Instead, the freemen would make their nomination by written ballot in November of each year, and the twenty names with the highest totals would be submitted to them the following May for acceptance or rejection, as under the law of 1640. This new statute, however, had a hooker: the names were submitted to the freemen in May according to the order of the number of votes received, the highest first, except that incumbents among the twenty were always placed at the head of the list. Consequently, when the names of the nominees were read off in the town meetings it would first be necessary for a voter to withhold his ballot from an incumbent before he could give it to a new candidate. While this did not make change impossible it did favor the existing leadership.[4] Indeed the court probably enacted (and the freemen probably accepted) this system because it did precisely this, the theory being that a magistrate should not be removed without cause even at a regular election. No one seems to have objected to the system except some modern historians and Edward Randolph, who objected to almost everything. In any case, no law prevented the freemen in the 1640s from nominating William Hawthorne in November and voting him into office the following May, while rejecting John Winthrop.

3. Ibid., pp. 332–33.
4. Ibid., 2 : 286–87.

The Merchants, the Moderates, and
Edward Randolph

The role of the merchant community in New England society remains
a controverted matter, especially for the stormy years between 1660
and 1690. Bernard Bailyn has argued in an influential work that the
merchants, by virtue of their profession, developed a modern ethos
in sharp conflict with the medieval one dominant in Puritan Massachusetts.[1] He maintains that "conflict between men who had risen
through the struggles of city life and the leaders of the puritan commonwealth was implicit from the start" (p. 40), and that, though
the faith of the first generation held that clash in check, the struggle
of Puritan magistrate and minister against modern merchant erupted
after 1660: "the business community represented the spirit of a new
age. Its guiding principles were not social stability, order, and the
discipline of the senses, but mobility, growth and the enjoyment of
life . . . To the Watchmen of the Holy Citadel nothing could have
been more insidious" (p. 139).

By 1675 the merchants were "emerging from the constrictions of a
medieval social order" (p. 134). Representing "the part of society
accustomed to wield political power in England" but denied it in
New England, the mercantile community joined with the English
authorities to overthrow the wilderness Zion of the old charter and
establish a royal government (pp. 160, 176–77). Several other writers, most notably Michael G. Hall, also identify the merchant class as
the base for an alleged "moderate party," a group of New Englanders
in the Restoration period willing to aid the British customs agent
Edward Randolph in substituting royal government for that of the

1. *The New England Merchants in the Seventeenth Century*, (New York:
Harper Torchbooks, 1964), passim.

the merchants had a very respectable representation among the magistracy. Governor John Leverett, Richard Russell, William Hawthorne, Edward Tyng, and Thomas Clarke qualify, both as merchants and as magistrates, and Bailyn would make Simon Bradstreet and Daniel Dennison merchants too (pp. 125, 163, 165), though most of their money was in land. Several other magistrates, while not merchants per se, were still tied to the mercantile community by personal and economic interest. John Pynchon was a large landowner who also operated as a supply merchant and investor in overseas trade. William Stoughton had close connections with various New England merchants through ventures in land speculation, as did his friend Joseph Dudley, elected in 1675, and both men were prominent "moderates."

The merchant contingent among the magistrates remained substantial to the very end of the old charter period. Between 1680 and 1686 thirty-one men served as magistrates, of whom about thirteen are classifiable as merchants. Besides those already mentioned, Humphrey Davy, James Russell, John Richards, John Hull, Bartholomew Gedney, Thomas Savage, William Brown, John Hawthorne, Elisha Hutchinson, and Samuel Sewall also gave the Massachusetts mercantile community ample voice in the colony's upper house. If the term *merchant* is stretched some, Elisha Cooke, related both by marital and financial connection to the Leveretts, and Peter Bulkeley, a supporter of Stoughton and Dudley, might also be included.[4]

The argument that merchants and moderates had a peculiar affinity for each other does not hold up much better under close scrutiny. It is all very well to note, as Bailyn does (p. 157), that the British agent Randolph named fourteen men in 1676 who "with many others . . . only wait for an opportunity to expresse their duty to his Majestie," and that nine of these fourteen were merchants. It might be advisable, however, to note as well, as Bailyn does not, that Randolph also named six men who "with some few others of the same faction, keep the country in subjection and slavery," of whom four (Leverett, Tyng, Clark, and William Hawthorne) were merchants too. In 1682,

4. Whitmore, *The Massachusetts Civil List*, pp. 25–26; James Savage, *A Genealogical Dictionary of the First Settlers of New England* (Boston, 1860–62), passim.; Robert Emmet Wall, Jr., *The Membership of the Massachusetts General Court* (Ph.D. diss., Yale University, 1964), passim.

Old Charter. *Moderation* for these writers has become not a tempera
ment, but a definite program of a party with a coherent economic an
social foundation.[2]

Bailyn's efforts to establish a distinct merchant outlook at varianc
with New England orthodoxy often seem rather strained. As ev
dence, for example, of growing worldliness in the merchants of th
second generation, he introduces a letter of the younger John Wir
throp cautioning his son Fitz-John against the obsessive fear of deat
(pp. 109–10). The younger Winthrop did write the warning, bu
only because too great a concern for mortality indicated a lack c
faith in God's providence. Winthrop's own father, the senior Johr
would hardly have disapproved of his son's advice:

> I perceive by your letter that you were much possessed wit
> the feare of Death, you must be [care]full that Sathan doth nc
> delude you, it is good to be alwaies mindful and prepared fc
> death, but take heede of distrusting, perplexed thoughts abou
> it, for that will encrease the sicnese; trust him with your lif
> that gave you life and being, and hath [the] only power ov
> death and life, to whom we must be willing to submitt to be
> the disposing of his good will and pleasure. Whether in life c
> death learne to know God and to serve him, and to feare hir
> and walke in his waies, and leave your selfe with him and ca
> your care on him who careth for all his servants and will nc
> forsake those that trust in his name.[3]

With literary evidence ambiguous at best, Bailyn's case for a sep
rate mercantile ethos rests on his polarization of the "merchants" c
the one hand and the "ministry" and "magistracy" on the other, an
on his assertion (p. 160) that few merchants gained political powe
under the old charter. To identify the New England merchant cla
would be very difficult, yet using Bailyn's own definitions, as of 167

---

2. Michael G. Hall, *Edward Randolph and the American Colonies* (Chap
Hill, N.C., 1960), pp. 58–60 and passim.; Perry Miller, *The New Englan
Mind, From Colony to Province*, chap. 10. Two studies which dissent from th
interpretation of the moderate party are Richard Dunn, *Puritans and Yankee*
pp. 212–28 and Paul Lucas, "Colony or Commonwealth: Massachusetts Ba
1661–1666," *The William and Mary Quarterly*, 3d ser., 24 (1967): 88–9

3. 5 *Coll. MHS*, 8 : 43.

when Randolph finally came around to enumerating "the faction," the moderates' opponents, his list included such prominent traders as John Richards, James Russell, Humphrey Davy, Bartholomew Gedney, Thomas Brattle, Anthony Stoddard, John Hawthorne, Elisha Hutchinson, and Richard Sprague.[5]

Randolph seems to have awarded his labels without much regard for consistency or precision. The embarrassing circumstance of Brattle and Gedney, both alleged moderates, appearing on the faction list, is merely one example. When Dudley and Stoughton finally came to power in 1686, they too took on characteristics remarkably like those of their enemies, the faction. Dudley, according to Randolph, was "a man of a base, servile and antimonarchicall principle," while Stoughton was described simply as "of the old leaven."[6]

Randolph was the ancestor of that long line of Englishmen residing abroad whose reports once prompted Lord Palmerston to remark that, when he wanted to be misinformed about a country, he went to a man who had lived there for ten years. If not quite someone whose "name and a lie goes for the same thing a thousand miles upon the continent of America" (William Penn's description), the royal customs collector certainly was a man who saw what he wanted to see and little else. In his report of 1676 he did not get so much as the details of the Harvard commencement correct, and he put the number of men able to bear arms in Boston at about four thousand, a neat trick for a town whose total population did not much exceed that number. Later, with equal extravagance, he offered to defeat the entire Massachusetts militia with five hundred of the king's guards.[7]

Merchants appeared frequently among Randolph's lists of those well affected to the king because he had decided that the whole of Massachusetts fitted that category, a small "faction" only excepted.

5. Robert N. Toppan and Thomas S. Goodrich, eds., *Edward Randolph* (Boston, 1898–1909), 2 : 254, 255; 3 : 130.

6. Randolph to the Archbishop of Canterbury, 27 October 1686, ibid., 4 : 131. John Richards, whom Randolph put on the faction list of 1682 and described as "a man not to be trusted in publique business" in this same letter of 1686, was "well principled" and a supporter of royal government in the report of 1676.

7. Ibid., 2 : 236, 257; Randolph to the Earl of Clarendon, 14 June 1682, ibid., 3 : 158.

Evcn the ministers were "for the most part very civill and inclining to his Majesties government, being held in subjection by the ruling elders, who govern all the affairs of the church." As for the inhabitants generally, Randolph reported them "well affected to his Majestie and his government, as well the merchants and farmers and the meaner traders and artificers, who groan under the yoake of the present government, and are in dayle hopes and expectations of a change."[8]

Randolph had ample leisure to contemplate his errors during his enforced residence in the Boston jail following the overthrow of his abortive Dominion of New England in 1689. More recent commentators on seventeenth-century Massachusetts, spared that experience, have continued to take his dubious reports at something very like face value and so to posit an organized moderate party, although they endow it gratuitously with a merchant base, as Randolph did not. Moderates there may well have been—there usually are. That they had sufficient cohesion to form a party remains unproven; that they drew their support mainly from a disgruntled merchant class shut out as a whole from political power is clearly false.

8. Ibid., 2 : 253, 255.

Family Connections of Merchants, Ministers, and Magistrates

Family histories illustrate strikingly the difficulties inherent in trying to establish the New England merchants as a coherent class separated by outlook and circumstances from the magistracy and ministry of the seventeenth century. Four genealogies, by no means exhaustive, give a good indication of the extent and complexity of the interconnections between the three groups.

THE FAMILY OF THE REV. JOHN HIGGINSON (1616–1708) OF SALEM

Higginson's two sons, John and Nathaniel, both became prominent merchants, the latter in India. His daughter Sarah married the merchant Richard Wharton, and he himself took as his second wife Mary Atwater, widow of Boston merchant Joshua Atwater and herself the daughter of an English minister.[1]

THE FAMILY OF GOVERNOR SIMON BRADSTREET (1603–97)

The governor himself was the son of a minister of Lincolnshire and became in Massachusetts both a merchant and a magistrate. He married the poetess Anne Dudley ("the twelfth muse lately raised up in the wilderness"), daughter of Governor Thomas Dudley and sister of Sarah Dudley Keayne, daughter-in-law of the notorious Boston merchant Robert Keayne. Anne and Simon's son, also named Simon, became a minister at New London, Connecticut, and married in his turn his first cousin once removed, Lucy Woodbridge, daughter of the Rev. John Woodbridge (whose mother Mercy was a daughter of Thomas Dudley and thus a sister of the Rev. Simon's mother Anne).

1. James Savage, *A Genealogical Dictionary of the First Settlers of New England*, 1 : 76; 2 : 413–14.

Another child of Governor Simon, Dorothy, married the Rev. Seaborn Cotton, and their son, also named Seaborn, after entering the
ministry himself took as his wife Ann Lake, daughter of Boston
merchant Thomas Lake.[2]

THE FAMILY OF RICHARD RUSSELL (1611–76) OF CHARLESTOWN

Russell, both a magistrate and a merchant, had a son, Daniel, who
became a minister. Daniel's widow, Mehitabel Willis, granddaughter
of Governor John Haynes of Massachusetts and Connecticut, married
as her second and third husbands two more ministers, the Rev. John
Hubbard and the Rev. Samuel Woodbridge respectively. Mehitabel's
mother, widow of magistrate Samuel Willis of Connecticut, married
Samuel Woodbridge's uncle, the Rev. Timothy Woodbridge, who was
in his turn a son of the Rev. John Woodbridge and brother to Lucy,
wife of the Rev. Samuel Bradstreet.[3]

THE FAMILY OF EDWARD TYNG (DIED 1681) OF BOSTON

Tyng was the son of a merchant and himself both a merchant and
a magistrate. His daughter Hannah married the merchant Habijah
Savage, and their daughters Hanna and Mary married the Rev.
Nathaniel Gookin and the Rev. Thomas Weld respectively. Their
mother, the first Hannah Tyng, after Savage's death married the
magistrate Daniel Gookin, father of the Rev. Nathaniel. Another of
Edward Tyng's daughters, Deborah, married the magistrate Joseph
Dudley (son of Governor Thomas Dudley and brother of Anne
Bradstreet), while still another Tyng daughter, Eunice, married the
Rev. Samuel Willard, son of magistrate and fur trader Simon Willard.
Edward Tyng's brother William (died 1653), a merchant but not
a magistrate, had a daughter Elizabeth who married Thomas Brattle,
the wealthiest merchant in Boston. Their sons in turn were the fa-
mous pair Thomas, merchant and treasurer of Harvard College, and
William, minister of Cambridge, Massachusetts. Another of William
Tyng's daughters, Ann, married the Rev. Thomas Shepard; and still

---

2. Ibid., 1 : 463–64, 735–36; 4 : 631–32.
3. Ibid., 3 : 589–90, 593–94; 4 : 633; John Langdon Sibley and Clifford
K. Shipton, eds., *Sibley's Harvard Graduates* (Cambridge, Mass., 1873–   ),
5 : 131–32.

another, Berthia, became the first wife of Richard Wharton (later to marry Sarah Higginson); while a fourth daughter, Mercy, completed the circle by marrying Samuel Bradstreet, eldest son of Governor Simon and Anne Bradstreet.[4]

Other family connections, equally complicated, could easily be adduced.[5] Magistrate, minister, and merchant were anything but mutually exclusive social groupings in seventeenth-century New England.

4. Savage, *a Genealogical Dictionary*, 1 : 238–39; 4 : 356–58.
5. For further complications all lucidly set down, see Bernard Bailyn, *The New England Merchants*, pp. 135–38.

Bibliography

Almost anything thought, spoken, or written in New England between 1630 and 1730 could have served as source material for this book; to keep from being swamped by evidence, I had to restrict research almost exclusively to printed materials. I assumed that by reading widely in these I would gather as representative a sampling of normative thought and attitude in New England as I would obtain by extensive use of manuscript sources. Sewall, Hull, Wigglesworth, and Mather, for example, taken collectively, probably did not differ much in their opinions from the scores of lesser known diarists whose journals have never seen print. Subsequent experience in deciphering barely legible handwriting on badly preserved parchment has largely confirmed my original judgment, though I have gained a new appreciation of the difficulties of social history and a new respect for its successful practitioners.

The bibliography that follows lists only those items considered most useful and does not include everything used in the course of research or even everything cited in the footnotes. Each subgroup of sources opens with a brief bibliographical essay indicating the particular items I found most valuable. For complete listings of both primary and secondary sources consult the bibliographies in Perry Miller and Thomas H. Johnson, *The Puritans* (New York: Harper Torchbooks, 1963), especially those for sections 1 and 2.

1. Sermons, Treatises, Tracts

The forbidding nature of these works—their dryness, rigidly formal organization, and repetitive character—often obscures their real value. Every thousand-page folio seems only a slight variation on the thousand-page folio before it; every election sermon borrows heavily from every other election sermon, both overtly and implicitly, until the reader cannot help but believe that the whole body of formal statements of Puritan social ideology constitutes nothing more than the mindless reiteration of a meaningless litany. Yet the fact that the men of 1690 were content to hear the doctrine of 1600, that Samuel Willard often only echoed William Perkins, really gives some indication of the power of orthodox doctrines. The treatises did not go unread, the sermons unheard, no matter how much they imitated each other. Their contents might be mere commonplaces, but commonplaces became common by virtue of their widespread and unthinking acceptance.

Among the earlier treatise-makers the most readable and helpful is William Perkins (especially in his *Treatise of Callings* and his *Cases of Conscience*, both reprinted in his *Works*), and after him John Downame. Both men had at least some degree of literary skill, both wrote voluminously and comprehensively, and both produced books which have highly detailed tables of contents or indexes that add greatly to their usefulness. William Ames wrote the best short exposition of the point of view adopted by the New England Puritans, his *Medulla* becoming their standard statement of theology, his *Cases of Conscience* their authoritative work of casuistry. Unfortunately his very concision produced a kind of arithmetic aridity that Perkins and Downame managed to an extent to avoid, so that their works provide more interesting reading and more quotable material.

The first New Englanders were too busy putting social ethics into practice to write about them nearly as extensively as did their predecessors in England or their descendants in the New World. Also, given the limited capacity of the early press at Cambridge and the difficulties of sending manuscripts back to England for printing, the early New England ministers were obliged to assign priority to works explaining or defending their experiment in congregational polity rather than those concentrating on the niceties of social intercourse. For these reasons the works of a layman, John Winthrop, contain the most information, especially his *Model of Christian Charity* and the occasional reflective passages in his journal. Among the ministers, John Cotton produced the largest number of published works, and several of these deal with various aspects of Puritan social thought, especially *The Way of Life*. Thomas Hooker wrote almost as much as Cotton and surpassed him as a stylist, but his published works mainly center on church polity or on the path to regeneration.

Cotton gave the first election sermon in 1634, and other ministers served as election preachers annually thereafter, but the General Court did not begin printing election sermons until 1661. Before that date we have only the manuscript notes of Thomas Shepard's Massachusetts election sermon of 1638 and of Thomas Hooker's Hartford election sermon of the same year. By the time Massachusetts and Connecticut came around to printing these sermons regularly, they had begun to follow a fixed pattern which severely limited the amount of new material they might contain and which forbade any direct references to contemporary political events. Easily the most eloquent and the most interesting of the lot is William Hubbard's *The Happiness of a People*, the Massachusetts election sermon for 1676. Though I have read most of the Massachusetts and Connecticut sermons for the seventeenth century and for the first half of the eighteenth, I have included only a few of the more significant ones in the bibliography. Complete lists are available in Charles Evans's *American Bibliography* and in Robert W. G. Vail, "A Check List of New England Election Sermons," *Proceedings of the American Antiquarian Society* 45 (1935): 233–66.

Of later writers Cotton Mather produced far and away the largest bibliography and—thanks to his absorption in moralism and "practical divinity"—far and away the most detailed expositions on the moral conduct of life in the Puritan community. In exploring his mammoth collection of printed works, T. J. Holmes, *Cotton Mather, A Bibliography of His Works*, 3 vols. (Cambridge, Mass., 1940) is invaluable. Among other writers of the second and third generations Samuel Willard deserves the most notice. His *Compleat Body of Divinity* has all the advantages and disadvantages common to compendia: wide comprehension, systematic exposition, and chilling dullness.

AMES, WILLIAM. *Works*. London, 1643. Includes the *Medulla* and *Cases of Conscience*.

BAXTER, RICHARD. *A Christian Directory*. London, 1673.

BUKLEY, JOHN. *The Necessity of Religion in Society*. New London, Conn., 1713.

BURNHAM, WILLIAM. *God's Providence in Placing Men in their Respective Stations & Conditions Asserted & Showed*. New London, Conn., 1722.

COOKE, JOHN. *King Charls his Case.* London, 1649.

COTTON, JOHN. *A Brief Exposition on the Whole of Ecclesiastes.* Edinburgh, 1868.

———. "Certain Proposals Made by Lord Say, Lord Brooke, and other Persons of Quality, as conditions of their removing to New England, with the answers thereto." In Thomas Hutchinson, *History of the Colony and Province of Massachusetts-Bay,* edited by Lawrence S. Mayo, 1 : 410–13. Cambridge, Mass., 1936.

———. *Christ the Fountaine of Life.* London, 1651.

———. "Copy of a Letter from Mr. Cotton to Lord Say and Seal in the Year 1636." In Hutchinson, *History of the Colony and Province of Massachusetts-Bay,* 1 : 414–17.

———. *A Discourse About Civil Government in a New Plantation whose Design is Religion.* Cambridge, Mass., 1663. Sometimes attributed to John Davenport.

———. *God's Promise to His Plantations.* London, 1630. Reprinted in *Old South Leaflets,* no. 53.

———. "Moses His Judicials." Reprinted in Peter Force, ed. *Tracts and other Papers, Relating Principally to the Origin, Settlement, and Progress of the Colonies in North America,* vol. 3, no. 9. Washington, 1844.

———. *The Way of Life.* London, 1615.

DANFORTH, JOHN. *The Vile Prophanations of Prosperity by the Degenerate Among the People of God.* Boston, 1704.

DANFORTH, SAMUEL. *A Brief Recognition of New-England's Errand into the Wilderness.* Cambridge, Mass., 1671.

DENNISON, DANIEL. *Irenicon or a Slave for New-England's Sore.* In William Hubbard, *The Benefit of a Well-Ordered Conversation.* Boston, 1684.

DOWNAME, JOHN. *The Christian Warfare.* London, 1634.

———. *A Guide to Godlynesse.* London, [1622].

———. *The Plea of the Poore.* London, 1616.

FRAUNCE, ABRAHAM. The *Lawiers Logicke.* London, 1558.

GOODMAN, CHRSITOPHER. *How Superior Powers Ought to be Obeyed.* Geneva, 1558.

HILDERSHAM, ARTHUR. *CVII Lectures Upon the Fourth of John.* 2d ed. London, 1632.

HOOKER, THOMAS. *The Application of Redemption*. London, 1657.
————. *The Christians Two Chiefe Lessons, Viz Self-Deniall, and Selfe-Tryall*. London, 1640.
————. Hartford Election Sermon of 1638. In *Collections of the Connecticut Historical Society*, 1 (1860) : 20.
————. *Heautonaparnumenos, Or a Treatise of Self-Denyall*. London, 1646.
————. *A Survey of the Summe of Church-Discipline*. London, 1648.
HUBBARD, WILLIAM. *The Benefit of a Well-Ordered Conversation*. Boston, 1684.
————. *The Happiness of a People In the Wisdome of their Rulers Directing And in the Obedience of their Brethren Attending*. Boston, 1676.
JOHNSON, EDWARD. *The Wonder Working Providence of Sions Saviour in New England*, edited by J. Franklin Jameson. New York, 1910.
MATHER, COTTON. *Bonifacius*. Boston, 1710.
————. *The Christian at his Calling*. Boston, 1701.
————. *The Christian Philosopher*. London, 1721.
————. *Concio ad Populum*. Boston, 1719.
————. *A Conquest Over the Grand Excuse of Sinfulness and Slothfulness*. Boston, 1712.
————. *Durable Riches*. Boston, 1695.
————. *A Flying Roll for the House of the Thief*. Boston, 1713.
————. *Magnadia Christi Americana*. 2 vols. Hartford, 1855.
————. *Pascentius*. Boston, 1714.
————. *The Pure Nazarite*. Boston, 1723.
————. *The Servicable Man*. Boston, 1690.
————. *A Very Needful Caution*. Boston, 1707.
————. *The Wonderful Works of God*. Boston, 1690.
MATHER, INCREASE. *An Earnest Exhortation to the Inhabitants of New England*. Boston, 1676.
————. *The Great Blessing of Primitive Counsellours*. Boston, 1693.
MILTON, JOHN. *The Tenure of Kings and Magistrates*. London, 1649.
MOODEY, SAMUEL. *The Debtor's Monitor*. Boston, 1715.
MORTON, CHARLES. *Compendium Physicae, Publ*. CSM, vol. 33. Boston, 1940.

New England's First Fruits. London, 1643. Reprinted in Samuel Eliot Morison, *The Founding of Harvard College.* Cambridge, Mass., 1936, pp. 419–47.

NORTON, JOHN. *Sion the Out-Case Healed of her Wounds.* Cambridge, Mass., 1664.

————. A "small treatise" on the negative voice. *Proc.* MHS, 46 (1912–13) : 276–85.

OAKES, URIAN. *New-England Pleaded With.* Cambridge, Mass., 1674.

————. *A Seasonable Discourse Wherein Sincerity & Delight in the Service of God is Earnestly Pressed Upon Professors of Religion.* Cambridge, Mass., 1682.

OXENBRIDGE, JOHN. *New England's Freeman Warmed and Warned.* Cambridge, Mass., 1673.

PARSONS, THEOPHILUS. *The Essex Result.* In Theophilus Parsons, Jr., *Memoir of Theophilus Parsons.* Boston, 1859.

PEACHAM, HENRY. *The Compleat Gentleman.* Edited by G. S. Gorden. Oxford, 1906.

PEMBERTON, EBENEZAR. *The Divine Original of Government Asserted.* Boston, 1710.

————. *Sermons and Discourses on Several Occasions.* London, 1727.

PERKINS, WILLIAM. *Works.* Vol. 1, Cambridge, 1608.. Vols. 2, 3, London, 1631.

PONET, JOHN. *A Short Treatise of Politike Power.* [London], 1556. Reprinted in Winthrop S. Hudson, *John Ponet (1516–1556), Advocate of Limited Monarchy.* Chicago, 1942.

PRESTON, JOHN. *Four Godly and Learned Treatises.* London, 1633.

————. *The Golden Sceptor Held Forth to the Humble.* London, 1638.

SAFFIN, JOHN. *A Brief and Candid Answer to a Late Printed Sheet Entitled the Selling of Joseph.* Boston, 1700. Reprinted in part in George H. Moore, *Notes on the History of Slavery in Massachusetts,* pp. 251–56. New York, 1866.

SHEPARD, THOMAS. *Certain Select Cases Resolved.* London, 1648.

————. Massachusetts Election Sermon of 1638, *NEH&GR* 24 (1870) : 361–66.

————. *Three Valuable Pieces.* Boston, 1747.

————. *Wine for Gospel Wantons.* Boston, 1668.

SIBBES, RICHARD. *Works.* 7 vols. Edinburgh, 1862–67.

SMITH, SIR THOMAS. *De Republica Anglorum.* Edited by L. Alston. Cambridge, 1906.

STEELE, RICHARD. *The Trades-Man's Calling.* London, 1684.

STILES, EZRA. *A History of Three of the Judges of King Charles I.* Hartford, 1794.

STODDARD, SOLOMON. *An Answer to Some Cases of Conscience.* Boston, 1722.

————. *The Way for a People to Live Long in the Land that God hath Given Them.* Boston, 1703.

STUBBES, PHILLIP. *The Anatomy of Abuses.* Edited by F. J. Furnivall. London, 1882.

Tracts on Liberty in the Puritan Revolution. Edited by William Haller. 2 vols. New York, 1934.

WEST, SAMUEL. *A Sermon Preached before the Honorable Council and the Honorable House of Representatives of the Colony of the Massachusetts Bay.* Boston, 1776.

WILLARD, SAMUEL. *The Character of a Good Ruler.* Boston, 1694.

————. *A Compleat Body of Divinity.* Boston, 1726.

————. *The High Esteem Which God Hath of the Death of His Saints.* Boston, 1683.

WISE, JOHN. *A Vindication of the Government of the New England Churches.* Edited by Perry Miller. Gainsville, Florida, 1958.

WOTTON, SAMUEL. *The Art of Logick.* London, 1626.

2. LAW CODES, COLONY RECORDS, TOWN RECORDS, COURT RECORDS, CHURCH RECORDS

Official records and law codes give further information on a society's announced standards and also supply a beginning for examining the much more difficult problem of discovering what these standards actually mean to the people who hold them. The records of the county courts in particular provide detailed descriptions of the kinds of activity the colonies considered criminal and some indication of their relative success in suppressing these crimes. The *Essex County Court Records* and the *Suffolk County Court Records* also include lengthy extracts from the files of evidence which accumulated around many cases and which are a mine of information for social history.

Town and church records are important for similar reasons. Ministers might preach the word and magistrates wield the sword, but the

record of the actual influence of word and sword in the ordinary
course of life of the average New Englander appears most fully in the
local records. Those for Dedham and Watertown, and the Boston
Registry Department series are particularly full, others less so, while
some towns have detailed antiquarian histories, such as Frothingham's
of Charlestown, containing extensive citations from the mansucript
records.

Of the records of the New England colonies' central governments,
those of the Massachusetts Bay Company under the Old Charter are
the best. Taken together with the *Winthrop Journal* and the *Winthrop
Papers* they supply a highly illuminating account of the political and
constitutional development of the Bay Colony in its early years and of
the working out of Puritan political ideology in its first major test.
Plymouth Colony's records yield a good deal less information, those of
Connecticut still less. In neither of these two colonies is it possible to
trace the establishment and alteration of the governmental system in
as much detail as in Massachusetts Bay.

A.   COLONY RECORDS

*Records of the Governor and Company of the Massachusetts Bay in
New England.* 6 vols. Edited by N. B. Shurtleff. Boston, 1853–54.
*Acts and Resolves, Public and Private, of the Province of the Massa-
chusetts Bay.* 21 vols. Boston, 1869–1922.
*A Bibliographical Sketch of the Laws of the Massachusetts Colony
from 1630 to 1686.* Edited by William H. Whitmore. Boston,
1890. Contains the Body of Liberties of 1641.
The Book of General Laws and Liberties (1648). Edited by Max
Farrand. Cambridge, Mass., 1929.
*Records of the Court of Assistants of the Colony of the Massachusetts
Bay.* 3 vols. Edited by John F. Noble and J. F. Cronin. Boston,
1901–28.
The Massachusetts Civil Lists for the Colonial and Provincial Periods.
Edited by William H. Whitmore. Albany, N.Y., 1870.
Records of the Colony of New Plymouth in New England. 12 vols.
Edited by Nathaniel B. Shurtleff et al. Boston, 1855–61.
The General Laws and Liberties of New-Plymouth Colony. Cam-
bridge, Mass., 1672.
Public Records of the Colony of Connecticut. 15 vols. Edited by
J. H. Trumbull and C. J. Hoadly. Hartford, 1850–90.

The Book of the General Laws for the People within the Jurisdiction of Connecticut. Cambridge, Mass., 1673.

Acts and Laws, of His Majesty's Colony of Connecticut in New England. New London, Conn., 1715.

Acts and Laws of His Majesty's Colony of Rhode Island and Providence Plantations in America. Boston, 1719.

B. JUDICIAL RECORDS

Records and Files of the Quarterly Courts of Essex County Massachusetts. 8 vols. Edited by George F. Dow. Salem, Mass., 1911–21.

The Probate Records of Essex County Massachusetts. 3 vols. Salem, Mass., 1916–20.

Records of the Suffolk County Court, 1671–1680, Publ. CSM. Boston, 1933, 29–30.

Abstract and Index of the Records of the Inferiour Court of Pleas (Suffolk County Court) Held at Boston 1680–1698. Historical Records Survey. Boston, 1940.

Middlesex County Court Records. 4 vols., MS transcript. Office of the Clerk of Court, Middlesex County Court House. Cambridge, Mass.

Records of the Court of General Sessions of the Peace For the county of Worcester, Massachusetts, Form 1731 to 1737, Collections of the Worcester Society of Antiquity, 5 (1883), no. 10.

Colonial Justice in Western Massachusetts (1639–1702) The Pynchon Court Record. Edited by Joseph O. Smith. Cambridge, Mass., 1961.

Records of the Particular Court of Connecticut 1639–1663. Collections of the Connecticut Historical Society, vol. 22 (1928).

C. LOCAL RECORDS

Boston Registry Department, *Records Relating to the Early History of Boston.* 39 vols. Boston, 1876–1909. Vol. 4 includes the early town records of Dorchester; vol. 6, the church and land records of Roxbury.

The Records of the First Church in Boston, Publ. CSM. Edited by Richard D. Pierce. Boston, 1961, vols. 39–41.

The Records of the Town of Cambridge. Cambridge, Mass., 1901.

The Early Records of the Town of Dedham. 5 vols. Edited by Don Gleason Hill. Dedham, Mass., 1886–99.

Records of the First Church at Dorchester in New England 1636–1734. Boston, 1891.

Town Records of Salem. 3 vols. Salem, Mass., 1868–1934.
The First Century of the History of Springfield. 2 vols. Edited by
    Henry M. Burt. Springfield, Mass., 1898.
Watertown Records. 8 vols. Watertown, Mass., 1894–1939.

3. DIARIES, JOURNALS, LETTERS, ETC.

In general, the more informal the source, the more difficult it is to
use and the greater the amount of irrelevant material that must be
gone through before something significant turns up. When something
does, however, it often casts a brilliant light on the full meaning that
formal ideology held for living and breathing New Englanders.

Most useful of the works listed below is the *Winthrop Journal.* Not
really a diary, but the chronologically arranged notes for a projected
history of New England, it is informed by a constant and pervading
sense of the Bay Colony's destiny that probably tempted the author on
occasion to subordinate content to moral. Yet since he served as governor of the colony during many of its formative years, this heightened
self-consciousness also enhances the importance of the *Journal* because
it indicates quite clearly what the leader of the Massachusetts experiment thought he was doing. The *Winthrop Papers,* by contrast, are
mainly concerned with the shipment of hogsheads of peas and other
routine matters necessary for the survival and growth of a pioneer
community in a new and not particularly friendly environment. Useful
passages rarely occur outside of official statements of goals, deliberate
retrospects, or controversial pieces. The most important of these are
listed separately.

Samuel Sewall's diary was something of a disappointment for the
same reason. The judge wrote so straightforwardly and so unreflec-
tively that he included an immense amount on what happened to him
and very little on what he thought of it. His diary makes for more
pleasant reading than Mather's or Wigglesworth's to the same degree
as his personality was more appealing than theirs, but he leaves a tremendous amount implicit in the details of the routine events he de-
scribes. If Mather and Wigglesworth were insufficiently self-conscious
and literary in their journals, at least they provided a larger-than-life-
size picture of the selves of which they were conscious.

BRADFORD, WILLIAM. *History of Plymouth Plantation*. 2 vols. Boston, 1912.

HULL, JOHN. *The Diary of John Hull, Transactions and Collections of the American Antiquarian Society*, 3 (1857): 109–316.

HUTCHINSON, THOMAS, ed. *A Collection of Original Papers Relative to the History of the Colony of Massachusetts-Bay*. 2 vols. Publications of the Prince Society, 2–3. Albany, N.Y., 1865.

KEAYNE, ROBERT. *The Apologia of Robert Keayne, Publ.* CSM 42, 243–341. Edited by Bernard Bailyn. Boston, 1964.

MATHER, COTTON. *The Diary of Cotton Mather*, 7 *Coll.* MHS, 7–8 (1911–12).

———. *The Diary of Cotton Mather, D.D., F.R.S. for the Year 1712.* Edited by William R. Mannierre II. Charlottesville, N.C., 1964.

———. *Mather Papers*, 4 *Coll.* MHS, 8 (1868).

SEWALL, SAMUEL. *The Diary of Samuel Sewall*, 5 *Coll.* MHS, 5–7 (1878–82).

———. *Sewall Papers*, 6 *Coll.* MHS, 1–2 (1886–88).

WIGGLESWORTH, MICHAEL. *The Diary of Michael Wigglesworth, Publ.* CSM, 35 : 311–444. Edited by Edmund S. Morgan. Boston, 1951.

WINTHROP, JOHN. *The History of New England from 1630 to 1649.* 2 vols. Edited by James Savage. Boston, 1853.

———. *Winthrop Papers.* 5 vols. to date. Boston, 1929–
Includes:
Arguments for the Plantation of New England, 2 : 106–49.
A Declaration in Defense of an Order of Court Made in May, 1637, 3 : 422–26.
Defense of the Negative Voice, 4 : 380–91.
A Discourse on Arbitrary Government, 4 : 468–88.
The Humble Request of his Majesties loyall Subjects, the Governour and the Company late gone for New England, 2 : 231–33.
A Modell of Christian Charity, 2 : 282–95.

4. SECONDARY SOURCES

Students of the Puritans have so many satisfactory guides to secondary material currently available that an essay on historiography at the end of this kind of monograph can only have a very limited function.

Generally the author pretends he has never heard of previous bibliographies and proceeds to give a detailed if incomplete survey that functions as a kind of intellectual genealogy and apology. Favorable notices of friends locate him in some one of the contending camps of New England historians; favorable notices of potential critics hopefully draw the sting from the reviews that will issue from the opposing camps.

In my case the apology would probably come too late to repair the damage the text has done, but there is still a place to make some of my implicit assumptions explicit and to acknowledge a few intellectual debts. It goes without saying that the lesson I have learned from the work of another is not necessarily the one he intended and he is in no way responsible for my use or abuse of his material.

My methodology, such as it is, derives in part from the works of Edmund S. Morgan, particularly *Visible Saints*. The Puritan idea of a pure church, well articulated but untried in England, received its fullest definition in its actual establishment in New England. The same can be said of Puritan aspirations for society: the very existence of New England in itself indicates the inability of the Puritans to implement their social ideals in the mother country. As a historian of Puritan ideas, without pretending to be anything else, I felt obliged to discuss the institutional consequences of these ideas in New England simply in order to write an accurate and complete story.

The story as told is full of conflicts and contradictions. So are most histories of colonial New England, but I have been contending that the tensions of early New England resulted more from contradictions within Puritanism than from conflicts between unfulfillable Puritan goals and the unfulfilled needs of the flesh. This argument again owes something to Morgan, to his *The Puritan Dilemma*, and more still to Perry Miller, especially to *The New England Mind* series. Miller could construct some magnificent non sequiturs on occasion, his notion of social history often failed to transcend the works of James Truslow Adams, and he was a too frequent practitioner of that higher ambiguity some confuse with sophistication. Still his achievement remains, and it remains useful as well as remarkable. His exasperating thematic multivalence can have all the glitter and all the substance of a fourth of July fireworks display, but at his best he recreates the multifaceted, contradictory reality that eludes most of us in our study of the past and only confuses us in our attempts to comprehend the present.

Miller excelled also in his ability to locate American Puritanism within the moral and material battleground that was the civilization of early modern Europe. He was given to overdramatizing the conflicts and to exaggerating the originality of the American Puritans' solutions to them, but his was a perspective only just coming into its own among other historians. Too often even now the acknowledgment that New England history is a part of the history of Europe is largely verbal, a new introductory chapter on "the English background" tacked onto an old formula that depicts a provincial variant of the waning of the middle ages and the birth of the modern world. One of the few judicious assimilations of European history and European historiography into a New England theme is Kenneth Lockridge's *The First Hundred Years of A New England Town, Dedham, 1630–1730*. Quite apart from its considerable substantive value, Lockridge's history stands out for its ability to classify social processes in a vocabulary neither uniquely American nor restricted to rise and fall, medieval and modern.

The most fruitful recent examples of New England social history (Richard Bushman's *From Puritan to Yankee* excepted) have, like Lockridge's work, concentrated on a single town. Two have had particular importance for my own study: Sumner Chilton Powell's study of Sudbury, *Puritan Village*, and Darrett Rutman's *Winthrop's Boston*. Since my text takes issue with some of the conclusions of the latter work, it is worth noting that I still think Rutman asks all the right questions, particularly in his insistence on knowing what part of New England culture was in fact merely European and not specifically Puritan at all. Rutman also places renewed emphasis on New England communitarianism (an emphasis seconded by Lockridge for Dedham), and this has left an obvious mark on my own chapter on the same subject.

A list of some other secondary works I have used follows. First, however, I really ought to note the more significant recent books I have *not* read. Several important studies appeared after my text was all but complete, and I was reluctant to attempt to incorporate their conclusions into my own, a process likely to become so extensive that still more relevant new works would have come out by the time it was completed. At some point every author has to stop reading if he is ever to start writing, but my own work is undoubtedly the poorer for omitting, among other books: John Demos, *A Little Commonwealth*

(Cambridge, Mass., 1970); Phillip J. Greven, Jr., *Four Generations* (Ithaca, N.Y., 1969); David E. Little, *Religious Conflict, Law and Order* (New York, 1969); Robert Pope, *The Half-Way Covenant* (Princeton, N.J., 1969); Darrett B. Rutman, *American Puritanism* (Philadelphia, 1970); and Michael Zuckerman, *Peaceable Kingdoms* (New York, 1970). Lockridge's *First Hundred Years* and Timothy Breen's *The Character of the Good Ruler* are fortunate exceptions because I was familiar with their contents before publication, through personal acquaintance with the authors.

ADAMS, GEORGE BURTON. *Constitutional History of England*. 2d ed. New York, 1962.

ALLEN, J. W. *A History of Political Thought in the Sixteenth Century*. Reprinted with revised bibliography. London, 1957.

ANDREWS, CHARLES M. *The River Towns of Connecticut*. Baltimore, 1889.

BAILYN, BERNARD. "The Apologia of Robert Keayne." *The William and Mary Quarterly*, 3d ser., 7 (1950): 568–87.

————. *Education in the Forming of American Society*. Chapel Hill, N.C., 1960.

————. *The New England Merchants in the Seventeenth Century*. New York: Harper Torchbooks, 1964.

————. *The Origins of American Politics*. New York, 1968.

BARKER, ARTHUR. *Milton and the Puritan Dilemma*. [Toronto], 1942.

BARNES, VIOLA. *The Dominion of New England*. New Haven, Conn., 1923.

BENTON, JOSIAH HENRY. *Warning Out in New England*. Boston, 1911.

BREEN, TIMOTHY. *The Character of the Good Ruler*. New Haven, Conn., 1970.

BRENNAN, ELLEN. "The Massachusetts Council of the Magistrates." *The New England Quarterly* 4 (1931): 54–93.

BRIDENBAUGH, CARL. *Cities in the Wilderness*. New York, 1955.

BROWN, B. KATHERINE. "A Note on the Puritan Concept of Aristocracy." *Mississippi Valley Historical Review* 41 (1954); 105–12.

————. "Puritan Democracy: A Case Study." *Mississippi Valley Historical Review* 1 (December 1963): 377–96.

————. "Puritan Democracy in Dedham, Massachusetts: Another Case Study." *William and Mary Quarterly*, 3d ser., 24 (July 1967): 378–96.

BUSHMAN, RICHARD L. *From Puritan to Yankee.* Cambridge, Mass., 1967.

COLLINSON, PATRICK. *The Elizabethan Puritan Movement.* London, 1967.

DAWES, NORMAN H. "Social Classes in Seventeenth Century New England." Ph.D. dissertation, Harvard University, 1941.

————. "Titles as Symbols of Prestige in Seventeenth-Century New England." *The William and Mary Quarterly*, 3d ser., 6 (1949): 69–83.

DEXTER, FRANKLIN B. "On some Social Distinctions at Harvard and Yale before the Revolution." Proceedings of the American Antiquarian Society, N.S., 9 (1893): 34–59.

FROTHINGHAM, RICHARD. *The History of Charlestown, Massachusetts.* Boston, 1845–49.

GEORGE, CHARLES H., and GEORGE, KATHERINE. *The Protestant Mind of the English Reformation, 1570–1640.* Princeton, N.J., 1961.

HALL, MICHAEL G. *Edmund Randolph and the American Colonies.* Chapel Hill, N.C., 1960.

HALLER, WILLIAM. *The Elect Nation, The Meaning and Relevance of Foxe's Book of Martyrs.* New York and Evanston, Ill., 1963.

————. *Liberty and Reformation in the Puritan Revolution.* New York: Columbia University Press paperback, 1963.

————. *The Rise of Puritanism.* New York: Harper Torchbooks, 1957.

HEIMERT, ALAN. *Religion and the American Mind: from the Great Awakening to the Revolution.* Cambridge, Mass., 1966.

HILL, CHRISTOPHER. *Puritanism and Revolution.* London, 1958.

————. *Society and Puritanism in Pre-Revolutionary England.* New York, 1964.

HOLMES, THOMAS J. *Cotton Mather, A Bibliography of His Works.* 3 vols. Cambridge, Mass., 1940.

HUDSON, WINTHROP. "Puritanism and the Spirit of Capitalism." *Church History* 18 (1949): 3–17.

HUTCHINSON, THOMAS. *History of the Colony and Province of Massachusetts Bay.* 3 vols. Edited by L. S. Mayo. Cambridge, Mass., 1936.

JAMES, MARGARET. *Social Problems and Policy During the Puritan Revolution 1640–1660.* London, 1930.

JORDAN, WILBUR K. *Philanthropy in England 1480–1660.* London, 1959.

KELSO, ROBERT. *The History of Public Poor Relief in Massachusetts 1620–1920.* Boston, 1922.

KELSO, RUTH. *The Doctrine of the English Genteman in the Sixteenth Century. University of Illinois Studies in Language and Literature* 14 (1929).

KNAPPEN, M. M. *Tudor Puritanism.* Chicago, 1939.

LOCKRIDGE, KENNETH A. *A New England Town: The First Hundred Years.* New York, 1970.

LOVEJOY, ARTHUR O. *The Great Chain of Being.* New York, 1960.

MACPHERSON, C. B. *The Political Theory of Possessive Individualism.* Oxford, 1962.

MAINE, JACKSON TURNER. *The Social Structure of Revolutionary America.* Princeton, N.J., 1965.

MICHAELSEN, ROBERT S. "Changes in the Puritan Concept of Calling or Vocation." *The New England Quarterly* 26 (1953): 315–36.

MILLER, PERRY. *Errand into the Wilderness.* New York: Harper Torchbooks, 1964.

———. "From the Covenant to the Revival." In *Religion in American Life,* edited by James Ward Smith and A. Leland Jamison, 1 : 322–68. 4 vols. Princeton, N.J., 1961.

———. *Orthodoxy in Massachusetts.* Boston: Beacon Press paperback, 1959.

———. *The New England Mind, From Colony to Province.* Boston: Beacon Press paperback, 1961.

———. *The New England Mind, The Seventeenth Century.* Boston: Beacon Press paperback, 1961.

———, and Johnson, Thomas, eds. *The Puritans A Sourcebook of their Writings.* 2 vols. New York and Evanston, Ill.: Harper Torchbooks, 1963.

MORGAN, EDMUND S. *The Puritan Dilemma, The Story of John Winthrop.* Boston, 1958. Reference is to the paperback edition.

————. *The Puritan Family*. Boston, 1956. 2d ed., rev. New York: Harper Torchbooks, 1966.

————. *Visible Saints*. Ithaca, N.Y.: Cornell paperback, 1965.

MORISON, SAMUEL ELIOT. *Builders of the Bay Colony*. Boston, 1930.

————. *The Founding of Harvard College*. Cambridge, Mass., 1935.

————. *Harvard College in the Seventeenth Century*. 2 vols. Cambridge, Mass., 1936.

————. "Precedence at Harvard College in the Seventeenth Century." Proceedings of the American Antiquarian Society, N.S., 42 (1932): 371–431.

————. *Three Centuries of Harvard, 1636–1936*. Cambridge, Mass., 1942.

MORRIS, RICHARD B., and CROSSMAN, JONATHAN. "The Regulation of Wages in Early Massachusetts." *The New England Quarterly* 11 (1938): 470–500.

O'BRIEN, GEORGE. *An Essay on Medieval Economic Teaching*. London, 1920.

OWEN, DAVID. *English Philanthropy, 1660–1960*. Cambridge, Mass., 1964.

POCOCK, J. G. A. *The Ancient Constitution and the Feudal Law*. Cambridge, 1957.

POWELL, SUMNER C. *Puritan Village*. Garden City, N.Y.: Doubleday paperback, 1965.

DE ROOVER, RAYMOND. "The Concept of Just Price: Theory and Economic Policy." *Journal of Economic History* 18 (1958): 418–38.

RUTMAN, DARRETT B. "The Mirror of Puritan Auhority." In *Law and Authority in Colonial America*, edited by George Billias, pp. 149–67. Barre, Mass., 1965.

————. *Winthrop's Boston*. Chapel Hill, N.C., 1965.

SAVAGE, JAMES. *A Genealogical Dictionary of the First Settlers of New England*. 4 vols. Boston, 1860–62.

SHIPTON, CLIFFORD. "Ye Mystery of Ye Ages Solved." *Harvard Alumni Bulletin* 57 (December 1954): 258–63.

————, and SIBLEY, JOHN L. *Sibley's Harvard Graduates*. 13 vols. to date. Cambridge, Mass., 1873–

TAWNEY, R. H. *Religion and the Rise of Capitalism*. New York: Mentor paperback, 1963.

TILLYARD, E. M. W. *The Elizabethan World Picture*. New York, 1944.

TOWNER, LAWRENCE. " 'A Fondness for Freedom,' Servant Protest in Puritan Society." *William and Mary Quarterly*, 3d ser., 19 (1962): 201–19.

————. *A Good Master Well Served: A Social History of Servitude in Massachusetts 1620–1750*. Ph.D. dissertation, Northwestern University, 1955.

WALL, ROBERT EMMETT. *The Membership of the Massachusetts General Court*. Ph.D. dissertation, Yale University, 1964.

WALZER, MICHAEL. *The Revolution of the Saints*. Cambridge, Mass., 1965.

WATERS, JOHN J. "Hingham, Massachusetts, 1631–1661: An East Anglian Oligarchy in the New World." *Journal of Social History* 1 (1967–68): 350–70.

WEBER, MAX. *The Protestant Ethic and the Spirit of Capitalism*. Translated by Talcott Parsons. New York: Scribners' paperback, 1958.

WEEDEN, WILLIAM B., *Economic and Social History of New England*. 2 vols. Boston, 1890.

WINSLOW, OLA. *Meetinghouse Hill*. New York, 1952.

WOODHOUSE, A. S. P. *Puritanism and Liberty*. n.p., 1951.

ZANGER, JULES. "Crime and Punishment in Early Massachusetts." *William and Mary Quarterly*, 3d ser., 22 (July 1965).

Index

Adams, John, and democracy, 169n
Affliction: and acquisitiveness, 124–25; and poverty, 129–32; and economic depression, 132–34
Ames, William, 5; on frugality, 109–10; on wealth, 110; on social mobility, 114n; on just price, 117n; on poverty and sin, 129; writings of, 192
Anabaptists, 18–19
Andover, poor relief in, 144
Andros, Sir Edmund, 92–93
Antinomians, 39–40; and Christian love, 55–56
Appleton, Nathaniel, on rulers, 97
Aquinas, St. Thomas, 116, 117, 119n
Aristocracy. See Rulers
Aristotle, 26, 34, 70, 108
Authority. See Government

Bailyn, Bernard, theories on merchants discussed, 182–86 passim
Bastards. See Poor relief
Belcher, Jonathan, 97
Belcher, Joseph, on poverty, 151
Bellingham, Richard, 84, 91, 139
Bodine, Jean, 72
Boston: and Hutchinsonians, 55; deputies of, 76n; merchants of, 117–19; poor relief in, 137, 145–46, 146n; charity in, 140–41, 148–51; increase of poor in, 144–45; workhouses in, 147–48; grain riot (1710) in, 151–52
Bradford, William: on deference, 38; on dispersion, 50; on merchants, 115
Bradstreet, Simon, 120, 184; family of, 187

Brattle, Thomas, 120, 185, 188
Brown, William, 184
Bulkeley, Peter, 184
Bushman, Richard, 203

Calling: defined, 99–100; limits of, 101–02; and inequality, 102–03; diligence in, 104–06; and recreation, 106; and efficiency, 107–08; Puritan ideal of contrasted with non-Puritan, 108–09; and frugality, 109–10; and wealth, 110–12; and social mobility, 114, 114n. See also Rationalization, economic
Calvin, John, on love, 44
Capitalism. See Puritanism, and capitalism
Charles I, 1, 2, 39, 160, 167
Charles II, 91
Charlestown, poor relief in, 137
Charity (*agape*). See Love, Christian
Charity (alms): and acquisitiveness, 110–11; forms of, 138–39; and New England churches, 139–41; in Boston, 148–51. See also Poor relief
Cheever, Ezekiel, on affliction, 131–32
Childe, Robert, 91
Church seating, 158–59
Civil War, English, xvi, 162
Clarke, Thomas, 184
Class. See Social classes; Social mobility
Coddington, William, on financial losses, 132
Communion, 60–61
Community. See Love, Christian
Congregationalism, xvi, 4, 57–58
Consent. See Voluntarism

Cooke, Elisha, 184

Cotton, John: on social class, 33; on hereditary aristocracy, 38–39; on theocracy, 46; on solitariness, 50; in Antinomian crisis, 55; on rulers, 67; on democracy, 72, 166–67; on life tenure for rulers, 79; on "negative voice," 80; on diligence, 104; on just price, 116, 117, 117n; on covetousness, 121; on declension, 123; on poverty and sin, 128, 129; on human nature, 169; writings of, 192

Council, Massachusetts. See Rulers

Covetousness, defined, 121; and social tension, 122–26

Cromwell, Oliver, xvi, 162

Danforth, John, on depressions, 132

Davenport, John, founds New Haven Colony, 2

Davy, Humphrey, 184, 185

Declension: and Puritanism, xvi–xvii; and acquisitiveness, 124–26, 123n

Dedham, 27, 31; Christian love in, 47–48; exclusiveness in, 53–54

Democracy: in Massachusetts political system, 72–75; distinguished from voluntarism, 157–58; and deference, 158–59; and ideology, 160; distinguished from radicalism, 165–66; Puritan contributions to, 166–71

Dennison, Daniel, 139, 184; on social order, 14; on deference, 25; on love, 53

Depression. See Affliction

Deputies: creation of, 75–76; authority of, 76–77; and theories of representation, 77, 95; compared to rulers, 77–78; contest "negative voice," 79–80, 81–84; claim executive powers, 84–85; question judicial powers, 86; impeach John Winthrop (1645), 87–88; become "representatives," (1692), 93

D'Ewes, Sir Simon, 73

Diaries, use of, 200

Dorchester, poor relief in, 137, 141

Downame, John: on order, 25; on aristocracy, 29; on diligence, 104–06; on recreation, 106; on wealth, 110–11; on affliction, 130

Dudley, Joseph, 92, 184, 185; attacks farmers, 17; controversy with Mathers, 93–94

Dudley, Thomas, 79, 139; on calling, 100, 101

Dyer, Mary, 56, 56n

Eaton, Theophilus, 2

Elections, meaning of, 71–72; of Massachusetts magistracy, 180–81

Eliot, Jared, on human nature, 95

Eliot, John, xvii, 164n; on poverty, 131

Endicott, John, 80, 139

England: contrasted with New England on social structure, 7, 32, 32n, 37–39, 38n; on ideal of order, 29–30; on ideal of love, 44; on government, 46–47, 70–71, 71n; on poor relief, 137–38; on revolution, 160–62

Family, regulation of, 24–25, 24n, 25n, 143–44

Ferrar, Nicholas, 16, 108

Fifth Monarchy Men, 47

Filmer, Sir Robert, 95

Fiske, Samuel, on councilors, 96

Franchise: in Connecticut, 32n; in Massachusetts, 32, 47, 70–71, 71n, 93, 173–79; in Plymouth Colony, 32n

Franklin, Benjamin, 113

Freemanship, Massachusetts. See Franchise, in Massachusetts

Gedney, Bartholomew, 184, 185

General Court, Massachusetts. See Deputies; Rulers

Gibbons, Edward, 120

Glorious Revolution, xv, 92–93
Goodman, Christopher, 162–63, 163–64
Government: before the Fall, 18–19; and subordination, 20–21; contempt of, 22, 22*n*. *See also* Rulers
Great Awakening, xv
Great Chain of Being, 13

Half-Way Covenant, 91, 164
Hall, Michael G., 182
Hawthorne, John, 184, 185
Hawthorne, William, 69, 181, 184; attacks magistrates, 84, 85
Henry of Langenstein, 117
Hierarchy. *See* Order
Higginson, John, on Pequot War, 58*n*; family of, 186
Hingham militia crisis, 87–88
Hobbes, Thomas, 161
Hooker, Thomas: founds Connecticut, 2; on social order, 15–16; on sin, 19; on covenants, 33*n*; uses Ramist logic, 35, 36; on Christian love, 43, 44; on elections, 67–68; on affliction, 130; writings of, 192
Hubbard, William, on social order, 12, 14; on unity, 51; on community of peril, 59, 60*n*; on rulers, 68; writings of, 193
Hull, John, 147, 184; on governors, 37; death of, 115; gives to charity, 148
Humphrey, John, 57
Hunting laws, 27
Hutchinson, Anne, 39, 55, 56, 56*n*, 80
Hutchinson, Elisha, 184, 185

Idleness: and calling, 106–07; and poverty, 134–36
Impeachment, 86–87
Inferiors, rights of, 17

James, Margaret, 128*n*
Judges. *See* Rulers, and judicial power

Just price: definition of, 116; significance of in New England, 117–18; enforcement of, 119*n*

Keayne, Robert, xvii, 187; and "sow's case," 81; and economic rationalization, 109; convicted of "oppression" (1639), 116, 117, 118; gives to charity, 139, 139*n*
King Philip's War, 59, 155

Labor. *See* Calling
Land: distribution of, 27, 27*n*, 31*n*; and deference, 37–38; and unity, 50–51, 51*n*
Land bank controversy (1741), 96–97
Laud, William, xv, 1, 2
Lawes and Liberties of Massachusetts, 86
Leete, William, on poverty, 136
Letters, use of, 200
Levellers, 47, 47*n*, 160
Leverett, John, 120, 184
Lilburne, John, 160, 162
Locke, John, influence in New England, 95–96
Lockridge, Kenneth, 203
Love, Christian: and inequality, 40; defined, 42–43; distinguished from natural love, 44; history of concept, 45–46; and unity, 49–50; and schism, 51–53; and conciliation, 53; and exclusiveness, 53–54; and peril, 58–59; changes in concept, 60–64 passim. *See also* "Tribalism"
Lovejoy, Arthur, 13
Luxford, James, 6

Magistracy. *See* Rulers
Mather, Cotton, xiii; on public service, 16; on human nature, 20*n*; on church membership, 61, 61*n*; on social organization, 62–63; on love, 64; on John Winthrop, 68–69; attacks Joseph Dudley, 93–94; on idleness, 107, 135, 137; on efficiency, 107–08; on calling, 112–13;

contrasted with William Perkins,
112–14; on covetousness, 121; on
depressions, 132–33; organizes
charities, 149–51; writings of, 193;
diary of, 200
Mather, Increase: on rulers, 69–70;
in Glorious Revolution, 92; attacks
Joseph Dudley, 93–94
Merchants, New England: and the
Puritan ethic, 114–15, 183; and
social conflict, 116–19; in Massa-
chusetts government, 119–20, 183–
84; and the moderate party, 184–
86; family connections of, 187–89
Miller, Perry, 201–02
Milton, John: compared to John
Winthrop, 160–61; on rights of
regenerate, 165–66
Ministry, New England: and life ten-
ure, 79; and executive power, 85;
and judicial power, 86; role in
Hingham militia crisis, 88
Mixed government: defined, 72–73;
and "negative voice," 83
Mobility, geographic. See Land
Mobility, social. See Social mobility
Mobs, 92, 151–52
Moderate party: defined, 182–83;
composition of, 184–86
Moral regulation, 22–25, 25n. See
also Sumptuary laws
Morgan, Edmund S., 202
Morton, Charles, on cosmology, 13

Natural law: and love, 42; and democracy, 167–71 passim. See also
Order
"Negative voice" (veto). See Deputies; Rulers
Norton, John, 164; on social order,
21; on aristocracy, 72–73

Oakes, Urian: on covetousness, 122–
23; on affliction, 124–25; on self-
hatred, 125
Official records, use of, 197–98

Order: and nature, 11–17; and sin,
18–29; changes in concept in New
England, 29–40; changes in eighteenth century, 60
Orphans. See Poor relief
Oxenbridge, John: on rulers, 69; on
merchants, 115

Paper money, 94; and affliction, 133–
34
Parsons, Theophilus, on human nature,
171
Peacham, Henry, on social order, 18
Pemberton, Ebenezer: on natural order, 19; denounces Boston poor,
152
Penn, William, 185
Pequot War, 58
Perkins, William, xiii; on chance, 11;
on inferiors, 17n; on love, 44; on
calling, 99–102; on social mobility,
110, 114n; compared to Cotton
Mather, 112–13; character of writ-
ings, 192
Peter, Hugh, on idleness, 106–07
Plena potestas, 77
Plenitude, 13
Ponet, John, on revolution, 162–63
Poor relief: and vagabonds, 134–36;
and the able-bodied, 136; English
and American compared, 137–38;
and the disabled, 137–44 passim;
and warning out, 141–42, 142n–
43n; and children, 143–44; and
urban poor, 144–52. See also Charity (alms)
Pope, Robert, 178n–79n
Poverty, and sin, 126–29. See also
Affliction; Charity (alms); Poor
relief
Powell, Sumner C., 203
Preston, John: on acquisitiveness, 11–
12; on covetousness, 121–22; on
affliction, 130
Providence Isle, 57
Prynne, William, 162

Public service, 16–17
Puritanism, problem of definition, xv–
    xvi; "decline" of, xvi–xvii, 123–26,
    123n; tensions in, xvi–xvii, 7, 171–
    72; and the past, 1, 4, 66; and
    English tradition, 4, 73, 75; and
    revolution, 39–40, 162–65, 164n;
    and capitalism, 103–14; and pov-
    erty, 127–29; and social cohesion,
    155–56; English and American
    compared, 161–62; and democracy,
    see Democracy
Pynchon, John, 184
Pynchon, William, 120

Rainborough, Thomas, 160
Ramist dialectic, 33–36
Ramus, Petrus, 33, 34, 35, 35n
Randolph, Edward, 181; reliability of,
    185–86
Rationalization, economic, 6, 108–10
Reformation, relation to American
    Puritanism, 45–46
Representation. See Deputies; Plena
    potestas; Rulers
Revolution. See Puritanism, and rev-
    olution
Richards, John, 184, 185, 185n
Riches. See Wealth
Rogers, Ezekiel, on merchants, 117
Rulers: dignity of, 25–29 passim;
    disunity among, 26, 164; and he-
    redity, 29, 38; in England and
    America, 30, 70–71; expenses of,
    37; and heresy, 39–40; source of
    authority, 67; character of, 68–70;
    and wealth, 69–70; and represen-
    tation, 71–72, 75; relation to depu-
    ties, 77–78; and life tenure, 79,
    80, 81, 90, 91–92; and "negative
    voice," 79–80, 81–84; and execu-
    tive powers, 84–85; and judicial
    power, 85–86; later history of ideal,
    92–98 passim; stability of in eight-
    eenth century, 96, 97; manner of
    electing, 180–81

Russell, James, 184, 185
Russell, Richard, 184; family of, 188
Rutman, Darrett B., 203
Ryece, Robert, 16

Saffin, John, defends slavery, 14
Salem, poor relief in, 137
Saltonstall, Richard, attacks powers of
    magistrates, 81, 84
Savage, Thomas, 184
Say and Sele, William Fiennes, Vis-
    count, 38, 40, 72
Separatists, 1
Sermons, use of, xi–xii, 191–92
Sewall, Samuel, 5, 120, 131, 184;
    attacks slavery, 14; on human na-
    ture, 20; on affliction, 124; on
    Boston grain riot (1710), 151–52;
    diary of, 200
Shepard, Thomas: on revolution, 40,
    164, 164n; on unity, 49; on diver-
    sity, 54; on calling, 105n; on
    affliction, 130–31
Sibbes, Richard, on poverty, 131
Simmons, Richard, 177
Sin, and natural order, 19–20
Slavery, 14–15
Smith, Adam, 113
Social classes: in New England, 32–
    33, 38n; and Ramist logic, 35–36.
    See also Social mobilty
Social ethic: defined, xi; distinguished
    from social history, xii; changes in,
    xiii–xv; and behavior, xvii, xviii,
    5–7, 159–60
Social mobility: and Ramist logic, 33,
    35–36; and doctrine of calling,
    110–12; legitimacy of, 114, 114n
"Sow's case." See Rulers, and "nega-
    tive voice"
Sprague, Richard, 185
Springe, Sir William, 49
Springfield, poor relief in, 137
Standing council. See Rulers, and life
    tenure
Stiles, Ezra, on democracy, 167–68

Stoddard, Anthony, 120, 185
Stoddard, Solomon: on order, 60–61; on just price, 118–19
Stoughton, Israel: on life tenure, 79; on John Winthrop, 122
Stoughton, William, 184, 185
Stubbes, Philip, on authority, 26
Sudbury, 52–53, 53*n*
Sumptuary laws, 23, 28, 29, 28*n*–29*n*; significance of, xii, 158, 158*n*
Symonds, Samuel, 37, 139; on property, 165

Tawney, R. H., 127*n*–28*n*, 128
Theocracy, 45, 46
Titles, 28, 158–59
Topsfield, poor relief in, 142
Town, New England, xvi; and land distribution, 27, 27*n*–28*n*, 31, 31*n*; and communitarianism, 47–48, 50; and poor relief, 141–44; and social cohesion, 156; records of, 197–98; historiography of, 203
"Tribalism," Puritan, 54–58
Tyng, Edward, 184; family of, 188–89
Tythingmen, 24, 25*n*

Unity. *See* Love, Christian
Utility, and Puritanism, 112–13

Vane, Sir Henry, 39, 70*n*
Voluntarism, 4; Puritan concept of, 30–31; and necessity, 31–32; and politics, 74; and social control, 156

Wall, Robert, 174–76
Ward, Nathaniel, 54*n*, 84, 165
Warning out, 141–43
Watertown, poor relief in, 137, 143
Wealth: and rulers, 69–70; uses of, 110–11; temptations of, 120–22; meaning of, 127–29, 127*n*–28*n*
Weber, Max, thesis discussed, 99, 103–14 passim, 127*n*
Welfare, public, 22

Wentworth, Peter, 21
West, Samuel, on democracy, 170
Wheelright, John, 55, 56
Wigglesworth, Michael, 122, 125; on covetousness, 121; diary of, 200
Willard, Samuel, xiv, 148; on fifth commandment, 18–19; on deference, 25; on "popularity," 71; on acquisitiveness, 111; on just price, 118; on poverty, 128; writings of, 193
Williams, Roger, 52
Williams, William, on rulers, 96–97
Willoughby, Francis, 91, 120
Wilson, John, 39–40
Winthrop, Fitz-John, 183
Winthrop, John, xi, xii, 1, 59, 68, 69, 122, 139; on temptation, 2; on mission, 3–4; on public service, 16–17; on Christian love, 41, 42, 43, 48–49; on exclusiveness, 54–64; on retribution, 57–58, 57*n*; on mixed government, 72; on English precedents, 73; on consent, 74; opens freemanship (1630), 74; on deputies, 76, 78, 78*n*; on judicial power, 80, 85–86; on the "sow's case," 81–82; defends "negative voice" (1642–44), 83; defends magistrates' executive powers (1644), 85; impeached (1645), 87–88; "little speech on liberty," 88–89; influence on Massachusetts government, 89–90, 91, 98; on affliction, 124; on "civil liberty," 157–58; compared to John Milton, 160–61; on natural law, 170; writings of, 192; letters of, 200
Winthrop, John, Jr., 120; on death, 183
Winthrop, Samuel, 101
Wise, John, 167
Workhouses, 147–48

Zwingli, Huldreich, on theocracy, 46